Topics and approaches to studying intelligence

Edited by

Andrew Macpherson
University of New Hampshire

Glenn P. Hastedt
James Madison University

Series in Sociology

VERNON PRESS

www.vernonpress.com

In the Americas:	*In the rest of the world:*
Vernon Press	Vernon Press
1000 N West Street, Suite 1200	C/Sancti Espiritu 17,
Wilmington, Delaware, 19801	Malaga, 29006
United States	Spain

Series in Sociology

Library of Congress Control Number: 2024934540

ISBN: 979-8-8819-0149-3

Also available: 978-1-64889-881-5 [Hardback]; 979-8-8819-0033-5 [PDF, E-Book]

Cover design by Vernon Press with elements from Freepik.

Table of contents

List of figures and tables

List of acronyms

AI	Artificial Intelligence
CAP	Career Analyst Program
CCP	Chinese Communist Party
CIA	Central intelligence Agency
DCI	Director of Central Intelligence
DCID	Director of Central Intelligence Directive
DIA	Defense Intelligence Agency
DNI	Director of National Intelligence
IAEA	International Atomic Energy Agency
IC	Intelligence Community
ICD	Intelligence Community Directive
IRTPA	Intelligence Reform and Terrorism Prevention Act of 2004
KGB	Soviet Komitet gosudarstvennoy bezopasnosti or Committee for State Security
MAPS	Membership Action Plans
NATO	North Atlantic Treaty Organization
NCTC	National Counterterrorism Center
NGA	National Geospatial-Intelligence Agency
NPT	Nuclear Nonproliferation Treaty
NSA	National Security Agency
ODNI	Office of the Director of National Intelligence
OPID	Official public intelligence disclosure
OSS	Office of Strategic Services
POA	Program of Analysis
SAT	Structured Analytic Technique
WMD	Weapons of mass destruction
WWII	World War II
WWW	World Wide Web

Preface

Andrew M. Macpherson

University of New Hampshire

Glenn P. Hastedt

James Madison University

Our goal in constructing *Topics and Approaches to Studying Intelligence* is to bring into sharper focus the evolving nature of intelligence studies, which is in the midst of a period of significant expansion taking place across a number of dimensions. This growth builds upon the foundational concepts and topics covered in early post-WWII writings on intelligence. It also extends the range of topics covered and the approaches and concepts used in these studies. Intelligence studies have moved from being a relatively small and self-contained silo of work into one now found in the mainstream of academic and professional writings. It has also moved from a field of study composed almost exclusively of U.S., Canadian, and British authors and professionals into one with worldwide authorship. We hope that *Topics and Approaches to Studying Intelligence* will serve as a platform for extending intelligence studies even further by bringing these trends together into a single volume.

The analytical study of intelligence is but one dimension of intelligence studies, and this has always been the case. Roger Hilsman (1956) identified four distinct attitudes toward the field of intelligence: 1) operational, 2) administrative, 3) working level, and 4) academic. Harry Ransom (1980) identified four categories of intelligence writing: 1) memoirs defending the intelligence system, 2) whistle-blowing exposés of the intelligence system, 3) scholarly analysis of intelligence, and 4) government reports. In terms of quantity, for much of the period, scholarly studies of intelligence lagged behind memoirs defending the intelligence system and whistle-blowing exposés, a combination Roy Godson (1993) characterized as popular studies rather than serious studies of intelligence.

Among the earliest post-WWII contributions to the analytical study of intelligence are those by George Pettee (1946) and Sherman Kent (1949). Pettee wrote of the deficiencies of U.S. intelligence immediately preceding and during WWII. He saw intelligence as a large-scale analytic task and called for creating a permanent intelligence unit within the government that was staffed by intelligence professionals and positioned such that intelligence and policy organizations would be in a relationship of mutual guidance. Kent (1949) argued that intelligence extended beyond providing information and giving warnings. It also involved analyzing policy problems. More was required than merely collecting data. Intelligence also entailed making projections into the future with an audience of elected officials, policy planners, and bureaucrats. In 1955, Kent would follow up his book *Strategic Intelligence* with the founding of a journal, *Studies in Intelligence*, published by the CIA's Center for the Study of Intelligence, which he hoped would help create a literature on intelligence.

A common theme running through commentaries on the analytic study of intelligence has been that it needs strengthening. Writing in 1964, Klaus Knorr noted that there was a general lack of either a descriptive or normative theory of intelligence. Such concerns continued into the 1980s. Reviewing writings on intelligence between 1977 and 1979, Hilsman (1981) concluded that, as a group, they were disappointing and did not make a serious contribution to the study of intelligence. A few years later, Ransom (1986) asserted that the relationship between information and action "remains tentative, and secrecy of evidence remains a formidable problem." In the early 1990s, Hastedt (1991) commented on the continued heavy focus placed on U.S. intelligence systems in intelligence studies and called for a greater emphasis on comparative intelligence analysis as well as a broadening of research strategies to include quantitative analysis.

Notwithstanding these critiques, this period also saw the beginnings of a breakthrough in the study of topics and approaches in the study of intelligence with the contributions made by such authors as Christopher Andrew, Richard Betts, Michael Handel, Loch Johnson, Mark Lowenthal, Kathy Pherson, Randy Pherson, Jennifer Sims, Michael Warner, Gregory Treverton, and Roberta Wohstetter. It also saw the founding of two new intelligence journals, *Intelligence and National Security* and the *International Journal of Intelligence and CounterIntelligence*. A much broader and deeper field of intelligence studies exists today and has emerged from this foundation. In November 2023, an online information session of intelligence studies journal editors organized by the Intelligence Studies Consortium brought together representatives from 14 journals with editors from North America, Europe, and Australia.

Working on this foundation of past and contemporary analytic intelligence studies, the chapters in *Topics and Approaches to Studying Intelligence* highlight areas of debate and disagreement, provide insight into new areas of study, and broaden the methodological toolset used by researchers. Many of the works in the book were presented as papers at the American Political Science Association, International Association for Intelligence Education, and other academic conferences. Working with the authors, we combined these works into this edited volume.

In Chapter One, "Beyond Information: Analysis, Analysts, and Intelligence," John J. Borek examines the process of creating intelligence using the concept of the intelligence cycle as a starting point for his analysis. He argues that the analysis is the critical component of the intelligence cycle and that the creation of intelligence is not a single transformation but a series of transformations. Borek calls for adopting a customer-analyst-centric approach as an alternative to the intelligence cycle model.

In Chapter Two, "Predicting Intelligence Alliances," Katharine Cunningham and Andrew M. Macpherson use a network science approach to predict intelligence alliances. Intelligence sharing is a critical activity that is often studied via qualitative approaches. Their novel quantitative work offers another approach to identifying intelligence alliances.

In Chapter Three, "Demystifying Private-Sector Security Intelligence Teams: Unlocking Their Value in Strategic Decision-Making," Angela Miller Lewis observes that strategic security intelligence teams have become an important part of the private-sector response to operating in the current volatile geopolitical and security environment, but they have received little attention in the intelligence studies literature. This chapter provides insight into their purpose, unique capabilities, the challenges they face, and their contributions to private-sector decision-making and risk management.

In Chapter Four, "Constructing Spies: Organizations, Gender, and Embodiment," Bridget Rose Nolan uses ethnographic data and declassified CIA documents to investigate how the gendered practices of intelligence organizations construct workers. Nolan's study illustrates that while the CIA and National Counterterrorism Center construct intelligence officers in ways that are presented as gender-neutral, they actually have gendered consequences for individual workers. Nolan calls upon the intelligence community to take steps to reorganize and rethink the workplace and its expectations of its employees more broadly.

In Chapter Five, "Analysis, Collection, Counterintelligence, and Covert Action, Oh My...: Evaluating Coverage of the Intelligence Disciplines in Academic Journals," Doug Patteson presents the results of a survey of academic national security intelligence journals from 2001 to 2021. Intelligence articles are divided into four categories: collection, counterintelligence, covert action, and analysis. The dominant intelligence topic covered in these journals was analysis, followed by covert action. Understudied is collection. Patteson concludes that broadening the literature on intelligence to include more on collection is a fundamental step in increasing our overall knowledge of intelligence.

In Chapter Six, "Advancing the Intelligence Profession: The Case for Accreditation in Intelligence Studies," James D. Ramsay and Barry A. Zulauf present an argument for the standardization of college-level intelligence studies through the process of accreditation and organized around outcome-based education. Accreditation is held to be necessary to ensure that intelligence studies programs offer quality assurance, legitimacy, and professionalism. They begin by reviewing arguments for and against doing so and then build their case around the academic and programmatic underpinnings of well-established professions such as medicine and law.

In Chapter Seven, "Official Public Intelligence Disclosure as a Tool of Foreign Policy," Ofek Riemer examines the authorized disclosure of secret intelligence information and assessments as a tool of foreign policy. He notes this is not a new development but one which is becoming increasingly prevalent. Riemer asserts that while not a silver bullet, under conditions where outright warfare has not yet broken out, official public intelligence disclosure allows a state to manipulate the decision calculus and perceptions of foreign governments and the public to obtain deterrence, compellence, and legitimacy for their foreign policy.

In Chapter Eight, "The IAEA and the Dynamics of Intelligence Sharing," Robert Reardon examines the complicated and politically sensitive process of intelligence sharing. His focus is on the three-way relationship between the International Atomic Energy Agency, the U.S.—upon which it is highly dependent for intelligence to carry out its mission—and the state that is the target of intelligence. Reardon outlines a framework to analyze this relationship and applies it to North Korea and Iran. His analysis sheds light on why cooperation is generally higher than expected and offers guidance for policymakers in deciding the pros and cons of sharing intelligence.

References

Godson, Roy. 1993. "Preface." In Abram Shulsky and Gary Schmidt, *Silent Warfare: Understanding the World of Intelligence.* 2nd ed. Washington, DC: Brassey's.

Hastedt, Glenn P. 1991. "Towards the Comparative Study of Intelligence." *Journal of Conflict Studies* 11 (3). Available at: https://journals.lib.unb.ca/index.php/JCS /article/view/14966.

Hilsman, Roger. 1956. *Strategic Intelligence and National Decisions.* Glencoe, IL: Free Press.

Hilsman, Roger. 1981. "On Intelligence." *Armed Forces and Society* 8: 129-41.

Kent, Sherman. 1949. *Strategic Intelligence for American World Policy.* Princeton: Princeton University Press.

Knorr, Klaus. 1964. *Foreign Intelligence and the Social Sciences.* Princeton: Center for International Studies.

Pettee, George. 1946. *The Future of Strategic Intelligence.* Gaithersburg, MD: Infantry Journal Press.

Ransom, Harry Howe. 1980. "Being Intelligent About Secret Intelligence Agencies." *American Political Science Review* 74: 141-48.

Ransom, Harry Howe. 1986. "Review Essay." *American Political Science Review* 80: 990-91.

Chapter 1

Beyond information: Analysis, analysts, and intelligence

John J. Borek
University of New Hampshire

Abstract: John J. Borek examines the process of creating intelligence using the concept of the intelligence cycle as a starting point for his analysis. He argues that the analysis is the critical component of the intelligence cycle and that the creation of intelligence is not a single transformation but a series of transformations. Borek calls for adopting a customer-analyst- centric approach as an alternative to the intelligence cycle model.

Keywords: Alternative analysis, intelligence analysis, intelligence cycle, open source, structured analytical techniques

***

Creating intelligence: Analysis and the role of analysts

As the U.S. completes its transition in national security focus from the Global War on Terrorism to an era of great power competition, there is a corresponding need for intelligence practitioners to transition the type of intelligence it provides. While "actionable intelligence," the type used to disrupt terror cells and prevent imminent attacks, will always be needed, the requirement for well-reasoned analytic forecasts looking beyond the immediate timeframe has again become necessary. In this progression of knowledge past mere information, a review of how intelligence is created and who is responsible for doing it is a necessary component of any discussion. Unfortunately, intelligence analysis—that is, "the process by which information is transformed into intelligence" (Office of the Director of National Intelligence 2013b, 71)—is acknowledged to be one of the least understood and most understudied aspects of the national security intelligence enterprise (Borek 2017). A primarily cognitive function, other actants, and variables ranging from workplace policies to the types of tools and technology available all play a role in the process, making it difficult to develop a comprehensive description of the activity.

At its core, we understand intelligence analysis to be the analysis (breaking down into components for detailed study) and synthesis (combining disparate elements into a new whole) of information in response to a question. But that merely scratches the surface of the analytic process. As we move past this macro level of understanding, we quickly recognize that analysis and the analysts that accomplish it are *the* critical components of the entire intelligence cycle, with duties and responsibilities driving the intelligence enterprise.

This chapter will approach the creation of intelligence, that is, the process of intelligence analysis, not as a single transformation but as a series of transformations, each resulting in unique products (both tangible and intangible). It will begin with a review of the intelligence cycle and present the case that the analytic component is the driving element within it, offering a customer-analyst-centric alternative to the current model. It begins with a brief discussion of the customer component of that relationship, reviewing the wide range of analysis the national security enterprise requires and continues with a discussion of the influence that post-9/11 legislation and policy had on the process. The majority of the chapter will detail the different transformations that define the analytic process and conclude with some thoughts on the future of intelligence analysis and the analytic process.

The intelligence cycle and the analyst

The use of the intelligence cycle as a model of the process of collection, analysis, and dissemination in response to customer requirements can trace its origin to the U.S. military in WWII, with roots likely further back (Wheaton 2011, January 4). It was explicitly discussed as the model of how the post-WWII intelligence community (IC) operated in the 1976 Church Committee Report, although the committee found the model "barely recognizable" when compared to actual operations (Select Committee to Study Governmental Operations with Respect to Intelligence Activities 1976, 17-19). This early description of the cycle begins with consumers first identifying the information they need, resulting in senior intelligence managers translating those needs into requirements, which are used to cue the collection system; the collected information is then turned into finished intelligence by the analysts; the finished product is then provided to the consumer, resulting in additional information needs and beginning the cycle again.

This depiction of the intelligence cycle has undergone slight modifications over the years, with categories being reworded, added, subtracted, or combined to reflect the emphasis of the agency or organization developing it.

However, it has remained generally consistent with the Church Committee's understanding of it (see Figure 1.1). The model currently promulgated by the Office of the Director of National Intelligence (ODNI) contains six steps: planning and direction, collection, processing and exploitation, analysis and production, dissemination, and the added sixth step reflecting a legislated mandate of the ODNI, evaluation (Office of the Director of National Intelligence 2013b, 4) (see figure 1.2).

Figure 1.1. The intelligence cycle

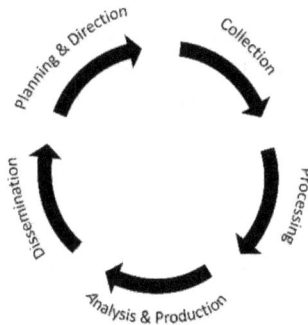

A graphic depiction of the intelligence cycle.

Figure 1.2. The ODNI six step intelligence cycle

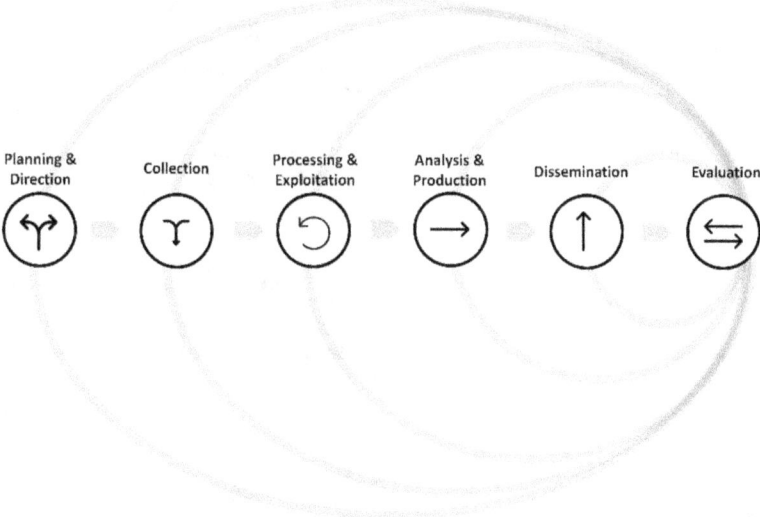

The ODNI intelligence cycle, including the sixth step of evaluation (Office of the Director of National Intelligence 2013, 4).

With only superficial differences in the number and description of elements, current models all feature a linear flow of activity with equal pieces of the cycle pie allotted to all the elements of the intelligence enterprise. As previously noted, however, it is not a completely accurate portrayal of the intelligence process. Criticisms of the cycle range from its roots in a twentieth-century military hierarchal system to its overall inaccurate portrayal of intelligence as a cycle.[1] Despite these critiques, this model of the intelligence cycle has been adopted by the separate agencies of the intelligence community and the ODNI as the basis for conducting intelligence operations.

In this author's experience, a more authentic depiction of the intelligence cycle would show the analyst at the center of a dynamic series of relationships, the primary one between the consumer and the analyst—essentially, the individual who asks the question and the one who answers it. It would more accurately portray the analyst as the element that cues the all-source collection system either through new requirements or evaluations of existing collection in response to any gaps in knowledge needed to answer the question. It also more clearly identifies the role of managers in establishing priorities and providing resources to the collectors and analysts (see Figure 1.3).

Figure 1.3. A reinterpretation of the intelligence cycle

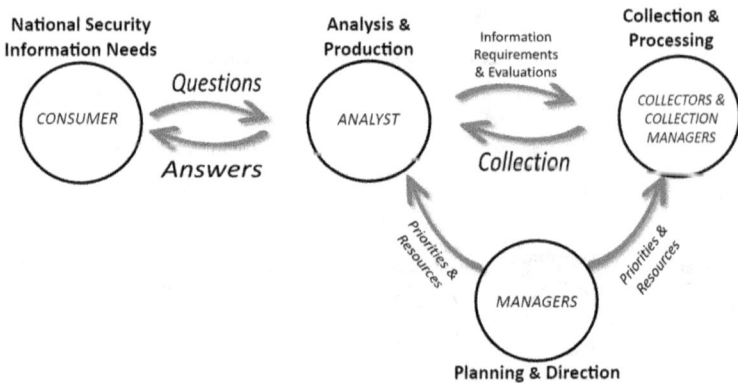

An interpretation of the intelligence cycle portraying the consumer-analyst relationship as the central element of the cycle.

---

[1] For examples of critiques of the intelligence cycle, see Wheaton (2011, May 20); Phythian (2013); Hulnick (2006); and Krohley (2017).

As with any model of a complex series of events, figure 1.3 necessarily simplifies the process and may not be applicable in every situation. However, it does provide a more accurate and humanizing contextual understanding of the intelligence cycle and will provide the framework for further discussion of the analytic process and the role of the analyst.

Types of analysis

As the consumer's requirement is the driving force for all intelligence production, it is necessary to acknowledge the wide range of requirements analysts, collectors, and managers will face. In the 2019 National Intelligence Strategy, the ODNI identified three foundational mission objectives, which it said are the "broadest and most fundamental of the IC's intelligence missions" (Office of the Director of National Intelligence 2019, 7). The three analytic categories of strategic intelligence, anticipatory intelligence, and current operations intelligence highlight that different customers will have different requirements and depths of analysis at different points in the national security process.[2]

The IC provides intelligence support at all levels of the U.S. national security enterprise. If we look at a model of how national security goals are achieved, we can identify corresponding analytic products. At its widest aperture, when policy is determined and supporting strategies are developed, the analysis itself is necessarily broad. The time horizon for an analytic forecast can span several years; assumptions are used to fill in gaps in knowledge, and a range of possible outcomes may be provided with indicators that can be used to narrow the forecast as time progresses and events unfold.

Once a strategy to achieve the policy goal is completed, executive branch agencies and departments begin to develop support plans. The time horizon used by planners is likely to be much less than that of the overall strategy, requiring greater fidelity in the intelligence also. Ideally, at this point, the analyst relies on fewer assumptions, conflicting evidence begins to resolve itself, and the range of possible outcomes narrows as indicators are either observed or not.

---

[2] The *National Intelligence Strategy* (2019) defines strategic intelligence as that meant to "identify and assess the capabilities, activities, and intentions of states and non-state entities to develop a deep understanding of the strategic environment, warn of future developments on issues of enduring interest, and support U.S. national security policy and strategy decisions"; anticipatory intelligence is that meant to "identify and assess new, emerging trends, changing conditions, and underappreciated developments to challenge long-standing assumptions, encourage new perspectives, identify new opportunities, and provide warning of threat to U.S. interests"; and current intelligence as that which "supports planned and ongoing operations."

As the plans are executed, the intelligence needed becomes even more precise and time-sensitive; at this stage, information may become more valuable than the analysis driving the plan. The IC will be expected to provide actionable intelligence or targeting data, which can run the gamut from the time-sensitive location of an individual to specific computer network parameters. As activities progress, analysts will also be expected to provide an assessment of the operation and its effects, regardless of whether the operation was a drone strike on a terrorist compound or economic sanctions against a foreign government.

Figure 1.4 represents this model of the national security decision making and the supporting intelligence information needed. Obviously, there will be times when the most senior policymakers will rely on the IC to provide them with detailed information for warning and to aid in decision-making, and those planning and executing operations will benefit from long-range forecasts or must work with less than precise information. However, figure 1.4 is useful in demonstrating the range and depth of analysis and analytic products that fall under the concepts of the intelligence cycle, analytic requirements, intelligence analysis, and the three foundational mission objectives of the ODNI.

Figure 1.4. Intelligence support to national security decision making

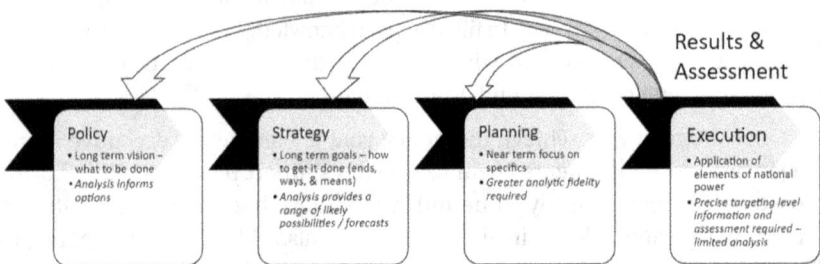

A graphical depiction of the varying intelligence needs at different phases of national security planning and operations.

The influence of legislation and policy on analysis

One direct result of the back-to-back intelligence failures surrounding the 9/11 attacks on the U.S. and the flawed assessment of the status of Iraqi weapons of mass destruction has been legislated community-wide analytic and tradecraft standards. While Congress has had an ongoing interest in the IC since its inception in 1947, its ability to directly influence the analytic element of the intelligence cycle was limited, given the nonphysical, almost idiosyncratic nature of analysis.

Legislative branch oversight and reform efforts were instead focused on the more tangible components of the IC and the intelligence cycle, such as the organizational structure, means of collection, and personnel management (Warner and McDonald, 2005). Within the IC itself, the Director of Central Intelligence (DCI), simultaneously serving as head of the Central Intelligence Agency and titular head of the IC, had limited control over analysis outside of the agency. Community-wide management was exercised through the use of the Director of Central Intelligence Directives (DCID), which focused on high-level policy issues, not the mechanics of individual agency analytic procedures (Federation of American Scientists 2017).

With the passage of the Intelligence Reform and Terrorism Prevention Act of 2004 (IRTPA 2004), two legislatively mandated changes were made to the IC which have directly influenced how analysts work. First was the establishment of a Director of National Intelligence (DNI) as a distinct position separate from that of DCI, with specific responsibilities to "encourage sound analytic methods and tradecraft throughout the elements of the intelligence community" and "to ensure that analysis is based upon all sources available" (Intelligence Reform and Terrorism Prevention Act 2004, 118). Second was the establishment of the analytic and tradecraft standards themselves and the requirement for the DNI to submit an annual review of IC analytic products using those standards as the basis for their evaluation (Intelligence Reform and Terrorism Prevention Act 2004, 118-119). With this mandate to address analysis within the IC, the DNI implemented the IRTPA 2004 using a series of Intelligence Community Directives (ICDs), replacement policy documents to the DCIDs, in combination with a program of sampling finished intelligence products against an established tradecraft rubric.[3]

The two directives with the most immediate impact on the analytic process are ICD 203, *Analytic Standards*, and ICD 206, *Sourcing Requirements for Disseminated Analytic Products*. In addition to reiterating and describing the legislatively mandated analytic and tradecraft standards, ICD 203 also established a common lexicon within the IC for expressing likelihood or probability, improving communication and coordination between analysts in the IC, and reducing the possibility of confusion among consumers. ICD 206, in support of ICD 203, established community-wide standards for sourcing information used as the basis for analytic judgments.

---

[3] Also included in this program was an education and training program for analysts, senior analysts, and managers throughout the IC.

Box 1.1

Analytic and Tradecraft Standards, as established in the Intelligence Reform and Terrorism Prevention Act of 2004 and promulgated in Intelligence Community Directive 203

IC Analytic Standards:

- Objective
- Independent of political considerations
- Timely
- Based on all available sources of information
- Implements and exhibits Analytic Tradecraft Standards

Analytic Tradecraft Standards:

- Properly describes quality and credibility of underlying sources, data, and methodologies
- Properly expresses and explains uncertainties associated with major analytic judgments
- Properly distinguishes between underlying intelligence information and analysts' assumptions and judgments
- Incorporates analysis of alternatives
- Demonstrates customer relevance and addresses implications
- Uses clear and logical argumentation
- Explains changes to or consistency of analytic judgments
- Makes accurate judgments and assessments
- Incorporates effective visual information where appropriate (this tradecraft standard is not in the IRTPA 2004 but was added in a 2015 update to ICD 203)

These mandated community-wide standards and the supporting program of evaluation have established a degree of consistency among analysts. While the analytic and tradecraft standards have not necessarily changed the analytic process itself, they have introduced a more stringent requirement for analysts to be able to "show their work" and document their progress through the transformation process that is intelligence analysis.

The analytic process

Now that we have a better understanding of the role of the analyst in the intelligence cycle, the range of products an analyst can be expected to provide, and the legislative and policy mandates governing analytic production, we can take a more in-depth look at the analytic process itself. As previously described, the process of intelligence analysis is a series of transformations, a change or metamorphosis from one form to another, where the analyst takes their inputs (questions from consumers and information available to them) and provides answers and additional requirements and evaluations to the collectors—all in an environment where management provides resources and establishes priorities.

The first transformation occurs when the analyst (or analytic team) refines the question from the consumer into a more concise and answerable question. The focus of the analytic effort is established at this point. In an all-source analytic environment, questions are likely to be broad and open-ended. Many times, the question itself may be in the form of a standing requirement at the national or agency level. The National Intelligence Priorities Framework, for example, communicates "overarching national intelligence priorities" to ensure "the IC is focusing its collection, analysis, and operational resources" (Office of the Director of National Intelligence 2021, 1). As a result, an analyst must be able to parse the question into more manageable bites or portions or relate how recently obtained information influences the broader question. Exceptions to this transformation, where an analyst would likely have a clear and concise question at the start of the process, would be at the very far right end of the continuum in Figure 1.4, where the policy, strategy, and planning decisions have already been made.

An analyst will be expected to understand the nuances of a consumer's question or a standing requirement and be able to translate it into a specific question or question. For example, a seemingly simple and straightforward national security concern—will China invade Taiwan?—belies a simple yes or no response. For this example, an analyst might first bound the question with a time horizon: say, will China invade Taiwan in the next 12 months? At that point the analyst might begin to consider what is reasonably known to happen in the next 12 months that would be different from the previous 12 months in which China didn't invade Taiwan. What are the political, economic, and demographic factors exerting pressure on the Chinese leadership to act, and will they reach a critical point? What military capability that didn't exist last year is scheduled to be fielded—by any actor in the scenario—that would change the calculus for an invasion? What cultural or historic milestone or anniversary will occur that might require the Chinese Communist Party (CCP) to demonstrate strength and resilience? Each one of those known components of a decision to launch an invasion is substantial enough to warrant an analytic effort and would contribute to an overall IC assessment of whether China will invade Taiwan in the coming year or not.

To be able to refine the question, an analyst must understand their agency's role in the IC and their program of analysis (POA) (McIntosh, Nelson, and Shackelford 2018). A Department of State Bureau of Intelligence and Research analyst might focus on the political aspects of a CCP decision to invade Taiwan, while a Defense Intelligence Agency naval analyst would concentrate on how the fielding of additional amphibious warfare ships impacts the decision. Further, being grounded in their agency's POA allows an analyst to interpret and apply the information they read every day. One intelligence report on China's industrial output can contain information that analysts in different IC agencies working on different elements of the same portfolio would find applicable to standing requirements and their POA.

Having a clear and concise question at the beginning of the process is crucial to the analytic effort. A vague question or one that is too broad in scope will not allow the analyst to focus their research, analysis, and synthesis. Analysts will waste time and energy bouncing around a problem, essentially trying to retroactively frame it with available information. They will let the information they are finding carry them to different aspects of the problem instead of finding and focusing on the information they need to answer the question.

The second transformation occurs as the analyst begins to identify and collect the information available in relation to the question developed in the first transformation. While the intelligence cycle model shows this coming from collectors in the IC, in fact, information can and should come from any available source. This includes prior analytic products on the issue, open source/media reporting, academic research, and publications, conversations with subject matter experts, etc. The advantage IC analysts have over academic and think tank researchers is access to otherwise denied information collected through national resources, but analysts can't consider that as the sole source of information or give it greater credence. As researchers and critical thinkers, analysts need to aggressively collect all information available that is relevant to the question they are answering.

Box 1.2

The skills, talents, and personality traits of a successful analyst have been the subject of discussion and debate and include, but are certainly not limited to, imagination, self-awareness of biases, self-confidence, obsessiveness, tenaciousness, logical, and an understanding of intelligence collection methods (Bruce and George 2008; QRO Global 2020). However, a crucial skill for analysts, especially in this second transformation, is the ability to conduct research. While on the surface this may sound like an obvious prerequisite, underdeveloped and sloppy research skills will cause an analyst to waste time and miss important messages in the tremendous volume of material published daily. The vast majority of databases, whether the highly classified single-source type or public libraries and internet search engines, use Boolean logic as the basis for queries. Referring to our example of the analyst developing an answer to whether China will invade Taiwan in the next 12 months, a message profile built around the operators CHINA <AND> TAIWAN will result in a bottomless message queue. A strong understanding of Boolean logic and the specifics of the database they are accessing (e.g. the use of wild cards and other operators), familiarity with the intelligence disciplines (INTs) and their unique reporting characteristics, available data bases, and a solid understanding of their portfolio and the key words (people, places, things) associated with it are fundamental and the first step in successfully filtering the torrent of data analysts are exposed to.

As the second transformation progresses, the analyst will also begin to have an idea of what information is needed but isn't available to answer the question. At this point, the time available to provide the answer becomes a deciding factor. The intelligence community analyst isn't limited to the information already collected and available; they have the ability, in fact, the responsibility, to cue the collection system on the information gaps. Depending on the agency and echelon in which the analyst is working, they will have access to a collection manager, a subject matter expert on collection system assets and procedures to update requirements or enter new ones, or they can tweak the system themselves by submitting evaluations to existing reporting or contacting producing agencies directly through secure means. Even if the gap the analyst identified is something that can be collected, there will be a time lag between the request, collection, processing, and dissemination of the information that can run the range from days to weeks or months.

In some instances, analysts may have identified gaps in knowledge and may be aware of relevant expertise outside of the IC. ICD 205, *Analytic Outreach*, recognizes the need to occasionally approach outside experts "to explore ideas and alternative perspectives, gain insights, or generate new knowledge" (Office of the Director of National Intelligence 2013a). However, ICD 205 also acknowledges that reaching outside of the IC for this expertise incurs risk. Analysts must coordinate their analytic outreach with management and security personnel with the understanding that the gain of gathering information must be measured against the risk of compromise.

Within this transformation, the analyst must also begin the process of cataloging the information they are finding and will use. During this research phase, the analyst will be flooded with information from multiple sources. Bits and pieces of message traffic, open-source reporting, phone calls, conversations, and prior finished intelligence will all be synthesized later into an answer. However, to aid in critically evaluating the evidence and to be compliant with ICD 206 and ICD 203 (Office of the Director of National Intelligence 2015a, 2015b), analysts must know exactly which sources of information they used to make the judgments they made. They must be able to map their logic and thought processes and source all the information they use, and it is much easier to start that process early than try to recreate it afterward. Further, when working in an all-source environment and synthesizing multiple sources of information into one answer, it is the analyst's responsibility to ensure correct classification and handling markings are carried over to the finished product. How the analyst does this, what this looks like, and what tools are used are a matter of experience, personal preference, and agency policy.

The second transformation only ends when the time available has run out, and the analyst must prepare the final product for the consumer. This is when the analyst has completed their research using all available means and parsed and cataloged the information available to answer the question. Conversely, the analyst also understands what information isn't available and where assumptions will have to be made.

The third transformation occurs as a direct sequel to the second. All the information the analyst identified as relevant to the question is not created equally and must be assessed individually as part of the critical thinking process. The most basic questions, such as when the information was collected, whether the source was witting or not, the source motivation or bias, the access of the source, the reliability of the source, etc., need to be answered for each piece of information used. This scrutiny is crucial to being able to provide an honest assessment of the likelihood and confidence levels of analytic judgments in accordance with ICD 203 and the sourcing requirements of ICD 206.

Additionally, information the analyst receives from different sources can often be contradictory, requiring the analyst to make judgment calls on which source will be given more credence and how to incorporate the conflicting information into their confidence level and any alternative analysis. Analytic biases, as well as collection biases for or against any particular intelligence discipline (e.g., signals intelligence, geospatial intelligence, open-source intelligence, etc.), must also be examined at this point. Suppose the majority of information appears to come from one discipline. Is that because of the adversary's security practices, a lack of collection requirements, or an analyst's bias in the second transformation (whether an intentional or unintentional result of the databases chosen to query)? All must be taken into consideration as part of the critical thinking process.

The need for the analyst to have some sort of personal spreadsheet, catalog, or database of information collected in the second transformation is obvious at this point. In addition to evaluating the information, the analyst must be able to take notes and highlight information for later consideration. Evaluation is an iterative process, and analysts can quickly get overwhelmed with information and ideas.

It is important for the analyst to remember that this is not a quest for the perfect roster of sources that represent all intelligence disciplines, are current, and complement each other's reporting, or to find that one missing piece of high-confidence information. All sources of information have strengths and limitations and contribute to the overall understanding of a situation. This is the time for an honest appraisal of the information analysts have available to form the basis of their judgments so they can accurately assess their confidence in it.

Box 1.3

Source Evaluation Framework

While there are several established source evaluation frameworks adapted from open-source research, such as CRAAP (Currency, Relevance, Authority, Accuracy, Purpose) and Alexander-Tate (Accuracy, Authority, Objectivity, Currency, Coverage, Appearance), the essential evaluation criteria for an analyst revolve around the basic interrogatives:

- Who: Who said it, saw it, collected it ... how reliable are they.

- What: What was collected ... physical evidence, fact, opinion, conjecture.

- When: When was it collected ... not reported or read but first collected.

- Where: Where was it collected ... detention center or cocktail party, personal blog or government document.

- How: What intelligence discipline was used ... witting or unwitting source, strengths and limitations of the collection platform.

- Why: What are the source motivations/biases.

At the completion of this third transformation, the analyst has information that has been organized and evaluated and is ready to be synthesized into an analytic judgment.

The fourth transformation occurs as the analyst takes the evaluated information and begins the process of answering the initial question. If, as we identified earlier, intelligence analysis is the combination of analysis (breaking down) and synthesis (combining), then the first three transformations are the analysis of the question and available information, and the fourth transformation begins the process of synthesizing what is known and assumed into an answer. It is at this point that the analyst is able to provide "the truth, or a closer approximation to the truth than we now enjoy" (Kent 1949, 155).

It is also important to remember that the questions all-source analysts are likely to get are mysteries, not puzzles. Mysteries resist an early arrival at one correct answer given with confidence; they require forecasts of possible outcomes that can be narrowed as time progresses and options are reduced. A meteorologist's "spaghetti map" of hurricane tracks, which get progressively tighter as time passes, is a useful analogy. Puzzles, on the other hand, can be compared to a Sudoku or crossword puzzle where there is one right answer, and the more data collected to fill in the blank spaces, the more confident the analyst can be in the answer.

The focus of this transformation must be directed toward the restated question from the first transformation. It is probably due to human nature, compounded by an analyst's innate curiosity, that many analysts at this point become sidetracked with providing the information they found most interesting or the conclusion that is supported by the best information instead of answering the question that was asked (Neris Analytics n.d.). The second and third transformations are an immersion into information that can cause even the most disciplined analyst to lose track of the initial question as ideas for follow-up assessments and additional collection requirements are identified. It is helpful at this point for the analyst to start any process of synthesis by reminding themselves of the question driving the analytic requirement.

Unless we are on the far right of Figure 1.4 executing tactical operations, analysts are usually providing forecasts, a range of possible outcomes. This range of outcomes can be characterized using qualifiers such as "most likely" to "least likely," "most dangerous" to "least dangerous," etc. The analyst should be able to identify unique indicators that would confirm or deny the discrete outcomes. If unique indicators can't be identified, the analyst may want to rethink the actual differences between the forecasts and the range of options available. Importantly, the analysts shouldn't limit themselves to what they believe the collection system is able to provide at this point, only that indicators leading to the adoption of one forecast over another exist.

If the analyst chooses, this transformation is where structured analytic techniques are likely to be used. Structured analytic techniques (SATs) are not a tool, but a number of different tools designed to assist in developing analytic rigor and working through complex analytic issues (United States Government 2009). It is important to emphasize that SATs will not provide an answer to the analytic question and are not a guarantee that the answer you arrive at is correct. They may help in making analysis and synthesis more transparent and may help in determining an overall confidence level in an assessment. Conversely, very little research on the efficacy of SATs has been done, and the limited research that has been done shows, at best, mixed results and may indicate that SATs are potentially harmful to analysis (Coulthart 2017; Whitesmith 2019). Ultimately, the decision to use an SAT or not is up to the analyst and may depend on such variables as time available, personnel availability, experience level, and the type of question asked.

Regardless of whether an SAT is used or not, the analyst must now draw a conclusion from the totality of information available. This totality includes the mix of things known to be true, things believed to be true to varying degrees based on source evaluation, and things that must be assumed to fill in the gaps of knowledge. Again, returning to our example of a Chinese invasion of Taiwan, we may know the official leadership structure of the CCP, and we may have high confidence in our assessment of how the People's Liberation Army would execute an invasion based on written doctrine and our observation of exercises, but we would likely have to assume the precise arrangement of variables that would have to fall into place for the release of an invasion order.

How the analyst blends this mix of information is an individual process that resists a simple explanation or model. However, once it is developed, the analyst must be able to clearly articulate how the answer was arrived at and provide a clear trail of the evidence used and assumptions made to be compliant with ICD 203.

The fifth and final transformation occurs when the analyst takes the answer arrived at in the previous step and turns it into a product best suited to answer the question asked and to the consumer who requested the product. This can range from a formal, peer-reviewed written assessment to an in-person briefing or any combination of products.

What is important for the analyst to remember is that the most perceptive analysis is useless unless it can be clearly and concisely delivered to the correct decision-maker in a timely manner. The mass of ideas occupying the head of the analyst from the first four transformations, the available evidence and evaluation of its reliability, the assumptions, the conclusions, and associated likelihood and confidence must all come together in a coherent package that meets IC standards.

This transformation is also where any peer review and/or managerial review of the analyst's work would occur. Peer reviews, at a minimum internal to the analyst's agency and ideally externally to analysts of other agencies working the same portfolio, are done to avoid surprises involving information that may have been missed in the second transformation and for the opportunity to familiarize the rest of the community with your findings. Managerial reviews are done to ensure compliance with policies, standards, and the agency's POA and to ensure that analytic conclusions are consistent within the agency—or, if divergent, that it is purposeful and supported with evidence.

Analytic issues identified during a peer review can generally be resolved at the analyst level and can generate stimulating and enlightening conversations. If significant differences between analytic assessments arise and can't be resolved, it may present an opportunity for an alternative analysis segment to be included in the final product. This will likely be managed at the senior analyst or managerial level since a true alternative analysis is not a simple "we don't think you're right" position. It is the presentation of a viable, alternative forecast based on the same evidence, a different synthesis of information in the fourth transformation.

The use of graphics and other presentation tools is often an overlooked element of this transformation. Incorporating effective visual information was included as an analytic tradecraft standard when ICD 206 was updated in 2015; however, many analysts struggling through the first four transformations can neglect the inclusion of graphics until they have completed the written elements of their product, resulting in the graphics being superficial additions, not supporting overall comprehension and retention of the analysis. Graphics can take the form of photographs, infographics, illustrations, tables, charts, or videos. As just one group of researchers attempting to "define and compile existing visualization methods" identified 100 unique visualization techniques grouped into six visualization groups, it can be difficult for an analyst to know which type of graphic to include to enhance their final product (Lengler and Eppler 2007, 1). Ideally, the agency would have a graphics specialist on staff who can work with the analyst from the start to integrate graphics early into the product development for the best effect. When a specialist is not available, the analyst should be comfortable in reaching out early to peers for suggestions and advice on the type of graphics that would best support their analysis.

As the final product is being reviewed, staffed, and edited, the analyst must budget time to update collection requirements. At this point, they will be the most current on what has been collected, what the information gaps are, and what collection disciplines are not being effectively used in their portfolio. Failing to update collection requirements means that assets will continue to collect against targets that are no longer valid, other assets won't be used to their fullest potential, and the indicators needed to refine and update the forecasts won't be collected. While the classic intelligence cycle shows the collection assets being cued in the planning and direction phase, this is clearly an analyst's responsibility and should occur at the completion of an analytic project in addition to its outset.

At the conclusion of this transformation, the analyst will have a complete product as a response to the question driving the analytic effort and an updated requirements deck with the collection manager.

A summary of the analytic process

While the five analytic transformations are sequential, as described, it should be obvious that loops are an inherent part of the process. Consumers will modify their requirements to meet changing conditions, new information will be collected and must be evaluated, assumptions will be refined, and peer reviews will provide new insights into the situation; in short, the totality of information described in Transformation four will be in flux until the final product is released. Loops in the process are expected; however, the sequence of transformations remains fixed.

Figure 1.5. Graphic representation of the five analytic transformations

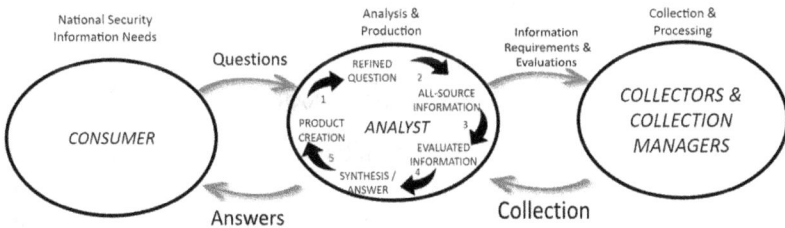

Graphic representation of the five analytic transformations embedded in the Analysis and Production element of the intelligence cycle (the Planning and Direction element is omitted from the intelligence cycle for clarity).

This process—the five transformations described above and depicted in Figure 1.5—is the same, whether for a single analyst or a multidisciplinary, multiagency team of analysts. However, an analytic team, especially one that spans several IC agencies, obviously introduces complexity to the process. In any analytic team, it is crucial that, early on, a standard operating procedure is established, including software to be used, data management, meeting schedules, and a timeline for product development. While no one likes meetings for the sake of meetings, true analytic synergy is only achieved when there is an open exchange of ideas and information. Contact and communication between analysts is key and is the difference between a true team effort bringing forward the best possible analytic product and a cobbled-together collection of products on a similar theme.

An obvious question is how much time the analyst should allot to complete this process. The answer is as much as they have, based on customer requirements. ***These five steps are the analytic process.*** If given a day to complete them, it will take a day; if given a year, it will take a year. The analyst must consider these five steps as part of a backward-planning process when given a new analytic assignment. Begin by establishing the due date for the final product on the calendar and then work backward to incorporate the five transformations.

A note about analytic design. *Analytic design* is a term generally used for an agency-specific approach to capturing this process and likely includes the identification of specific offices or actions—for example, approval chains, planning factors for the use of a graphics department, or specific agencies with which products are to be coordinated. The development and adoption of analytic design by agencies and departments is a positive trend, indicating an effort across the IC to capture and refine the broad analytic process described above. It can be useful in training new analysts and new hires to an agency, as it represents the analytic process brought down from a macro level discussion into a specific work environment. One consideration is that an analytic design developed for one agency may not be readily adaptable to another; the specifics that make an agency's analytic design useful also limit its transferability.

The future of analysis

With the process described above in mind and the role of the analyst in the intelligence cycle, it becomes easier to see where developments are likely to occur that will have an impact on analysis in the future or issues that will need to be addressed.

The volume of information that analysts are expected to read, process, and evaluate has reached the point where no one can any longer honestly say that they've completed their research on an intelligence problem. In 2010, the volume of information in the world created, captured, and consumed was two zettabytes (a zettabyte is one trillion gigabytes); in 2022, it was 97 zettabytes, and it is estimated that by 2025 it will be 181 zettabytes (Statista n.d.). The specter of missing a fragment of information that could make the difference in an assessment, especially when it can be pieced together after the fact, can cause an analyst to be frozen in the second transformation, reach "analysis paralysis," and be unwilling or unable to move forward with the assessment. Tools that are able to filter and manage the information analysts receive without unnecessarily or unintentionally blocking sources are crucial.

Open-source and crowd-sourced information will continue to compete with professional analysts providing reasoned, analytically sound, and defendable assessments. As discussed earlier, following the 9/11 attacks and the commencement of anti-terrorist campaigns worldwide, highly perishable and usually single-source actionable intelligence was prized over the need for analytic forecasts. A generation of consumers conditioned to expect live video feeds and instant commentary may find crowd-sourced intelligence more alluring and, unfortunately, more deserving of their time than assessments created in accordance with ICD standards.

The use of artificial intelligence (AI) in all-source analysis may help in managing the incredible volume of information analysts will be expected to work through as described above. AI should be able to condense large volumes of information identifying trends and summarizing key points, relieving the analyst of having to wade through the traffic themselves. However, the ability of AI to provide reliable, discrete source evaluations as it compiles volumes of data is yet to be determined.

- Project Maven, an effort by the U.S. Special Operations Command to automate the analysis of full-motion video in Iraq, has integrated AI into single-source analysis and reporting since 2017 and has been successfully used in combat operations, the far right-hand side of Figure 1.4 (Shultz and Clarke 2020).

- AI is machine learning, and it has been proven that AI will become biased as it processes information because it learns from the biases inherent in the data. Biases can also be unwittingly introduced in the algorithms of the AI software itself (Mehrabi et al. 2021). This susceptibility makes AI vulnerable to manipulation by an adversary and to deception operations.

An allure of AI is the ability to manage and glean insight from "big data."[4] However, the very creation of these data sets for all-source analysis is

---

[4] Big data is commonly defined as complex data sets containing "the three Vs": variety, volume, and velocity.

problematic in an environment where analysts must scrupulously manage source information (e.g., classification, foreign releasability, U.S. persons' information, declassification dates, etc.) and data spillovers from various silos can result in security violations and disciplinary actions. Legislative and policy changes will be required to address the way the IC manages data if the complete benefits of AI are to be realized. Further, an update to ICD 203 and 206 to reflect the use of AI in managing data and compiling source material is necessary if these requirements are to maintain their relevance in an environment where the use of AI and big data becomes as common as recommended in the 2021 National Security Commission on Artificial Intelligence final report (2021, 10).

Adversary use of AI may have confounding effects on analysts and analysis. On the one hand, it can reduce the time available for analysis and decision-making in a dynamic situation—that is, the ability of an analyst to get into an adversary's decision cycle. On the other hand, if it removes or reduces the human element from adversary decision-making, replicating or manipulating an adversary's information feeds and AI algorithms can result in better insight into their courses of action.

AI has been used to compose simple newsfeeds (e.g., financial reports, sports scores, etc.) since at least 2014. The release to the public in 2022 of ChatGPT and other generative artificial intelligence applications has demonstrated the increasing sophistication of these programs to generate text and images (Peiser 2019). The need for analysts to report information—that is, to simply compile data and produce it in a user-friendly format—will soon be a thing of the past. As tactical operations on the right side of Figure 1.4 become more automated, the information needed to support those operations will also become automated. AI will likely replace analysts at the tactical level, where operations are supported with time-sensitive, often single-source information. Alternatively, an analyst at this level may be required to monitor and tweak the analytic algorithms as analytic biases are identified or an adversary changes the behavior, which was the basis for the algorithmic model.

Optimistically, as long as humans are still making decisions, human analysts will be needed. While AI can identify trends and anomalies and help visualize data, it can't yet identify why those trends and anomalies are occurring; as of the writing of this chapter, reasoning is still a uniquely human attribute.[5] The ability of narrow AI to fill in gaps in collection with reasoned assumptions and

---

[5] Narrow AI is the current state of AI development; it is the use of algorithms to perform tasks mimicking human intelligence. Artificial General Intelligence is the hypothetical next step in AI development. It is the point where the algorithms will be capable of reasoning and planning, not just learning within narrow prescribed parameters.

provide a range of possible outcomes with unique identifiers is still undetermined, and the use of AI in analysis where questions reflect mysteries rather than puzzles and the quality of data is weak or suspect may be particularly risky (Goldfarb and Lindsay 2022).

Conclusion

At the center of the intelligence machine lies the analyst, and he is the
fellow to whom all the information goes so he can review it and, think
about it and determine what it means. –William Colby (DCI 1973-1976)
(Colby 1992)

As the stated mission for the U.S. IC is to provide "timely, rigorous, apolitical, and insightful intelligence and support to inform national security decisions," an understanding of how this intelligence is developed is needed by both practitioner and scholar (Office of the Director of National Intelligence 2023). From a simple reinterpretation of the intelligence cycle, we see how crucial the role of the analyst is in accomplishing this mission, and through a broad review of the type of intelligence the national security enterprise needs, the influence of legislation and policy on analysis, and a detailed examination of the analytic process itself, we can take the steps needed to break discussions of analysis out of the level of the anecdote and into the realm of evidence-based scholarship (Borek 2019).

Concurrently, the IC faces the task of integrating new and emerging technologies into the analytic process, including AI and machine learning. If this task is to be successful, the models used to build these neural networks and the data used to train them must be based on as accurate an understanding of the intelligence cycle and the analytic process as possible. Analysts, collectors and collection managers, and intelligence managers must be included in the development of these models, as they are in the best position to describe what they do and how they do it. Consumers at all echelons of the national security enterprise already have almost unlimited access to single-source information, from unclassified social media feeds to highly classified and caveated message traffic. The value added by analysts is the skilled transformation of that data into intelligence.

References

Borek, J. J. 2017. *Analytic Tradecraft in the U.S. Intelligence Community.* Minneapolis, MN: Walden University.

———. 2019. "Developing a Conceptual Model of Intelligence Analysis." *International Journal of Intelligence and CounterIntelligence,* 805-828.

Bruce, J. B., and R. Z. George. 2008. "Intelligence Analysis: The Emergence of a Discipline." In R. Z. George, *Analyzing Intelligence: Origins, Obstacles and Innovations*, 1-15). Washington, DC: Georgetown University Press.

Colby, W. 1992. "Retooling the Intelligence Industry." *Foreign Service*, 21-25.

Coulthart, S. J. 2017. "An Evidence-Based Evaluation of 12 Core Structured Analytic Techniques." *International Journal of Intelligence and CounterIntelligence* 30 (2): 368-391.

Federation of American Scientists. 2017, January 5. *DCIDs: Director of Central Intelligence Directives*. Retrieved June 11, 2023, from https://irp.fas.org/offdocs/dcid.htm.

Goldfarb, A., and J. R. Lindsay. 2022. "Prediction and Judgment." *International Security* 46 (3): 7-50.

Hulnick, A. S. 2006. "What's Wrong With the Intelligence Cycle." *Intelligence and National Security*, 959-979.

Intelligence Reform and Terrorism Prevention Act. 2004, December 17. Pub. L. 108-458. *Intelligence Reform and Terrorism Prevention Act of 2004*, 118 STAT.3650-3651. Washington, DC: U.S. Government Printing Office.

Kent, S. 1949. *Strategic Intelligence for American World Policy*. Princeton, NJ: Princeton University Press.

Krohley, N. 2017, October 17. *The Intelligence Cycle Is Broken. Here's How to Fix It*. Retrieved September 20, 2023, from https://mwi.westpoint.edu/intelligence-cycle-broken-heres-fix/.

Lengler, R., and M. J. Eppler. 2007. "Towards a Periodic Table of Visualization Methods for Management." *Proceedings of the International Association of Science and Technology for Development Conference on Graphics and Visualization in Engineering*. Clearwater, FL. Retrieved from https://www.visual-literacy.org/periodic_table/periodic_table.pdf.

McIntosh, R., K. Nelson, and C. Shackelford. 2018. "The Army Intelligence Program of Analysis." *Military Intelligence Professional Bulletin*, 25-28.

Mehrabi, N., F. Morstatter, N. Saxena, K. Lerman, and A. Galstyan. 2021. "A Survey on Bias and Fairness in Machine Learning." *ACM Computing Surveys* 54 (6): 1-35.

National Security Commission on Artificial Intelligence. 2021. *Final Report*. Washington, DC: NSCAI. Retrieved from https://www.nscai.gov/wp-content/uploads/2021/03/Full-Report-Digital-1.pdf.

Neris Analytics. N.d. *Roles: Analysts*. Retrieved May 20, 2023, from https://www.16personalities.com/articles/roles-analysts.

Office of the Director of National Intelligence. 2013a. *Analytic Outreach*. Washington, DC: ODNI.

———. 2013b. *US National Intelligence: An Overview*. Washington DC: ODNI.

———. 2015a. *Analytic Standards*. Washington, DC: ODNI.

———. 2015b. *Sourcing Requirements for Disseminated Intelligence Products*. Washington, DC: ODNI.

———. 2019. *National Intelligence Strategy of the United States of America 2019*. Washington, DC: ODNI.

———. 2021. *Roles and Responsibilities for the National Intelligence Priorities Framework*. Washington, DC: ODNI.

————. 2023. *National Intelligence Strategy 2023.* Washington, DC: ODNI.

Peiser, J. 2019, February 7. "The Rise of the Robot Reporter." *New York Times.*

Phythian, M. 2013. *Understanding the Intelligence Cycle.* New York: Routledge.

QRO Global. 2020. *Thoughts on Analysis: The Role of the Analyst in the Intelligence Cycle.* Retrieved September 19, 2023, from https://qro-global.co.uk/the-role-of-the-analyst-in-the-intelligence-cycle/.

Select Committee to Study Governmental Operations with Respect to Intelligence Activities. 1976. *Foreign and Military Intelligence.* Book 1. Washington DC: U.S. Government Printing Office.

Shultz, R. H., and R. D. Clarke. 2020, August 25. *Big Data at War: Special Operations Forces, Project Maven, and Twenty-First Century Warfare.* Retrieved May 30, 2023, from https://mwi.usma.edu/big-data-at-war-speci al-operations-forces-project-maven-and-twenty-first-century-warfare/.

Statista. N.d. *Volume of Data/Information Created, Captured, Copied, and Consumed Worldwide from 2010 to 2020 with Forecasts from 2021 to 2025.* Retrieved May 15, 2023, from https://www.statista.com/statistics/871513/worldwide-data-created/.

United States Government. 2009. *A Tradecraft Primer: Structured Analytic Techniques for Improving Intelligence Analysis.* Washington, DC: CIA.

Warner, M., and K. J. McDonald. 2005. *US Intelligence Community Reform Studies Since 1947.* Washington, DC: Center for the Study of Intelligence.

Wheaton, K., and M. Beerbower. 2006. "Towards a New Definition of Intelligence." *Stanford Law & Policy Review* 17 (3): 319-330.

Wheaton, K. J. 2011, January 4. *RFI: Who Invented the Intelligence Cycle.* Retrieved September 20, 2023, from https://sourcesandmethods.blogspo t.com/2011/01/rfi-who-invented-intelligence-cycle.html.

————. 2011, May 20. *Let's Kill the Intelligence Cycle.* Retrieved September 20, 2023, from https://sourcesandmethods.blogspot.com/2011/05/lets-kill-int elligence-cycle-original.html.

Whitesmith, M. 2019. "The Efficacy of ACH in Mitigating Serial Position Effects and Confirmation Bias in an Intelligence Analysis Scenario." *Intelligence and National Security* 34 (2): 225-242.

Chapter 2

Predicting intelligence alliances

Katharine Cunningham
University of New Hampshire

Andrew Macpherson
University of New Hampshire

Abstract: Katharine Cunningham and Andrew M. Macpherson use a network science approach to predict intelligence alliances. Intelligence sharing is a critical activity that is often studied via qualitative approaches. Their novel quantitative work offers another approach for identifying intelligence alliances.

Keywords: Alliances, network analysis, Ford-Fulkerson Maximum Flow Minimum Cut algorithm, intelligence alliance dynamics

***

Introduction

Examples of alliances between political groups are found throughout history. The Delian League, in the fifth century BCE, was an alliance of various city-states led by Athens (Kagan 2103). More recently, alliances played a central role in both World Wars of the twentieth century. The Cold War between the United States and the Soviet Union resulted in the realignment of World War II's international alliances. In 1953, U.S. Secretary of State John Foster Dulles noted that "America's alliances are at the heart of the maintenance of peace" (Walt 1987, 3). Today, alliances remain a key element of international affairs. In 2021, Secretary of State Anthony Blinken wrote that alliances stand for "a world that's more secure, more peaceful, more just, more equitable, a world with greater health, stronger democracies, and more opportunity for more people" (Blinken 2021). For many countries, alliances are among their most important foreign relations activities.

In the international relations literature, scholars seek to understand why states support each other's foreign policy. Walt (1987, 1) defines an "alliance" as "a formal or informal relationship of security cooperation between two or more states." The alliance relationship entails some form of commitment and an exchange of benefits for the parties involved. A similar definition is proposed by Barnett and Levy (1991, 310). Definitions have been expanded or reduced to facilitate research. For example, Weitsman (2004, 27) describes alliances as "bilateral or multilateral agreements to provide some element of security to the signatories."

Security studies researchers are interested in understanding the relationships among countries' intelligence services. There is no single generally accepted definition for "intelligence." Hastedt and Macpherson (2023) note practitioners and academics propose at least 37 published definitions. For this chapter, we define "national security intelligence" as a secret state activity to understand, influence, or defend against a threat to gain an advantage. Using this definition, we are purposefully excluding the activities of private-sector organizations, such as investment firms' collecting and analyzing information to limit risk for their decision-makers, law enforcement agencies' collecting criminal intelligence to facilitate their investigations or proactively prevent illicit activity, terrorist entities' conducting anti-government "intelligence" to plan their violent actions and other forms of intelligence. We are interested in the government agencies practicing intelligence domestically and internationally and the alliances they form. Previous research has primarily used qualitative case studies to describe relationships. In this paper, we begin to address this lacuna by quantitatively investigating intelligence agency alliances.

The paper proceeds as follows: Our literature review utilizes categories from the international relations literature to place relevant intelligence studies literature on a contextual map. We note that almost all of the intelligence studies in this area of study are qualitative. We describe the network science approach that we employ and our rationale in the theoretical framework section. The methodology section details our operationalization of variables and how we collected and analyzed these data. In the results section, we provide our findings. The meaning of the findings and some ideas for additional lines of research are presented in our discussion section. We conclude that while the approach we took is applicable to bipolar international systems, more robust models may be utilized in future research.

Academic works review

International relations scholars are responsible for many works examining the scope and characteristics of alliances. Duffield (2012, 4) notes that works in this literature may be categorized into those examining alliance formation, alliance dynamics, alliances and state behavior, and alliances and war. These categorical distinctions offer a link between the international relations and intelligence studies literature. The two primary intelligence studies journals are *Intelligence and National Security* and *The International Journal of Intelligence and CounterIntelligence*. Both journals contain a small set of articles on intelligence alliances. From 1986 to 2023, *Intelligence and National Security* published approximately 1,374 articles.[1] Of these, at least 13, or just under 1%, of the total articles primarily concerned intelligence alliances. *The International Journal of Intelligence and CounterIntelligence* published approximately 1,049 articles from 1986 through 2023. We found approximately 2%, at least 18 articles, to be primarily concerned with intelligence alliances.

Alliance formation

In his book *The Origins of Alliance*, Walt (1987) identifies five explanations for international alliances. These are balancing, bandwagoning, ideology, foreign aid, and transnational penetration. *Balancing* is defined as a country allying with other countries against an external threat. *Bandwagoning* is a term used for a country that aligns with an external threat. *Ideological* alliances may form between countries as a result of "states sharing political, cultural, or other traits" (Walt 1987, 33). *Foreign aid* may help create or strengthen alliances. *Transnational penetration*—the manipulation of one country's political system by another country—is the final reason for alliance formation. Walt uses a series of case studies from the Middle East, from 1955 to 1979, to demonstrate that states most often use balancing against threats compared with other reasons. Ideology was important; however, when an imminent or ongoing threat is present, ideological factors may be set aside.

The Five Eyes intelligence network is a frequent subject in intelligence studies literature. This alliance comprises Australia, Canada, New Zealand, the United Kingdom, and the United States (FIORC n.d.). An example of an article on the Five Eyes is Gee and Patman's "Small State or Minor Power? New Zealand's Five Eyes Membership, Intelligence Reforms, and Wellington's Response to China's Growing Pacific Role" (2021). In this article, the authors detail the 1955 agreement to create the Five Eyes alliance and its purpose: to collect information against the common threat of the Soviet Union. The lesser-known Maximator alliance is a partnership among Denmark, France, Germany, Sweden, and the Netherlands (Jacobs 2020). The article "Maximator: European Signals Intelligence Cooperation, from a Dutch Perspective" provides a window into the Danish-initiated partnership focused on signals intelligence. As of 1978, the alliance comprised Denmark, Sweden, Germany, and Holland and was focused

---

[1] To approximate the articles published, we used the R rcrossref package to download information from https://www.crossref.org/ for both journals. We edited the downloaded information to exclude book reviews, letters to the editor, and the like.

on the military threat from the Soviet Union. The alliance remained secret for slightly less than 50 years. Both the Five Eyes and Maximator alliances illustrate a convergence of balancing and ideological reasons for alliance creation. Both broad security cooperation to limit risk and more specific technical intelligence sharing seem to be reasons for states to align their intelligence agencies.

Alliance dynamics

The dynamics of European intelligence cooperation are seen in the works of Cross and Palacios. In her 2013 article "A European Transgovernmental Intelligence Network and the Role of IntCen," Cross argues that a European intelligence agency may be created due to advances in open-source intelligence that would elevate the need for sharing state secrets. Palacios (2020, 483), who worked at IntCen, argues that threats across Europe continue to put pressure on European leaders to develop an "autonomous European intelligence capacity." These papers highlight the dynamics of political (ideological) and economic integration as a vehicle for intelligence alliance.

Another example of alliance dynamics is seen in Ginter's article, "Truth and Mirage: The Cuba-Venezuela Security and Intelligence Alliance" (2013). The purpose of the Cuba-Venezuela alliance seems on the surface to be the desire to share information for internal security; however, the alliance may be an example of transnational penetration: the manipulation of one country's political system by another country. According to the author, Cuban advisors were embedded in Venezuela's military intelligence service at the time, the *Dirección de Inteligencia Militar,* and they may have had direct access to then-President Hugo Chávez, influencing his decisions. These examples seem to indicate that multiple variables in play impact the dynamics of alliances across intelligence agencies.

Alliances and state behavior

Alliances may cause countries to follow the norms and behaviors of their partners. One example may be found in the transparency activity of intelligence agencies. Conrad et al. (2023, 1) define government transparency as the "principle and practice of openness, accountability, and accessibility of government actions, decisions, and information to the public, including the disclosure of information, processes, and decision-making mechanisms by the government to ensure that citizens have access to relevant and reliable information about the government's activities." This study found that the intelligence agency websites of Estonia, Latvia, and Lithuania all offered transparency-related documents following their transformation from Soviet Bloc states to European Union members (Conrad et al., 2023, 8). It seems these states' intelligence agencies are following the behaviors required by their alliance membership.

Another example of behavioral transformation is found in "Intelligence Reform in Europe's Emerging Democracies" (Watts 2001). In this article, Watts discusses cooperation among the former Soviet states and the Russian KGB and the reorientation of these countries toward the West. Many of the countries reformed their intelligence agencies and now have relationships with Western intelligence organizations. Watts notes that while NATO played a role in driving security sector reform through the Partnership for Peace and Membership Action Plans (MAP), no similar organization exists for cooperation across Europe. In both of these examples, the behavior of a country's intelligence agencies is driven by their alliances.

Alliances and war

Scholars also study the impact of alliances on the probability of war and prospects for victory (Duffield 2012, 5). Security is often the primary driver of alliances. While it is not war in a traditional sense, fighting terrorism seems to be a unifying issue across countries with substantive differences in their national governments' political orientations. Rudner's 2004 article "Hunters and Gatherers: The Intelligence Coalition against Islamic Terrorism" details the collaboration of governments of many orientations to defeat a common threat posed by terrorism. The article mentions a number of intelligence alliances, including the UKUSA (United Kingdom and United States), the Shanghai-6 (China, Russia, Kazakhstan, Kyrgyzstan, Tajikistan, and Uzbekistan), NATO, the Kilowatt Group (Belgium, Canada, France, Germany, Ireland, Israel, Italy, Luxembourg, the Netherlands, Norway, South Africa, Switzerland, Sweden, the United Kingdom, and United States), the Egmont Group, the Middle Europe Conference, and the South Asia Center for Counter-Terrorism. Another case study examining the ways that intelligence organizations cooperate to combat terrorism is Guttmann's (2018) "Combatting Terror in Europe: Euro-Israeli Counterterrorism Intelligence Cooperation in the Club de Berne (1971–1972)." The Club de Berne, an informal forum of Western security and intelligence agencies established in 1969, focused on intelligence and terrorist threats. The countries added Israel to the club in 1971. The members all had a vested interest in preventing terrorism on their soil and in protecting their citizens, and the relationship with Israel brought "agents with the required language skills and the capacity to infiltrate terrorist groups," which the Europeans did not possess (Guttmann 2018). In Lefebvre's (2003) "The Difficulties and Dilemmas of International Intelligence Cooperation," the author notes that when countries face a common threat, they may form alliances that transcend traditional alliances. Terrorism is one such threat. The author identifies a balance that must be evaluated: gaining unique capabilities and access via intelligence alliances and "protecting their own sources, methods, and information" (Lefebvre 2003, 537).

Qualitative vs. quantitative literature

The works presented here are a theoretical map of the scholarly activity outlining what we know about intelligence alliances. What is clear is that these works are overwhelmingly qualitative in nature. That is, they involve the investigation of phenomena where the authors describe the unit of analysis and then provide insights, often without numerical results. Qualitative analysis emphasizes context, interactions, and perspectives in order to explore and understand the complexities of social phenomena. It often involves the use of theoretical frameworks and concepts to guide the analysis and interpretation of data.

In 1991, Hastedt argued that the comparative method is essential for gaining a true understanding of political ideas, institutions, and processes. According to Hastedt, studying a subject in isolation from similar phenomena hinders the ability to recognize unique or shared characteristics. In his article "Towards the Comparative Study of Intelligence," Hastedt (1991) pointed out the existing imbalance between case studies on intelligence in the United States and those conducted in the rest of the world. Clearly, the articles we have described in this paper contribute toward the progress of meeting the research goals Hastedt proposed.

Hastedt (1991) proposed a research agenda that encompassed several key elements. These included establishing a clear definition of "intelligence," conducting case studies on counterintelligence and covert action and investigating the factors that drive intelligence activities based on a country's security priorities. Hastedt's objective was to promote a comprehensive and comparative understanding of intelligence across different contexts. He wrote, "The challenge is not to get qualified academics interested in intelligence. It is to find meaningful points of comparison that do not place unrealistic data demands upon researchers." He noted that "rather than treat data limitations due to government-imposed secrecy and conflicting memoir accounts of events as reasons for not engaging in a research effort. They might also be viewed as starting points" (Hastedt 1991, 60). In this paper we attempt to meet Hastedt's challenge and build on the qualitative work already completed by offering a quantitative analysis of intelligence alliances. We use a network science approach and numerical data to predict intelligence alliances between countries.

Theoretical framework

In many sciences, researchers are interested in what information is transmitted from one unit of analysis to another. Neural networks, food webs, and metabolic networks are areas of study for network science researchers (Girvan and Newman 2002). The World Wide Web (WWW) may be represented as a network of computers maintaining billions of web pages and other resources for information sharing (Newman 2010). The structure of the WWW is frequently studied for optimization, security, and scholarship. Similarly, individuals, groups, and organizations may be represented as networks to study information flow (Newman 2010). Across the academy, mathematicians, physicists, and sociologists, among others, have developed statistical methodologies for the empirical study of networks (Girvan and Newman 2002).

What Is a network?

In its simplest form, a network is a collection of points joined by lines. The points are referred to as nodes or vertices by network scientists. The lines connecting the nodes are called edges. As seen in Figure 2.1, a small network may be represented by six nodes and seven edges. A mathematical representation, called an adjacency matrix, of this small network is seen in Figure 2.2. In the adjacency matrix A, the relationship occurring in the i-th row and the j-th column is called the (i, j)-th entry of the matrix A and will represent the defined relationship between the (i,j)-th members. A zero in any i row and the j column signifies there is no relationship between the member nodes. If there is a one in any i row and the j column, then the member nodes do have some type of relationship. The first row in the matrix represents the relationships for node 1. Reading the first row, left to right, we see that in the first column, there is a zero, indicating that node 1 does not have an edge connecting to itself. Reading the first row, left to right, we see that in the second column, there is a one, indicating that node 1 does have an edge connecting it to node 2. The third, fourth, and sixth columns are zeros, indicating that node 1 does not have edges between it and nodes 3, 4, or 6. The fifth column has a one, indicating that node 1 does have an edge between it and node 5. A visual inspection of the small network in Figure 2.1 confirms this representation. Another characteristic of the adjacency matrix is its symmetry. Note that column one (vertically) contains the same data that row one does (horizontally). Also note that there is a diagonal of zeros from the top left to the bottom right of the matrix, signifying that no node can connect with itself. The edges in this matrix all have the same value of one. Additional data can be added to the matrix in the form of weights. A *weight* is the term used to describe edges that may have different values. For example, if the edges were data transmission lines for a computer network, the maximum bandwidth of the pipes could be represented by numbers. Networks with different edge weights are referred to as weighted networks.

Figure 2.1. A small network

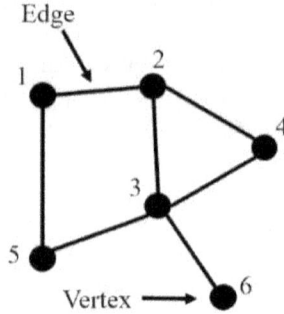

Edge

Vertex ⟶

Figure 2.2. A small network as an adjacency matrix

$$A = \begin{pmatrix} 0 & 1 & 0 & 0 & 1 & 0 \\ 1 & 0 & 1 & 1 & 0 & 0 \\ 0 & 1 & 0 & 1 & 1 & 1 \\ 0 & 1 & 1 & 0 & 0 & 0 \\ 1 & 0 & 1 & 0 & 0 & 0 \\ 0 & 0 & 1 & 0 & 0 & 0 \end{pmatrix}$$

Zachary's karate club

In this paper, we draw upon and are inspired by the sociological method used in the 1977 study by W. W. Zachary titled "An Information Flow Model for Conflict and Fission in Small Groups." Also known as the karate club, this research captured data on interactions between 34 members of a university karate club over three years. The group's members split into two factions following a disagreement between the dojo owner, with the pseudonym Mr. Hi, and the student club leader, with the pseudonym John A, over the price of the lessons.

Zachary hypothesized that the friendship ties in the karate club network might be conceptualized "as channels across which information may flow" (1977, 458). He recorded information on the locations where members met both during and outside of club events. Activities outside the club included individual meetings at karate studios, tournaments, classrooms, or restaurants.

Zachary theorized that these interactions were contexts or additional channels of information flow for sharing information. Further, the political crisis strengthened the friendship bonds between the members in each faction and weakened the bonds between the factions via "the pattern of selective reinforcement" (Zachary 1977, 454). Zachary compiled this data into an adjacency matrix (the existence matrix of club member interactions) and a capacity matrix (the strength of club member interactions based on additional contexts). Using the data in these matrices and a network science flow algorithm, Zachary predicted the faction each member of the club would belong. He compared the predicted outcome with the actual factions the members separated into. Zachary found that this approach predicted the outcome with 97% accuracy (based on a hit/miss rate).

We hypothesize that similar channels exist in the formal alliance relationships between countries. Countries share national security information and related artifacts that allow researchers to observe their interactions over time. As Walt (1987) notes, alliances may form to balance against or bandwagon with a threat for ideological reasons as a result of foreign aid or the transnational penetration of a country's government. We propose using physical activity, which we define as security-based contexts where information exchange may occur, as an indicator of alliances. Physical events may allow us to develop contexts for information sharing that we can operationalize to construct a mathematical matrix and predict the alliance the country belongs to. We can compare the predicted outcome with the real-world intelligence-sharing alliances we know exist from open sources.

Applying a parallel approach and conceptual setup as that accomplished by Zachary, we utilize the Ford-Fulkerson Maximum Flow Minimum Cut algorithm to predict the alignment of 18 countries with either the United States or Russia for intelligence sharing. We develop security-based contexts where information exchange may occur. Real-world intelligence-sharing networks from open sources are utilized to construct an existence and capacity matrix, which we then compare to the predicted network. We hypothesize that we can predict with 95% accuracy the community into which each country will be categorized.

Methodology

Our unit of analysis is country. We selected 18 countries that belong to intelligence alliances with either Russia or the United States. We identified these alliances via open sources. The countries included in the study are Armenia, Australia, Belarus, Canada, France, Germany, Iran, Israel, Japan, Kazakhstan, New Zealand, People's Republic of China, Russia, Saudi Arabia, South Korea, Syria, United Kingdom, and the United States of America. We gathered data from 2015 to 2021.

In accordance with Zachary, we will look to determine the division of these countries into their respective factions. This will be accomplished by focusing on congruent hypotheses: first, the division of the countries will be defined by the minimum cut of the network model. The minimum cut may be thought of as a "bottleneck" of information flow across the network. Second, given the minimum cut, the resulting factions will represent the actual factions the countries split into based on knowledge of open-source intelligence-sharing alliances associated with Russia and the United States (Zachary 1977, 466).

The Ford-Fulkerson Maximum Flow Minimum Cut algorithm

Utilizing a mathematical technique called the max-flow min-cut labeling procedure, a theorem discovered by Ford and Fulkerson in 1962, we can address the two proposed hypotheses (Zachary 1977, 464). The Ford-Fulkerson Maximum Flow Minimum Cut algorithm finds the maximum flow in a network. A flow network is a graph defined mathematically as a matrix whose edges have the capacity for flow, or movement, across the network. "Capacity" is defined as the weighted flow allowance of each edge. The maximum flow is calculated from the source to the sink, or s and t, in network flow theory. In network architecture, "data sources and sinks can help provide directionality to flows. A data source generates a traffic flow, and a data sink terminates a traffic flow" (McCabe 2007, 175). The definition of the source and the sink are set based on how the network should break apart into factions, with the source aligned with one faction and the sink with the other. For our countries, the source and the sink are indicated by Russia and the United States, respectively, and are mathematically represented as the start and end nodes from which information flows and upon which information lands.

A series of steps are used to find the maximum flow of a network. We start with a flow of zero and the given capacity of each edge; we then initiate a process of finding augmenting paths. An augmented path has the capacity for flow. At each iteration, we increase the end-state flow value and update the remaining capacity of each edge. If certain paths reach their maximum flow, the algorithm will continue to find other available paths until no further information can flow from the source to the sink. This process is accomplished using a depth-first search approach. This approach is a recursive search algorithm that visits every node in a forward and backward process to determine the best path across the network. See a generalized example of this setup in Figure 2.3 (Fiset 2018).

Figure 2.3. Max flow network

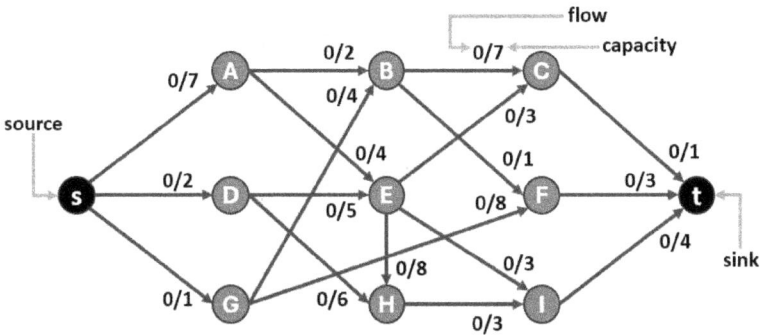

The result of this algorithm is a maximum flow that has passed through the network. Once the maximum flow of the network is established from *s* to *t*, we can cut the network. A cut across a network partitions the graph into two pieces. The minimum cut is used here as the "best" set of edges to disconnect *s* and *t*. The minimum cut is made up of the edges for which the max flow equals the capacity of the cut. This cut is also understood as the set of edges that transport the flow at their max capacity, or the "bottleneck" of the network. The minimum cut will define the partitions—*s*, and everything you can reach from *s* after all the flow has passed through will be on one side of the cut, and everything you can't reach from *s* will land on the other. In this regard, the result of the algorithm run will result in a network division.

Representing countries in matrix form

Our research presents data on interactions between 18 countries (nodes) and their alliance existence (edges). The matrix we constructed represents the existence of at least one security-based information exchange between countries. The matrix has a symmetrical structure, with dimensions of 18 x 18, and each country representing a row and column. The source and the sink nodes were set as the first and last nodes, row/column 1 and 18, respectively.

If we reference this matrix as *F*, we can understand that the relationship occurring in the *i*-th row and the *j*-th column is called the (i, j)-th entry of the matrix *F* and will represent the defined security alliance relationship between the (i,j)-th countries. A zero in any *i* row and the *j* column means there is no relationship between the countries. If there is a one in any *i* row and *j* column, then physical activity exists between the countries. The one signifies physical activity, a security-based context where information exchange may occur, as an indicator of alliance; these may be conceptualized as edges between countries or nodes. The relationships (edges) represented within the matrix are undirected, meaning information can flow both ways across an edge, and therefore, the matrix is also symmetric. An undirected graph is not a necessary setup to perform the Ford-Fulkerson Maximum Flow Minimum Cut algorithm, though it is utilized in our setup to mirror Zachary (1977). The undirected nature implies that we are not so much interested in the direction of physical activity between the countries (e.g., who is providing military exchange to whom), but rather that activity exists. As seen in Figure 2.4, we create this matrix as our "existence matrix."

Figure 2.4. Existence matrix: intelligence alliances

	Russia	Armenia	Australia	Belarus	Canada	France	Germany	Iran	Israel	Japan	Kazakhstan	New Zealand	People's Republic of China	Saudi Arabia	South Korea	Syria	United Kingdom	United States of America
Russia	0	1	0	1	0	1	1	1	0	0	1	0	1	1	0	1	0	0
Armenia	1	0	0	1	0	1	1	0	0	0	1	0	1	0	0	0	0	0
Australia	0	0	0	0	1	1	1	0	1	1	0	1	0	1	1	0	1	1
Belarus	1	1	0	0	0	1	0	0	0	0	1	0	1	0	0	0	0	0
Canada	0	0	1	0	0	1	1	0	1	1	0	1	0	1	1	0	1	1
France	1	1	1	1	1	0	1	0	1	1	1	1	1	1	1	0	1	1
Germany	1	0	1	0	1	1	0	0	1	1	0	1	1	1	1	0	1	1
Iran	1	1	0	0	0	0	0	0	0	0	0	0	1	0	0	1	0	0
Israel	0	0	1	0	1	1	1	0	0	1	0	0	0	0	0	1	1	1
Japan	0	0	1	0	1	1	1	0	1	0	0	1	0	0	1	0	1	1
Kazakhstan	1	1	0	1	1	1	0	0	1	0	0	0	1	1	0	0	1	1
New Zealand	0	0	1	0	1	1	1	0	0	1	0	0	0	0	1	0	1	1
People's Republic of China	1	1	0	1	0	1	1	1	0	0	1	0	0	1	0	0	0	0
Saudi Arabia	1	0	1	0	1	1	1	0	0	0	1	0	1	0	1	0	1	1
South Korea	0	0	1	0	1	1	1	0	1	1	0	1	0	1	0	0	1	1
Syria	1	0	0	0	0	0	0	1	0	0	0	0	0	0	0	0	0	0
United Kingdom	0	0	1	0	1	1	1	0	1	1	1	1	0	1	1	0	0	1
United States of America	0	0	1	0	1	1	1	0	1	1	1	1	0	1	1	0	1	0

Military exchanges, security alliances, arms sales, and military bases

We selected four variables to add detail to our existence matrix, therefore representing additional contexts for the sharing of national security information and related artifacts: military exchanges, security alliances, arms sales, and military bases. The military exchange variable formed the structure of our network and the initial existence matrix referenced in Figure 2.4, equivalent to the friendship structure of the karate club that formed Zachary's existence matrix. We defined "military exchanges" as formal exchanges of military personnel between countries for training and exercises.

Data was collected on military exchanges via open sources, including books, media articles, press releases, and videos. As seen in Figure 2.4, a zero in any i row and the j column means there are no military exchanges between the countries. If there is a one in any i row and the j column, then the members conduct military exchanges. As noted in the discussion section, a categorical or numeric variable could provide additional options to researchers.

We added detail to our existence matrix by adding other interactions between the countries. Interactions included security alliances, arms sales, and military bases. These interactions are seen as context or additional channels of information flow. The "security alliances" variable is defined as "formal alliance[s] between at least two states that fall into the classes of defense pact, neutrality or non-aggression treaty, or entente agreement" (Gibler 2009). We used the Correlates of War Formal Alliances data set (v4.1), which details "formal alliances among states between 1816 and 2012, including mutual defense pacts, non-aggression treaties, and ententes" (Gibler 2009). The arms sales variable data is compiled from the Stockholm International Peace Research Institute (SIPRI) Arms Industry Database (2001). "Arms sales" are defined as sales of military goods and services to military customers, including both sales for domestic procurement and sales for export. Buyer and seller data from 2015 to 2021 was used. We define the "military base variable" as a country operating at least one military base in a foreign country. As seen in Figure 2.5, we increased the values in any i row and the j column based on the number of additional contexts between countries. These additional context layers add weight or scale to each of the edges of the network.

Figure 2.5. Capacity matrix: intelligence alliances

	Russia	Armenia	Australia	Belarus	Canada	France	Germany	Iran	Israel	Japan	Kazakhstan	New Zealand	People's Republic of China	Saudi Arabia	South Korea	Syria	United Kingdom	United States of America
Russia	0	4	0	4	0	1	3	2	0	0	3	0	3	2	0	3	0	0
Armenia	4	0	0	2	0	1	0	1	0	0	2	0	1	0	0	0	0	0
Australia	0	0	0	0	2	2	2	0	2	2	0	2	0	1	2	0	3	4
Belarus	4	2	0	0	0	1	0	0	0	0	2	0	2	0	0	0	0	0
Canada	0	0	2	0	0	3	4	0	2	1	0	2	0	2	1	0	4	3
France	1	1	2	1	3	0	4	0	4	2	2	2	2	2	2	0	3	3
Germany	3	0	2	0	4	4	0	0	2	2	2	2	2	2	2	0	4	4
Iran	2	1	0	0	0	0	0	0	0	0	0	0	3	0	0	4	0	0
Israel	0	0	2	0	2	1	2	0	0	1	2	0	0	0	2	0	2	3
Japan	0	0	2	0	1	2	2	0	1	0	0	1	0	0	1	0	2	4
Kazakhstan	3	2	0	2	0	2	2	0	2	0	0	0	3	1	0	0	1	2
New Zealand	0	0	2	0	2	1	2	0	0	1	0	0	0	0	2	0	2	2
People's Republic of China	3	1	0	2	0	2	2	3	0	0	3	0	0	2	0	0	0	0
Saudi Arabia	2	0	1	0	2	2	2	0	0	0	1	0	2	0	2	0	2	3
South Korea	0	0	2	0	1	2	2	0	2	1	0	2	0	2	0	0	2	4
Syria	3	0	0	0	0	0	0	4	0	0	0	0	0	0	0	0	0	0
United Kingdom	0	0	3	0	4	3	4	0	2	2	1	2	0	2	2	0	0	4
United States of America	0	0	4	0	3	3	4	0	3	4	2	2	0	3	4	0	4	0

This capacity matrix represents our "capacitated network," a network that has the capacity for information flow. The capacity matrix depicts all 18 countries (as nodes) and their security contexts (as weighted edges). As in the existence matrix, the matrix structure remains the same, with dimensions of 18 x 18 and an undirected and symmetrical construction. For illustrative purposes, the source and the sink nodes were set as the first and last nodes. Russia is row/column 1, and the United States is row/column 18.

The Ford-Fulkerson Maximum Flow Minimum Cut algorithm was used to calculate the maximum flow that passed through the capacitated network. The output of the code produced an *s* and *t* cut as well as the maximum flow of the network. The max flow was used to cut the network. The minimum cut defined the two partitions we used to compare with the known intelligence-sharing network based on research from open sources. The predicted intelligence alliances are visualized as a network diagram in Figure 2.6.

Figure 2.6. Predicted intelligence networks

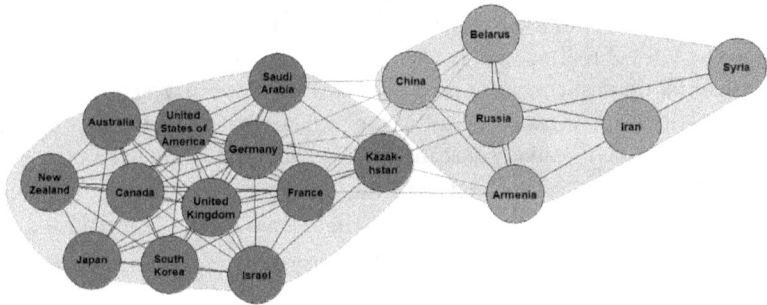

To measure the success of our predicted community membership, we created a similar hit/miss rate prediction summary to compare the actual alliance membership, determined from our real-world intelligence-sharing networks derived from open sources, to our predicted alliance membership, determined from our algorithm run on our capacitated network. We utilized a confusion matrix, a performance-measuring summarization matrix, to visualize the accuracy of our two-dimensional community predictions.

In coding our algorithm and producing our network graph results, we used R version 4.2.2 for our algorithm run and network visualization with packages graph (1.4.2), graph data (1.0.1), dplyr (1.1.2), clustAnalytics (0.5.2), knitr (1.42), and Python version 3.7.1 for our data manipulation, matrix build, and additional network visualizations with numpy (1.21.5), pandas (1.3.5), networkx (2.6.3), matplotlib (3.5.2), seaborn (0.12.1), and sklearn (1.0.2).

Findings

Figure 2.6 is a network diagram of the predicted intelligence-sharing alliances. The cut resulting from the Ford-Fulkerson Maximum Flow Minimum Cut algorithm created two communities, the first consisting of the United States of America and 11 other countries: Australia, Canada, France, Germany, Israel, Japan, Kazakhstan, New Zealand, Saudi Arabia, South Korea, and the United

Kingdom. There are 112 edges connecting the 12 nodes (countries) in this community. The node with the greatest overall degree and the greatest number of connected edges is France, with 15. The average degree, which is a connectivity metric that can signify the strength of the social ties within the network, is calculated as 9.33 for this community allied with the United States. Russia and 5 countries—Armenia, Belarus, China, Iran, and Syria—form the second community. There are 22 edges connecting the 6 nodes (countries) in this community. The node with the greatest overall degree is Russia, with 9. The average degree of this community is less connected than the United States community, with an average measurement of 3.67. Twelve edges don't fall completely inside either of the two communities and instead connect the two communities; these are represented in Figure 2.6.

Figure 2.7 is a network diagram of the real-world intelligence-sharing alliances. The first community consists of the United States of America and 10 other countries: Australia, Canada, France, Germany, Israel, Japan, New Zealand, Saudi Arabia, South Korea, and the United Kingdom. There are 100 edges connecting countries in this community. The node with the greatest overall degree is the United States of America, with 11. The second community consists of Russia and 6 countries: Armenia, Belarus, China, Iran, Kazakhstan, and Syria. There are 22 edges connecting the countries in this community. The node with the greatest overall degree is Russia, with 8. There are four edges connecting the two communities; these are illustrated in Figure 2.7. The average degree of the United States–allied community is 9.09 compared to the average degree of the Russia-allied network, which is 3.04.

Figure 2.7. Real-world intelligence networks

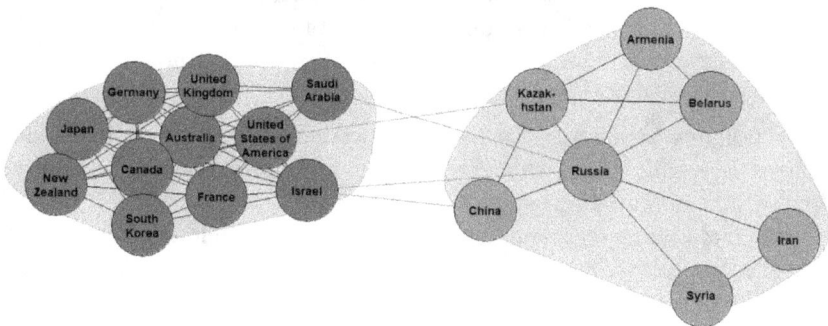

In order to determine the accuracy of our model, we compared our predicted results to the real-world intelligence-sharing network. We used a confusion matrix as a prediction summary representation of the hit/miss rate to illustrate model accuracy with a focus on the positive membership predictions. The

Ford-Fulkerson Maximum Flow Minimum Cut algorithm approach allowed us to predict the real-world network with a hit/miss rate of 94%. We predicted 17 of the 18 relationships accurately. In the real-world network, Kazakhstan is grouped with Russia, while in the predicted network, it is aligned with the United States. The results are shown in Figure 2.8.

Figure 2.8. Hit/miss rate predicted vs. real-world intelligence networks

Community Predictions 17 Hits, 1 Miss 94% Hit, 6% Miss		Predicted	
		Russia	United States
Actual	Russia	6	1
	United States	0	11

Discussion

Our model predicted the real-world relationship with 94% accuracy. While we did not achieve our accuracy objective (95%), we believe our research adds to our understanding of intelligence alliances. Walt (1987) noted that balancing is the most frequent form of alliance. Our predicted network with the United States as the key node displays the balancing countries undertook during the Cold War.

Intelligence alignment and ideology

Walt (1987) wrote that there is only a moderate association between ideology and alignment. As we noted in the Alliances and War section of the literature review, terrorism is a security threat that seems to facilitate interstate cooperation of countries with different forms of government. Counter to the terrorism example, both the predicted and real-world networks appear to be ideologically aligned in our study.

To test this hypothesis, we used the Economist Intelligence Unit (EIU) Democracy Index score, which provides a numerical measure of a country's polity from authoritarian regime to full democracy (Economist 2019). The EIU Democracy Index scores range from 0 to 10. More authoritarian countries have lower scores (China: 2.26), and more democratic countries have higher scores (New Zealand: 9.26). As seen in Figure 2.9, the countries aligned with the United States, excluding Saudi Arabia, have an average score of 8.47. The countries aligned with Russia have an average score of 2.88. When we examined these countries, it appears that ideology is highly correlated with alignments with the United States or Russia during the Cold War.

Figure 2.9. Economist intelligence unit 2019 democracy index scores

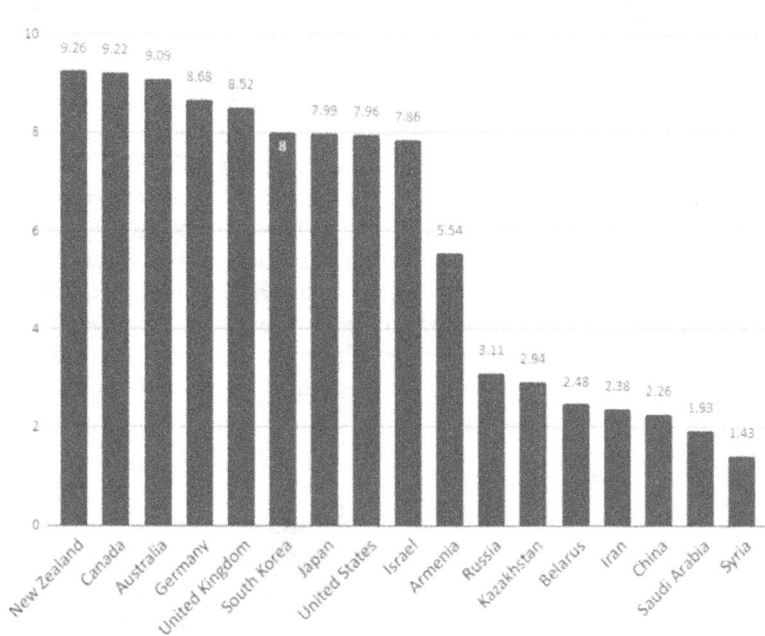

Intelligence alliance dynamics

The issue of alliance dynamics may also play a role in intelligence alliances. The countries aligned with Russia have significant military ties with Russia and, in some cases, are in existential relationships. We believe this may be a form of transnational penetration. The Bashar regime in Syria, in all likelihood, owes its existence to Russia's intervention in its civil war. Belarus serves as a vassal state to Russia. Russian troops trained and staged in Belarus and attacked Ukraine from its military bases in February 2022. Russia's transnational penetration of these states likely plays a key role in their intelligence alliances.

Value of network prediction

As we noted in the theoretical framework, mathematicians, physicists, and sociologists, among others, use statistical methodologies to empirically investigate networks. Our work demonstrates that networks existing in the real world may be mathematically represented as an adjacency matrix with or without additional capacity context. Researchers may apply network science approaches to detect community structure in alliances. The ability to detect community structures in networks has practical applications. Identifying the variables and approaches that can be used to predict intelligence networks may give researchers new insights. For example, adding countries to our model could provide preliminary evidence of intelligence alliances that are not confirmed via open sources. Open-source data on intelligence sharing may not allow us to build the real-world adjacency matrix to which we could compare a future predictive model.

There are two limitations to our study. The first limitation is the scope of the states in the study. We were interested in expanding our network beyond the 18 countries; however, the time and resources required to acquire these data were prohibitive. A second limitation is the structure of the predictive model. We chose the Ford-Fulkerson Maximum Flow Minimum Cut algorithm for its simplicity and relatively straightforward application to our research. The current approach is a bipolar model with one source and one sink. Network science literature contains some research on flow networks defining multiple sources and sinks. Perhaps a multiple source and sink model would yield interesting sub-alliances. Further, researchers may choose to use weighting to add detail to the relationships in the model.

Community detection approaches

A single source and sink approach is likely insufficient for more complex intelligence-alliance analysis. For example, students of intelligence studies are surely interested in the three key players in international relations: China, Russia, and the United States. Further, how should an alliance such as the European Union be accounted for in the model? Girvan and Newman (2002) propose using centrality indices to find community boundaries. They found their approach detects community structures with high sensitivity and reliability. The use of more advanced network detection approaches may allow us to add other variables to the networks. Alternatively, future research could make this more of an unsupervised machine-learning exercise. If the goal is to partition networks rather than predict community membership, then we can use other clustering methods such as k-means, spectral, agglomerative, or affinity clustering (Kuofos and Martin, n.d.).

Conclusion

The common element in all intelligence alliances is the sharing of information. In many sciences, researchers are interested in what information is transmitted from one unit of analysis to another. We found that for a bipolar network, a labeling procedure accomplished with the Ford-Fulkerson Maximum Flow Minimum Cut algorithm could be used to predict national security intelligence alliances. The capacitated model we constructed provides a novel quantitative approach to understanding and predicting intelligence alliances. Future research could employ other network science approaches to explore the structure and nature of intelligence-sharing networks.

Bibliography

Barnett, M., and J. Levy. 1991. "Domestic Sources of Alliances and Alignments." *International Organization* 45 (3): 369-395.

Blinken, Anthony. 2021. "Reaffirming and Reimagining America's Alliances." Speech to NATO. US Department of State. https://www.state.gov/reaf firming-and-reimagining-americas-alliances/.

Conrad, N., P. Embury, T. Gaumont, E. Hunt, A. Macpherson, T. Nydam, and A. Villela. 2023. "An Examination of Post-Soviet Intelligence Agencies and Public Transparency." Accepted for publication in *American Intelligence Journal*.

Cross, Mai'a K. Davis. 2013. "A European Transgovernmental Intelligence Network and the Role of IntCen." *Perspectives on European Politics and Society* 14 (3): 388-402. https://doi.org/10.1080/15705854.2013.817805.

Duffield, John S. "Alliances." 2012. *Political Science Faculty Publications* 28. https://scholarworks.gsu.edu/political_science_facpub/28.

Economist Intelligence Unit. 2019. Democracy Index 2019. https://www.eiu. com/topic/democracy-index/.

FIORC (Five Eyes Intelligence Oversight and Review Council). N.d. Office of the Director of National Intelligence. Accessed May 31, 2023. https://www. dni.gov/index.php/ncsc-how-we-work/217-about/organization/icig-pages/ 2660-icig-fiorc.

Fiset, William. 2018, August 29. *Max Flow Ford Fulkerson*. YouTube video, 13:24. https://www.youtube.com/watch?v=LdOnanfc5TM.

Gee, Austin, and Robert G. Patman. 2021. "Small State or Minor Power? New Zealand's Five Eyes Membership, Intelligence Reforms, and Wellington's Response to China's Growing Pacific Role." *Intelligence and National Security* 36 (1): 34-50. DOI: 10.1080/02684527.2020.1812876.

Gibler, Douglas M. 2009. *International Military Alliances, 1648–2008*. Washington, DC: CQ Press. Accessed May 31, 2023. https://correlatesofwar. org/data-sets/formal-alliances/#:~:text=Overview,aggression%20treaty%2C %20or%20entente%20agreement.

Ginter, Kevin. 2013. "Truth and Mirage: The Cuba-Venezuela Security and Intelligence Alliance." *International Journal of Intelligence and Counter Intelligence* 26 (2): 215-240. DOI: 10.1080/08850607.2013.758003.

Girvan, M., and M. E. J. Newman. 2002. "Community Structure in Social and Biological Networks." *Proceedings of the National Academy of Sciences* 99 (12): 7821-7826. https://doi.org/10.1073/pnas.122653799.

Guttmann, Aviva. 2018. "Combatting Terror in Europe: Euro-Israeli Counterterrorism Intelligence Cooperation in the *Club de Berne* (1971–1972)." *Intelligence and National Security* 33 (2): 158-175. DOI: 10.1080/026 84527.2017.1324591.

Hastedt, Glenn P. 1991. "Towards the Comparative Study of Intelligence." *Journal of Conflict Studies* 11 (3). https://journals.lib.unb.ca/index.php/JCS /article/view/14966.

Hastedt, Glenn P., and Andrew Macpherson. 2023. "Defining Intelligence: Advancing the Conversation." Studies in Intelligence 67(3): 7-14. https://ww w.cia.gov/resources/csi/studies-in-intelligence/studies-in-intelligence-67-n

o-3-extracts-september-2023/what-is-intelligence-a-new-quantitative-appr
oach-to-an-old-question/

"Igraph R Manual Pages." N.d. R Documentation. Igraph.org. Accessed May 30, 2023. https://igraph.org/r/doc/cluster_edge_betweenness.html.

Jacobs, Bart. 2020. "Maximator: European Signals Intelligence Cooperation, from a Dutch Perspective." *Intelligence and National Security* 35 (5): 659-668. 10.1080/02684527.2020.1743538.

Kagan, D. 2013. *The Outbreak of the Peloponnesian War.* Ithaca, NY: Cornell University Press. https://doi.org/10.7591/9780801467219

Koufos, Nikos, and Brendan Martin. N.d. "Review of K-Means and Other Clustering Algorithms: A Quick Intro with Python." *Learn Data Science.* Accessed May 31, 2023. https://www.learndatasci.com/tutorials/k-means-clustering-algorithms-python-intro/.

Lefebvre, Stéphane. 2003. "The Difficulties and Dilemmas of International Intelligence Cooperation." *International Journal of Intelligence and Counter Intelligence* 16 (4): 527-542. DOI: 10.1080/716100467.

McCabe, James D. 2007. *Network Analysis, Architecture, and Design.* 3rd ed. Burlington, MA: Morgan Kaufmann / Elsevier.

Newman, Mark E. J. 2010. *Networks: An Introduction.* Oxford, UK: Oxford University Press.

Palacios, José-Miguel. 2020. "On the Road to a European Intelligence Agency?" *International Journal of Intelligence and CounterIntelligence* 33 (3): 483-491. DOI: 10.1080/08850607.2020.1754670.

Rudner, Martin. 2004. "Hunters and Gatherers: The Intelligence Coalition against Islamic Terrorism." *International Journal of Intelligence and CounterIntelligence* 17 (2): 193-230. DOI: 10.1080/08850600490274890.

Stockholm International Peace Research Institute. Stockholm International Peace Research Institute SIPRI. United States, 2001. Web Archive. https://www.loc.gov/item/lcwaN0011225/.

Walt, Stephen M. 1987. *The Origins of Alliance.* Ithaca, NY: Cornell University Press. http://www.jstor.org/stable/10.7591/j.ctt32b5fc.

Watts, Larry L. 2001. "Intelligence Reform in Europe's Emerging Democracies." *Studies in Intelligence* 48 (1). https://www.cia.gov/static/6a5dba328a4abc38b f12d8b3c02d406c/Intel-Reform-Europes-Democracies.pdf.

Weitsman, Patricia A. *Dangerous Alliances: Proponents of Peace, Weapons of War.* Stanford: Stanford University Press, 2004.

Zachary, Wayne W. 1977. "An Information Flow Model for Conflict and Fission in Small Groups." *Journal of Anthropological Research* 33 (4): 452-473. https://doi.org/10.1086/jar.33.4.3629752.

Chapter 3

Demystifying private-sector security intelligence teams: Unlocking their value in strategic decision-making

Angela Miller Lewis

Georgetown University

Abstract: Angela Miller Lewis observes that strategic security intelligence teams have become an important part of the private- sector response to operating in today's volatile geopolitical and security environment, but they have received little attention in current intelligence studies literature. This chapter provides insight into their purpose, unique capabilities, the challenges they face, and their contributions to private- sector decision-making and risk management.

Keywords: Competitive advantages, decision theory, risk management, strategic security intelligence teams

***

Introduction

Strategic security intelligence teams have emerged in the private sector as a response to an increasingly dynamic geopolitical and security environment in order to enhance strategic decision-making. In today's rapidly changing world, these teams play a critical role in helping organizations navigate complex global landscapes as they face multifaceted challenges that include concerns related to political stability, regulatory changes, trade policies, security threats, health and safety trends, and regional conflicts. This rapidly changing world, exemplified by the COVID-19 pandemic, has been referred to as a VUCA environment:

> VUCA (Volatility, Uncertainty, Complexity, Ambiguity) has been in the business vocabulary for over 30 years, and yet we've seldom been confronted with the degree of uncertainty we're now facing with the COVID-19 pandemic. Where next? How bad? How long? Who can we rely

on for the latest and most reliable information? How will our organization—our employees, customers, partners, supply chain—be impacted? How should we respond? ... The threat is evolving, and leaders are recognizing that they will have to respond and make adjustments in real-time. (Foster 2020, paras 1-2)

This is equally true of other types of threats, as well. Geopolitical and security threats such as crime, terrorism, and economic and political instability all pose significant risks to global businesses and require business leaders to choose their sources of information wisely, remain flexible, make effective decisions, and communicate clearly amidst uncertainty (Hackman and Johnson 2013). The COVID-19 pandemic exacerbated this uncertainty and highlighted the need for accurate, reliable, and timely information to mitigate uncertainty so that business decision-makers can operate effectively in this complex environment.

To navigate this challenging landscape, private-sector organizations are increasingly establishing and leveraging strategic security intelligence teams. These teams leverage their expertise in geopolitical analysis, risk assessment, and strategic forecasting to provide valuable insights and recommendations to decision-makers. However, because these teams often operate behind the scenes, there are myriad misconceptions regarding how they operate, given the mysterious cloak-and-dagger ethos associated with their public-sector counterparts. Moreover, for the most part, these teams exist within organizational security elements and thus focus the majority of their work on security implications associated with these developments, though their utility and insights can—and often do—extend beyond a corporate security function. This chapter, which is expanded from, and based in part, on a doctoral dissertation entitled "Thriving in a VUCA World: A Case Study Exploring Geopolitically-Focused Intelligence Teams in the Private Sector Through a Systems Theory Lens" (Lewis 2022), aims to demystify private-sector security intelligence teams, shedding light on their purpose, functions, methodologies, and value. It explores the unique capabilities of these teams, the challenges they face, and their contributions to strategic decision-making and risk management in the private sector.

What are the functions of strategic private-sector security intelligence teams?

Geopolitical dynamics have a significant impact on business operations and strategies. To address this, private-sector organizations rely on specialized intelligence teams with a focus on geopolitical and security analysis. However, the roles and functions of these teams are often misunderstood. Strategic security intelligence teams within the private sector are specialized units composed of professionals with expertise in geopolitical analysis and security risk assessment. They are responsible for collecting, analyzing, and interpreting information related to geopolitical, economic, social, and security factors that shape global landscapes and impact global business operations. These teams provide timely and accurate intelligence to support strategic decision-making processes and provide valuable insights to organizations, enabling them to make informed decisions, mitigate risks, and seize opportunities. These teams monitor and analyze geopolitical events and security incidents, assess their implications relative to a specific organization, and some also provide actionable recommendations. Their functions include geopolitical risk assessment; country, regional, economic, and security analysis; and scenario planning. The overall aim of these functions is to effectively contribute to strategic decision-making, risk management, and operational planning within organizations, which some teams do to greater effect than others.

These intelligence teams employ a range of methodologies and tools to analyze a variety of security-related dynamics. These include data collection from diverse sources, open-source intelligence analysis, in-depth research, trend analysis, geopolitical mapping, and scenario modeling. They leverage technology, data analytics, and visualization tools to process and interpret information efficiently. These methodologies and tools enable the teams to generate actionable insights and strategic foresight.

Strategic intelligence teams possess a unique focus that differentiates them from other intelligence functions. They combine geopolitical expertise, regional knowledge, security awareness, and business acumen to provide tailored insights to organizations. These teams have an understanding of political and cultural nuances, geopolitical risks, emerging trends, social and economic shifts, and the interconnectedness of global systems. They are adept at translating complex geopolitical dynamics into practical implications for business strategies.

Strategic security intelligence teams contribute to strategic decision-making by providing a comprehensive understanding of the external environment. They help organizations identify and assess geopolitical risks, anticipate potential disruptions, and identify emerging opportunities. Their insights can inform market entry strategies, investment decisions, and supply chain management, as well as geopolitical and security risk mitigation measures. By incorporating geopolitical and security intelligence into decision-making processes, organizations enhance their competitiveness and resilience and are better able to seize opportunities that may present themselves in an ever-changing environment.

Strategic security intelligence teams also play a crucial role in risk management within private-sector organizations. They help identify and assess geopolitical risks that may impact business operations, supply chains, investments, or reputations. These teams provide early warnings, develop risk mitigation strategies, and support crisis management efforts. By proactively managing geopolitical risks, organizations can protect their interests and navigate complex environments more effectively.

Despite the clear advantages of leveraging intelligence provided by these teams for strategic business decision-making, these intelligence teams face various challenges in their work. These include the complexity of geopolitical dynamics, the rapid pace of change, information overload, access to reliable sources, and balancing strategic foresight with operational requirements. Additionally, teams may encounter challenges in effectively communicating their insights to decision-makers and ensuring the integration of geopolitical intelligence into organizational processes. Successful private-sector strategic security intelligence teams collaborate closely with other functions within organizations. They work with business units, risk management, external communications, operations, legal, compliance, and executive leadership to ensure that geopolitical analysis is integrated into strategic planning and decision-making. This collaboration facilitates a holistic understanding of risks and opportunities, fosters alignment, and enhances the utilization of intelligence insights.

These intelligence teams bring significant value to private-sector organizations. They enable proactive risk management, enhance strategic decision-making, support market entry and expansion strategies, identify emerging trends and opportunities, and safeguard organizational reputation. By leveraging geopolitical and security intelligence, organizations can gain a competitive edge, anticipate changes, and navigate global uncertainties more effectively.

These intelligence teams are valuable assets for organizations operating in a globalized world. By demystifying their role and functions, their contribution to strategic decision-making, risk management, and organizational resilience is more easily recognized. Understanding the capabilities and value proposition of these teams allows organizations to leverage geopolitical intelligence effectively and thrive in a rapidly changing global landscape.

What is strategic private-sector security intelligence?

Strategic security intelligence, as leveraged by multinational organizations in the private sector, is not a new field, but just as the rapid pace of globalization has required companies to work across geographic and cultural boundaries, adding complexity to the relationships between organizational and business sectors, it has also created growth opportunities in multiple business sectors.[1] This challenging environment has required multinational enterprises to be increasingly flexible, moving away from a myopic focus on classic cost minimization/profit maximization traditions and implementing a broader focus that includes capability development and opportunity identification, particularly in regions where understanding fast-moving geopolitical developments is paramount. For businesses to achieve continued success in uncertain times and a fast-paced and competitive environment, they need to stay ahead of geostrategic developments—one aspect of this is using intelligence to inform key business decisions.

In light of the growing complexity within the global business environment, business leaders are increasingly leveraging these strategic intelligence teams to capitalize on their deep content expertise and advisory capabilities to guide business decision-making. Effectively leveraging these intelligence teams allows organizations to be responsive and agile in addressing new problems as they arise, as well as identifying and capitalizing on emerging opportunities. However, although intelligence has been used within the private sector in some capacity for centuries, the field's development has been non-linear, and it remains in the nascent stages of professionalization. As such, there is limited understanding of how these teams operate and how they can most effectively support differing and evolving decision-maker needs within a single organization.

Many in the intelligence field have long perceived intelligence as falling primarily within the domain of a country's government. For example, Michael Warner argued that intelligence requires secrecy and falls solely in the domain of nation-state actors (Warner 2002), though he later acknowledged that the state "monopoly" of intelligence had ended by the 2010s (Warner 2014). Mark Lowenthal (2017, 10) defined intelligence as "the process by which specific types of information important to national security are requested, collected, analyzed, and provided to policymakers; the products of that process; the safeguarding of these processes and this information by counterintelligence

---

[1] A key distinction here is the term *strategic*. Many organizations have operational security elements that operate in a tactical capacity, as well, and these organizations may leverage intelligence in tactical decision-making. For the purposes of this chapter, the terms *strategic* and *tactical* are used in the context of planning, decision-making, and the execution of business priorities, with *strategic* referring to longer-term goals, objectives, and implications as identified by high-level executives and leaders, and *tactical* looking at shorter-term actions and plans. Tactical planning may entail the detailed steps required in order to implement a strategic plan, often under the purview of mid-level managers or leaders.

activities; [and] the carrying out of operations as requested by lawful authorities." Further, when defining strategic intelligence, Clough stated that strategic intelligence is a "mechanism to predict threats to a nation's stability and security, be they military, political, economic, environmental, or societal" (Clough 2004, 602).

However, these elements can also be applied to a multinational enterprise (MNE) operating in a volatile or uncertain political or economic environment. In expanding this understanding to the private sector, Fahey and Herring characterized an intelligence team as "a group of individuals who work together to develop a deep understanding of a specific business issue with the intent of developing strategy-relevant insights, action possibilities, and recommendations" (Fahey and Herring 2007, 15). Fahey and Herring further noted that team members are drawn from diverse functional departments or organizational units charged with generating insights that "add significant value to decision making" (2007, 17). Both Clark (2004) and Barnea (2020) also highlighted the role of intelligence in gathering information regarding changes taking place in the external environment to support the decision-making process in order to avoid surprises. Robson (2022, 5) later defined intelligence in the private sector as "applying intelligence analysis on external operating environments legally and transparently to facilitate strategic decision-making and mitigate geopolitical and security risks." Robson's definition aligns well with the definition espoused by Wheaton and Beerbower (2006), who argued that intelligence is an externally focused process that uses information from all available sources and is designed to reduce uncertainty for a decision-maker. Additionally, though focused on the public sector, Fingar noted the importance of contextualizing information for decision-makers: "The ultimate goal for intelligence is to provide insights and signposts for policymakers, providing as much color as possible, in order to facilitate better decisions" (2011, 99).

In short, intelligence is more than just information; it is something that is done to information that provides insight and context to decision-makers. In the case of private-sector intelligence teams—particularly those situated within security teams or focused on geopolitical developments—such intelligence may inform a corporate security-related decision but have implications that reach beyond security into operations, finance, sales, marketing, and so forth. Thus, while there is much variance in the field of intelligence, the overarching role of the intelligence professional is arguably to facilitate strategic decision-making by reducing the decision-maker's uncertainty, regardless of the domain in which that decision takes place (Gill, Marrin, and Phythian 2009). These insights should also take into consideration the potential secondary and tertiary effects of these decisions that may go beyond the primary domain of the decision itself.

This definition is most useful in understanding the utility of strategic intelligence in the private sector, particularly for MNEs. Defining intelligence more broadly by its purpose in facilitating strategic decision-making establishes the mission and purpose of these intelligence teams in the private sector to synthesize a broad array of externally focused information in such a way that it minimizes uncertainty to the extent possible and, therefore, supports decision-makers as they make reasoned, insightful, and context-specific decisions. It is important to note here that while most of these decisions are made by individuals who are responsible for mitigating risk, business leaders are also responsible for identifying new and viable opportunities, and geostrategic intelligence is an effective tool in both domains.

In early private-sector intelligence literature, Kilmann and Ghymn (1976) argued that an effective MNE must have a specially designed strategic intelligence system to monitor complex and changing international environments. More recently, Rice and Zegart highlighted that many businesses have been creating "political risk units whose mission is to identify political risks and opportunities and to work hand in hand with business unit leaders to mitigate losses and seize new opportunities" (2018, 81). Crucially, Rice and Zegart (2018, 81) noted that while many companies have found managing political risk elusive, it is still "seen as essential by everyone."

The history of private-sector security intelligence

Scholar-practitioner Lewis Sage-Passant has studied the history of the private-sector security intelligence field at length and has asserted that "the disjointed nature of the field's development has created a highly polysemic field—that is, one that appears as radically different to each observer depending on their experience and perspective (Sage-Passant 2023, 87). One challenge in understanding the history of the field is that many view intelligence in the private sector—in particular, as leveraged by security professionals—as a relatively new phenomenon, having developed largely in a post-9/11 world. While the professionalization of the field does remain relatively nascent (Robson 2022), the utility of intelligence in the private sector has existed as long as there have been existential threats with the potential to impact business decisions. Earlier forms of intelligence—in both the public and private sectors—have, of course, often been more basic and have lacked the refinement of intelligence processes and standards that have added to their value in their present state.

There are numerous examples of extensive information-gathering networks throughout history, including the Aztec use of merchant spies to conduct reconnaissance (Koontz 2015, 66). This type of activity persisted in Renaissance Europe in the merchant state of Venice as it sought to counter its European and

Ottoman rivals and in the activities of Augsburg-based banker and industrialist Jacob Fugger, who employed a wide network of sources that allowed him to learn of geopolitical and religious developments on a more timely basis than many of his competitors and thus gain the favor of client-patrons such as the Holy Roman Emperor Maximilian I. His investment in a well-developed network allowed him to become a key player in the foundation of the Austro-Hungarian Empire, the Protestant Reformation, and the modern financial system (Steinmetz 2015; Lozada 2015).

Challenges to developing effective intelligence in the private sector

If, as Rice and Zegart argue, companies are aware of the criticality of managing their risk, what impediments have they faced in developing meaningful geopolitical risk analysis? Why is effectively managing geopolitical risk so elusive?

Understanding the impact of uncertainty in decision-making

History tends to highlight the decisive leaders rather than those who struggled with making a difficult decision or developing strategy, and as such, there has been considerable research in the fields of decision theory and uncertainty avoidance, both in terms of national culture and in business and economic decision-making. Economist John Maynard Keynes (1931) argued that judgment about risk is possible when seeking a basis for action, and thus, much of Keynesian economic theory was based on reducing uncertainty through altering the economic environment and by implementing institutional change. From an economic perspective, business investment in a geopolitical intelligence function is much like the Keynesian implementation of institutional change, seeking to establish a framework that allows for greater certainty for business decision-making. Conversely, the Knightian uncertainty principle argues that there is a fundamental degree of ignorance and a limit to knowledge (Knight 1921). Efforts to quantify the impact and effects of this imperfect knowledge have led to research in the related but nuanced fields of ambiguity aversion and risk aversion (Ellsberg 2016).

Following the Knightian uncertainty principle—that there is an essential unpredictability of future events (Knight 1921)—if a business seeks to capitalize on the expertise of an intelligence team, which primarily exists to make sense out of an increasingly VUCA environment, it is critical that there be an understanding of the overall scope and limitations of such teams. This aligns with a nuance asserted by Friedman and Zeckhauser that the primary goal of intelligence is not to eliminate uncertainty but to assess it. In this regard, assessing uncertainty allows for an understanding of the likelihood and confidence of the intelligence being provided, rather than only sharing what is positively known (Friedman and Zeckhauser 2012).

Through an effective intelligence team, a company is able to reconcile the Knightian and Keynesian concepts. On the one hand, an intelligence team is able to provide relevant and context-specific insights that demonstrate what is known, thereby limiting uncertainty to the extent possible. At the same time, effective intelligence analysis also highlights gaps in knowledge and provides a framework for conceptualizing the risks associated with that which remains unknown, including the likelihood that specific events will occur and the potential impact should they occur, thereby allowing for forward thinking and strategic planning in order to mitigate potential risks before they occur. This is, however, an advanced function for these teams, and given the nascency of professionalization in this field, not all teams have the maturity and self-awareness to make these distinctions, though they may aspire to do so.[2]

As suggested by Gill et al., intelligence is intended to reduce a decision-maker's uncertainty, allowing them to make reasoned, insightful, and context-specific decisions. In this sense, private-sector intelligence is a strategic advantage in the fields of decision theory and, in particular, uncertainty avoidance (Gill, Marrin, and Phythian 2009). Decision theory provides a systematic framework for analyzing rational decision-making in situations involving uncertainty, multiple options, and conflicting objectives. This field of study combines insights from mathematics, economics, psychology, and philosophy to help individuals and organizations make informed choices. This includes utility theory, expected value, decision trees, and risk analysis. By incorporating risk analysis, decision theory aims to assess and manage uncertainties associated with different alternatives. Thus, risk analysis involves identifying potential risks, estimating their probabilities, and evaluating their potential impacts on outcomes and their implications for decision-making. Risk analysis as an element of decision theory can be applied in both the public and the private sector but has been most prevalent in fields where uncertainty

---

[2] Risk and uncertainty are related concepts often used in the context of decision-making and probability analysis, but they represent differing degrees of unpredictability, and are therefore not interchangeable. *Risk* refers to a situation where an outcome is uncertain but can be quantified or estimated using a variety of methodologies, including statistical analysis or historical trend data. *Uncertainty* generally represents a higher degree of unpredictability and describes a situation where an outcome is unknown, and there is not enough information available to assign probability. Risk also tends to be tied to negative outcomes, whereas uncertainty may lend itself to either positive or negative outcomes. An example of risk may include an investment decision where historical stock price data and financial indicators can be used to estimate the likelihood of different returns. Examples of uncertainty include situations where there are unknown factors, such as the impact of unprecedented events (e.g., a global pandemic) or geopolitical developments with unpredictable consequences.

can stymie decision-making, including economics, business, public policy, healthcare, and engineering. In economics, it provides insights into consumer behavior, investment decisions, and market dynamics. In business, it guides strategic planning, project management, and risk assessment. In public policy, it helps policymakers evaluate policy alternatives and their potential consequences. In healthcare, it aids in treatment decisions, resource allocation, and healthcare policy development. In engineering, it can inform design choices for complex systems.

Despite its contributions, decision theory—and risk analysis in general—has its limitations and has been subject to criticism. For example, when establishing an overall risk tolerance, risk analysis assumes decision-makers are fully rational and always seek to maximize expected utility, which may not always align with actual human behavior. Another limitation is the challenge of accurately estimating probabilities and assigning actual versus perceived value. Additionally, risk analysis may not adequately capture subjective factors such as emotions, social influences, and ethical considerations that impact decision-making. In short, risk analysis is inherently subjective, and despite significant efforts to quantify and apply rigor to risk methodologies, it remains, in many situations, speculative and is therefore heavily reliant on the credibility of the analyst. However, through effective risk analysis, decision-makers can more objectively evaluate options, assess potential outcomes, and make informed choices. Despite its limitations, decision theory continues to evolve, incorporating insights from various disciplines to enhance our collective understanding of decision-making processes and guide optimal decision-making in complex and uncertain environments.

Divergence with the public sector and a lack of standardization within the field

According to Robson, although intelligence tradecraft has been rapidly expanding in the private sector since the early 2000s, the field is still early in its development. Robson identified six key indicators of professionalization, including "(1) a shared identity, (2) a body of knowledge and knowledge advancement, (3) an accepted code of ethics, (4) agreement on competencies and standards, (5) training and education, and, finally, (6) certification and licensing" (3). Robson (2022) further noted that although some of these elements are emerging in the private-sector intelligence field, overall professionalization within the field remains in its nascent stages.

Matey (2013) argued that intelligence has evolved from a tool of national defense to a tool used by private-sector businesses, and thus, much of the literature on intelligence has historically been predicated upon the public sector. While this is useful in some regards, it neglects the divergent requirements of the private sector (Sage-Passant 2021). For example, according to Theodorou, "The fundamental difference between public- and private-sector intelligence lies not in the raw data and the analytical methodology, but rather in the interpretation for its end use" (Theorodou 1993, 147). Theodorou further explained that in the public sector, intelligence is focused on national security interests. In the private sector, however, the purpose of intelligence can range from personnel security interests for business persons and operations to brand and reputational risks (Crump 2015). Budgets can also vary quite widely, not only between the public sector and the private sector but also within the private sector, depending on business segment, size, and purpose. In the public sector, intelligence functions are publicly financed, operating in a not-for-profit setting. Meanwhile, in the private sector, intelligence professionals operate in a for-profit setting, though they typically exist in an organizational cost center (Ard 2022).

Ard further described the differences between intelligence in the public and private sectors, noting that in the public sector, intelligence teams typically operate in a bureaucratic and hierarchical structure, while private-sector teams tend to have a flatter hierarchy. Intelligence duties in the public sector are well-defined and predictable, and intelligence consumers comprise an established community of policymakers. In the private sector, however, duties are defined but highly flexible, and the consumer base in many firms is not well-established and may span multiple organizational segments. Differences also exist in the information sources leveraged, work environment, and job security in each sector. For example, in the public sector, both classified and open sources may be leveraged; the work environment is collaborative internally, but information sharing and cooperation are limited externally, and job security is stable. In the private sector, intelligence is derived almost exclusively from openly available (unclassified) sources; the work environment tends to be independent internally and collaborative externally; and job stability is contingent on providing intelligence that is timely and relevant to business needs (Ard 2022). Scholar-practitioner Sage-Passant has also noted significant differences in information sharing between the private and public sectors, noting that "where intelligence sharing and liaison between state intelligence agencies—especially those of other nations—is highly regulated and only occurs in specific circumstances given the often adversarial relationships states maintain with one another, in the private sector, intelligence sharing—even between companies that are bitter commercial rivals—is commonplace, albeit with secrecy restrictions maintained around commercially sensitive information" (Sage-Passant 2021).

Despite the overall commonality between the two sectors regarding the intent to reduce uncertainty for decision-makers, the numerous ways in which the two fields diverge create challenges in effectively using the framework of the more standardized public sector to move the private-sector intelligence field forward. Additionally, there is a general lack of consensus on the definition of intelligence within the private sector, which has led to significant variance in the roles and responsibilities of intelligence professionals in the private sector by business sector, objective, and organization. Without a standard definition of intelligence, titles are not always indicative of the actual skills and competencies that employees bring to the table. Many intelligence professionals carry the job title of "analyst" or "manager," though these job titles are often not truly indicative of the wide array of aptitudes an individual intelligence professional possesses or the job tasks they are asked to perform. For example, some professionals with "intelligence analyst" in their job title or job description are focused on investigative functions aligned with insider risk; some may have a degree of responsibility for cyber threat intelligence-related functions; others are focused externally on geostrategic threats; and still, others are asked to focus on more tactical incident reporting. Many are asked to do all of these and more.

The range of experience of those in the intelligence profession also varies greatly. Some hold management or project management responsibilities; some possess varying types of government or military experience; some have lived or worked abroad; some have foreign language skills; some hold advanced degrees (Robson 2022). As an example of this variation, in a 2021 study, when 126 private-sector intelligence practitioners were asked, "What is your job title?" their responses produced 98 different answers, which were standardized down to 72 distinct titles, meaning two-thirds of the titles were not shared by other respondents (Robson 2022). Robson contextualized this within the pathway to professionalization by comparing it with the well-established law profession, which has recognized levels across companies. In private-sector intelligence, however: "Practitioners' levels are set by their companies, which can confuse hiring and benchmarking. …When tested against survey respondents' years of experience … no correlation [was found] between the word 'senior' and years of experience. There was still no pattern when analyzed within industries" (Robson 2022, 10). Robson noted that common terminology is a critical step toward professionalization as it assists with entry into the profession, compensation benchmarking, and establishing "responsibilities to best apply intelligence in the private sector" (10).

The lack of a cohesive descriptor for intelligence professionals and their job requirements, in addition to the absence of an agreed-upon definition of intelligence, exacerbates the challenge of identifying appropriate professional and skills development for these teams. This lack of cohesion also presents a barrier to entry into the field, with many interested candidates uncertain of which terms to use to identify jobs that suit their particular skills or interests.

This challenge is underscored when these professionals seek to move upward in the field without an established trajectory (Robson, 2022).

This significant variation in private-sector intelligence teams, despite the challenges it presents to professionalization, is likely due in large part to the concept of equifinality—that there are many different means of reaching an optimal result, which allows for the nuances and flexibility that are necessary for the functioning of these teams. According to Cummings and Worley (2016), equifinality means that firms may use substantially different competencies to establish similar competitive advantages. The competitive advantage for intelligence teams—and thus the common objective of these teams—is supporting decision-maker needs by providing timely intelligence that mitigates uncertainty and informs decisions. This objective, however, has become both increasingly challenging and increasingly important in light of the evolving volatile, uncertain, complex, and ambiguous (VUCA) geopolitical environment in which global businesses are operating.

In private-sector intelligence teams, this equifinality can be seen within the differing processes and procedures that these teams employ in order to support their consumers. Regardless of the extent to which these teams leverage different resources, they aim to best address the needs of their executive stakeholders. In short, "there is no one process or tool that guarantees success [for these teams]" (Rice and Zegart 2018). Rather, it is the team's ability to provide relevant and context-specific analysis to the right consumers to support those consumers' decision-making needs—particularly those needs that are most specifically tied to critical business decisions—that determines these teams' success.

This objective begins and ends with a deep understanding of the consumer: what business decisions are they grappling with and what type of information will support them in making those decisions. This does not mean that intelligence should be cherry-picked to support a decision maker's intended course of action, but rather that it should help them make a decision. In many companies, despite the recognition that intelligence and risk mitigation have a critical role to play, intelligence teams may be brought in "after the fact" or as a "box-checking exercise" rather than to truly inform a decision. Worse, occasionally, leaders who do not truly understand the function of intelligence may completely disregard analysis that does not support their inclinations. This does not mean that intelligence analysts always "get it right" or that analysis should be accepted without question; it does, however, mean that intelligence teams are tasked with providing relevant and context-specific insights that help to inform a decision, and this cannot be done in a vacuum. It requires consistent engagement with business leaders in order for analysts to be attuned to their intelligence needs. While politicization, or the intentional slanting of analysis to influence a decision, is generally seen as unacceptable in the public sector, the concept of politicization has limited meaning in the corporate context because the intent of intelligence is tied to achieving corporate objectives (Ard 2022). That said, as these teams seek to develop a consistent consumer base that values their insights, there is a risk of smaller-scale politicization to the extent that information that supports or validates a leader's desired course of action may engender greater support from that leader. This risk is particularly prevalent in cost-cutting environments where intelligence teams must rely on the "protection" of specific segments or high-level leaders in order to maintain both relevance and necessary resources.

Understanding the requisite skill set for effective intelligence analysis

Given the lack of standardization within the field and the wide variation in roles and responsibilities, there are a number of skills that contribute effectively to a private-sector intelligence team. Because the roles and responsibilities of these intelligence teams typically involve monitoring domestic and global social and political developments and crime trends, conducting in-depth country and regional analyses, assessing risks and opportunities, and generating actionable intelligence reports in order to operate effectively, these intelligence teams must possess a diverse set of skills and expertise. As with the public sector, this includes not only effective communication skills in writing and briefing clearly and succinctly and distilling complex topics for clarity but also a deep understanding of international relations, political science, economics, regional studies, security concepts, risk assessment, data analysis, and at times, proficiency in languages relevant to their assigned regions.

Cross-cultural competence and the ability to interpret complex geopolitical dynamics are also crucial; however, for the private sector, this knowledge must also be combined with business acumen, which allows for contextualization of the information as it is relevant to a specific business or organizational decision. Because these teams must collaborate closely with internal stakeholders such as executives, strategy teams, risk management departments, and legal teams to provide insights that inform decision-making processes, they must understand the perspectives and needs of these consumers and develop a professional presence that leverages effective written and oral communication skills to engender trust, convey confidence, and project credibility.

For all intelligence teams, regardless of sector, beyond the thorough study of a particular topic, research understanding, and critical thinking, these professionals leverage analytic skills to accomplish their objectives. These "analytic skills" refer to the ability to analyze, synthesize, and contextualize data for a decision-maker or consumer. This embodies an ability to identify trustworthy sourcing and evaluate information sources for validity and relevance, going well beyond simple collation of data. Because these teams cannot be effective if they are not attuned to the needs of their consumers, they require a consistent, clear, and well-defined means of communication with their consumers in order to communicate intelligence and develop the requirements that guide their collection and analysis (Lewis 2022). While these communication procedures tend to be well-codified in the public sector, they are much less well-defined in the private sector. As such, many private-sector intelligence teams find themselves passing intelligence through multiple layers of organizational leadership or bureaucracy, which tends to undermine not only effective and timely communication but also the collection of useful feedback and the development of trusted relationships between intelligence analysts and their consumers.

A varied set of methodologies and tools

Strategic security intelligence teams employ a range of methodologies and tools to conduct their analyses. These may include open-source intelligence (OSINT), data mining, social media monitoring, expert interviews, trend analysis, scenario planning, and risk modeling. The teams must also have access to comprehensive databases and information sources to ensure accurate and up-to-date analysis. Due in large part to the lack of standardization across the field, a large number of tools, platforms, and vendors have cropped up that may be relevant and helpful in different contexts, and thus, the specific tools that are leveraged by a given intelligence team will likely differ on a case-by-case basis. This is also due in part to the wide variation in business interests depending on sector, geographic footprint, and overall objectives.

That said, Structured Analytic Techniques (SATs), which have long been popular within the public sector for establishing analytic rigor, are often leveraged to some degree in the private sector but tend to be used as a framework for critical thinking rather than in the crafting of an analytic product. In the private sector, leveraging Structured Analytic Techniques may entail a fully documented and very structured analysis, but more often than not, due in large part to the rapid pace of business, SATs are instead used in a more limited fashion, incorporating the concepts associated with the analytic techniques into the thinking behind building out an analytic product.

Structured Analytic Techniques are a set of systematic and disciplined methodologies used in intelligence analysis to improve the quality and reliability of analytical products. These techniques aim to enhance the objectivity, rigor, and clarity of analysis by providing a framework for organizing information, mitigating cognitive biases, and facilitating critical thinking. Key concepts associated with structured analytic techniques include defining the problem, gathering and evaluating relevant information, formulating hypotheses, conducting analysis using appropriate techniques, and drawing conclusions. By following a more structured process, analysts ensure consistency and rigor in their analytical approach. Analysis generally involves deconstruction—breaking complex issues or problems into smaller, more manageable components, allowing for each component to be individually examined. The analyzed components are then reconstructed to form a more comprehensive understanding of the whole. Deconstruction and reconstruction techniques help analysts identify patterns, connections, and gaps in their analysis. It also allows for alternative analysis, seeking multiple possible or plausible explanations or hypotheses for a given situation. As such, it helps to mitigate confirmation bias and encourages critical thinking.

By systematically examining different possibilities and assessing their plausibility and evidence, analysts aim to enhance the robustness and objectivity of their analysis. Structured analytic techniques also emphasize the explicit identification and evaluation of assumptions underlying analysis. Analysts are encouraged to make their assumptions explicit, assess their validity, and consider alternative assumptions or interpretations. Furthermore, Structured Analytic Techniques stress the need for evidence-based analysis, where assertions and conclusions are supported by reliable and verifiable information. Finally, Structured Analytic Techniques stress that collaboration is a key component of effective analysis. Analysts are encouraged to seek input and insights from their peers, subject matter experts, and stakeholders. Collaboration helps to challenge assumptions, validate findings, and ensure a comprehensive analysis. Additionally, feedback loops are incorporated to allow for continuous improvement and refinement of the analysis based on input from stakeholders. It also assists in strengthening communication with decision-makers as effective communication of analytic findings is crucial for decision-makers to understand and utilize the insights generated.

By incorporating these key concepts, Structured Analytic Techniques provide analysts with a systematic framework to enhance the quality, objectivity, and reliability of their analysis. These techniques promote critical thinking, collaboration, and evidence-based reasoning, ultimately leading to more robust and actionable intelligence products. Although most private-sector security intelligence teams do not embed detailed structured analytic techniques in their products, they do leverage the foundational critical thinking skills that these techniques entail.

Best practices for strategic security intelligence teams in the private sector: Moving the field forward

Organizations that exist in a complex and challenging global marketplace often struggle to operate effectively for a myriad of reasons, including acquiring and developing strong leaders (Bono et al. 2009; Douglas and Worley 2000), a scarcity of on-demand skills, and a rapidly changing and often uncertain business context (Foote et al. 2021). A 2021 McKinsey study that took place during the COVID-19 global pandemic showed that "responsive organizations outperformed their less agile peers by pivoting teams to solve new problems as they arose" (Handscomb et al. 2021). Private-sector intelligence teams typically have a skill set that supports this responsiveness and agility by operating across two disparate domains. In one sense, they serve as an advisor or business partner, working among multiple teams. Although these teams complete discrete projects, these projects are one element of a broader responsibility for providing continuing and trusted advice. The second domain that these teams operate in is that of the knowledge professional. These teams typically either have or quickly develop deep content expertise similar to that of a center of excellence. In this sense, they also operate across multiple teams, providing "targeted research and content expertise" (Foote et al. 2021, 4). However, in order for these organizations to effectively capitalize on this expertise, a number of concepts must be addressed.

Direct communication with key stakeholders

Private-sector intelligence teams are often stymied by organizational silos that impede their ability to reach key consumers more directly. As mentioned previously, an effective feedback loop is critical to providing the best possible intelligence. When an intelligence team is unable to liaise directly with business leaders, whether due to organizational factors, such as a rigid hierarchical structure or ineffective communication pathways, it is unable to inform the most critical business decisions, thus undermining its effectiveness.

Moreover, direct communication with key stakeholders is critical to building effective intelligence relationships that allow these decision-makers to understand the capability and scope of intelligence professionals and to understand the nuances of the intelligence being shared with them. So long as the mystique surrounding intelligence teams persists, so will the misperceptions regarding their work, leaving some leaders either hesitant to leverage their strategic capabilities or unaware of how to harness their insights most effectively.

Building trust and credibility

Equally critical is an intelligence team's ability to build credibility and trust with key consumers. Trust between decision-makers and intelligence analysts is essential for effective collaboration and informed decision-making. However, this trust is reliant on effective communication, transparency, expertise, credibility, and relationship-building. In this sense, intelligence analysts must know and understand their business and their consumers in order to develop such a relationship that business leaders rely on their insights collaboratively. Building strong relationships with decision-makers is crucial for establishing trust. Intelligence analysts must actively engage decision-makers, seeking opportunities to understand their priorities, preferences, and information requirements. By building rapport and demonstrating a genuine commitment to supporting their decision-making, analysts foster trust and collaboration with key stakeholders. This collaborative approach also entails analysts communicating their findings, insights, and assessments clearly and concisely and listening attentively to decision-makers' concerns and follow-on requirements. Following up on these requirements helps to demonstrate the value analysts' place on consumers' perspectives and input.

It also requires that analysts exercise intellectual honesty in sharing what is known factually, what underlying assumptions may be involved, what methodologies and sources were used in the analysis, and where intelligence gaps exist. Analysis must be contextualized for the consumer, and reasoning for any conclusions must be clear. Transparent and ongoing communication fosters understanding and alignment in the intelligence analysis process and encourages leaders to trust the information being provided to them. Because many business leaders may not be familiar with intelligence processes, analysts must be able to explain analysis effectively, including the scope of their work as well as what remains unknown. In order for intelligence analysts to showcase their knowledge, skills, and experience in a relevant domain and thus establish credibility, they must stay updated on emerging technologies and trends, new developments, and geopolitical factors influencing their analysis. By providing accurate, well-researched, and reliable analysis, intelligence analysts earn the trust and confidence of decision-makers. This information must also be timely and relevant so that decision-makers are able to make informed decisions.

Focusing on ethics

While in most cases, private-sector intelligence teams do not operate in the same secretive context as the public sector, maintaining confidentiality and demonstrating integrity is essential, both for building trust between decision-makers and intelligence analysts and for building the future of the field. Without an established ethical standard, most teams rely on business standards for information-sharing and handling of sensitive or business-critical data. Knowing and respecting ethical, legal, and regulatory boundaries, including avoiding conflicts of interest, mitigates reputational risk and builds trust in the confidentiality of intelligence sources and methods, while intellectual integrity supports the accuracy, credibility, and reliability of the analysis. Further ethical considerations that intelligence analysts must be cognizant of include respecting privacy rights, protecting human rights, and avoiding the misuse of intelligence for malicious purposes.

Getting it right

While intelligence analysis is neither magic nor crystal ball-gazing, in order to establish credibility, intelligence analysts must demonstrate value to decision-makers by providing unique insights, anticipating emerging risks, identifying opportunities, and offering actionable recommendations. Some involved in the field of intelligence analysis have used the term *predictive analysis*, which generally overstates the abilities of intelligence analysts. Analysts analyze past events, their causes, and their consequences. They assess trends; identify patterns, correlations, and relationships in events and data; understand nuances; evaluate indicators; consider alternative scenarios; provide insights; and anticipate future trends, events, and implications; and seek to apply concepts across functions and topics, where relevant; but rarely do they actually "predict" anything. It is important to note that while these approaches can provide valuable insights, the future is inherently uncertain, whereas the term *predict* suggests a level of certainty or foreknowledge that may not be accurate. Factors such as unexpected or black swan events and unforeseen circumstances can significantly influence a course of action. Therefore, a comprehensive approach that combines multiple methods, critical thinking, and ongoing analysis is essential for obtaining a more nuanced understanding of the future. As such, it is impractical to expect intelligence analysis to be *right* every time; however, what it should do is provide clarity and credibility, with analysis being relevant, insightful, and impactful so that analysts can establish themselves as trusted advisors to decision-makers.

Conclusion

Private-sector intelligence teams provide a significant advantage to the corporations who use them by providing an understanding of the geopolitical and security landscape. Though intelligence has historically evoked a mysterious cloak-and-dagger perception, the capabilities of these teams need not be shrouded in secrecy. While some do avail themselves of proprietary tools, more often than not, these units operate as strategic advisors rather than the classic "spook" perception. These teams afford their organizations a competitive edge in adapting to changing geopolitical environments and developing and aligning corporate strategy to identify and capitalize on new market opportunities while avoiding significant risk. They also provide a decision advantage to senior leaders through the valuable, actionable insights that they provide, which inform strategic decision-making. Intelligence analysis helps leaders assess potential risks and opportunities, make informed investment decisions, adapt business models, and develop robust contingency plans. These teams can also have a significant impact on a company's reputation by contributing to safeguarding a company's image and brand value.

In an increasingly interconnected and complex global landscape, strategic security intelligence teams have become indispensable for private-sector organizations. By leveraging their expertise, methodologies, and tools, these teams provide crucial insights that enable organizations to navigate security and geopolitical risks, make informed decisions, and secure a competitive advantage. As the world continues to evolve, these intelligence teams will play a vital role in shaping the strategies and operations of private-sector entities.

Bibliography

Ard, M. A. 2022. "Lessons Learned for the Private Sector Intelligence Analyst." In A. R. Martin and N. K. Drumhiller, *The Academic-Practitioner Divide in Intelligence Studies*, 129-145. Lanham, MD: Rowman & Littlefield.

Barnea, A. 2020. "Strategic Intelligence: A Concentrated and Diffused Intelligence Model." *Intelligence and National Security* 35 (5): 701-716.

Bono, J. E., R. K. Purvanova, A. J. Towler, and D. B. Peterson. 2009. "A Survey of Executive Coaching Practices." *Personnel Psychology* 62 (2): 361-404.

Clark, R. M. 2004. *Intelligence Analysis: A Target-Centric Approach.* Washington, DC: CQ Press.

Clough, C. 2004. "Quid pro quo: The Challenges of International Strategic Intelligence Cooperation." *International Journal of Intelligence and CounterIntelligence* 17 (4): 601-613.

Crump, J. 2015. *Corporate Security Intelligence and Strategic Decision-Making.* New York: Taylor & Francis.

Cummings, T. G., and C. G. Worley. 2016. *Organization Development and Change.* Toronto: Nelson Education.

Douglas, C. A., and W. H. Worley. 2000. *Executive Coaching: An Annotated Bibliography.* Greensboro, NC: Center for Creative Leadership.

Ellsberg, D. 2016. *Risk, Ambiguity and Decision.* London: Routledge.

Fahey, L., and J. Herring. 2007. "Intelligence Teams." *Strategy & Leadership* 35 (1): 13-20.

Fingar, T. 2011. *Reducing Uncertainty: Intelligence Analysis and National Security.* Stanford: Stanford University Press.

Foote, E., B. Hancock, B. Jeffery, and R. Malan. 2021. *The Key Role of Dynamic Talent Allocation in Shaping the Future of Work.* Boston: McKinsey & Company.

Foster, D. 2020, March 12. "Leading Through Uncertainty." *Harvard Business Review.* Retrieved March 15, 2023, from https://www.harvardbusiness.org/leading-through-uncertainty/.

Friedman, J. A., and R. Zeckhauser. 2012. "Assessing Uncertainty in Intelligence." *Intelligence and National Security* 27 (6): 824-847.

Gill, P., S. Marrin, and M. Phythian, M. 2009. *Intelligence Theory: Key Questions and Debates.* New York: Routledge.

Hackman, M., and C. E. Johnson. 2013. *Leadership: A Communication Perspective.* 6th ed. Long Grove, IL: Waveland.

Handscomb, C., D. Mahadevan, L. Schor, L. Sieberer, E. Naidoo, and S. Srinivasan. 2021. *An Operating Model for the Next Normal: Lessons from Agile Organizations in the Crisis.* Boston: McKinsey & Company.

Keynes, J. M. 1931. *Essays in Persuasion.* New York: Harcourt, Brace and Co.

Kilmann, R., and K.-I. Ghymn. 1976. "The MAPS Design Technology: Designing Strategic Intelligence Systems for MNCs." *Columbia Journal of World Business* 11 (2): 35-47.

Knight, F. 1921. *Risk, Uncertainty and Profit.* Boston: Houghton Mifflin Company.

Koontz, R. 2015. "Where Rulers Are Made: Warriors and Merchants on the Periphery." In *Memory Traces: Analyzing Sacred Space at Five Mesoamerican Sites,* edited by C. Kristan-Graham, L. M. Amrhein, and C. A. Kristan-Graham, 66. Denver: University Press of Colorado.

Lewis, A. 2022. "Thriving in a VUCA World: A Case Study Exploring Geopolitically-Focused Intelligence Teams in the Private Sector." PhD diss., Pepperdine University, Graduate School of Education and Psychology. ProQuest.

Lowenthal, M. 2017. *Intelligence: From Secrets to Policy.* 7th ed. Washington, DC: CQ Press.

Lozada, C. 2015, August 6. "He Remade Capitalism, Religion, and History. You've Probably Never Heard of Him." *Washington Post.* Retrieved September 15, 2023, from https://www.washingtonpost.com/news/book-party/wp/2 015/08/06/he-remade-capitalism-religion-and-history-youve-probably-nev er-heard-of-him/

Matey, G. D. 2013. "The Use of Intelligence in the Private Sector." *International Journal of Intelligence and CounterIntelligence* 26 (21): 272-287.

Rice, C., and A. Zegart. 2018. *Political Risk: How Businesses and Organizations Can Anticipate Global Insecurity.* New York: Grand Central Publishing.

Robson, M. 2022. "Private Sector Intelligence: On the Long Path of Professionalization." *Intelligence and National Security* 37 (1): 1-19.

Sage-Passant, L. 2021. "The Intelligence Language Problem: Towards New Definitions?" [Unpublished manuscript]. Department of International Relations, Politics, and History, Loughborough University, London.

Sage-Passant, L. 2023. *The Security Intelligence Services of the Private Sector.* London: Loughborough University.

Steinmetz, G. 2015. *The Richest Man Who Ever Lived: The Life and Times of Jacob Fugger.* New York: Simon & Schuster.

Theorodou, J. 1993. "Political Risk Reconsidered." *International Journal of Intelligence and CounterIntelligence* 6 (2): 147-171.

Warner, M. 2002. "Wanted: A Definition of 'Intelligence.'" *Studies in Intelligence* 46 (3): 1-13. Retrieved from https://www.cia.gov/static/72b2 d4c0d01e4e0 5c60ff7d37fdd68b1/Wanted-Definition-of-Intel.pdf.

Warner, M. 2014. *The Rise and Fall of Intelligence: An International Security History.* Washington, DC: Georgetown University Press.

Wheaton, K., and M. Beerbower. 2006. "Towards a New Definition of Intelligence." *Stanford Law & Policy Review* 17 (3): 319-330.

Chapter 4

Constructing spies: Organizations, gender, and embodiment

Bridget Rose Nolan

University of New Hampshire

Abstract: Scholars of organizations have thoroughly explored acculturation processes—the practices that bring people into organizations—but there is considerably less research on the ways in which organizations are brought into their people. This chapter uses ethnographic data and declassified CIA documents to investigate how the gendered organizational practices of intelligence agencies construct workers. I show that the organizational requirements of secrecy become embodied, such that intelligence officers internalize practices like surveillance on behalf of the organization. This organizational construction of the body has gendered consequences, including the symbolic erasure of the female body and the complication of officers' performances of masculinities/femininities.

Keywords: Gender, embodiment, organizations, division of labor, sociology of work, ethnography

***

Introduction

Sociology has a rich history of theorizing organizations as "gendered." Looking at an organization as "gendered" means looking past the characteristics of individual workers' bodies to see how gender is deeply embedded within organizational histories, structures, and practices. Although these practices are usually presented as gender-neutral, research suggests that the abstract notion of a "worker" in a "job" is actually a man and that formal organizations—in large and small ways—therefore primarily represent and reflect men's interests (Acker 1990).

If we accept that organizations tend to behave in gendered ways and that intelligence agencies are prime examples of such institutions, it follows that these gendered practices at the organizational level will affect individually gendered intelligence workers differently. When the analytic focus is on the level of the organization, we generally acknowledge that individuals have and perform a gender identity, but those individuals tend not to be the focus of the analysis. In this chapter, I first demonstrate that intelligence agencies are gendered organizations. I then ask questions about the consequences of organizational practices that are presented as gender-neutral but are, in fact, gendered. In essence, how do gendered organizational practices affect individually gendered people?

I find an explanation in conceptualizing intelligence officers as social constructs. Scholars of organizations have thoroughly researched acculturation processes—that is, processes by which people are brought into an organization—but there is substantially less research on how the organization is brought into its people. By exploring the internalization of the intelligence officer's role within a gendered organizational context, I shed light on how the organization constructs the embodied self in profoundly gendered ways. A key issue is what I call the social erasure of women's bodies, through which women minimize or deny their participation in reproduction and motherhood in order to maintain an edge at work.[1]

Methods and data

This is a mixed-methods approach that combines my ethnographic observations and interview data with the quantitative and qualitative data available in three declassified documents. The first declassified document is a 1953 internal study the CIA did on gender in the organization called "Career Employment of Women in the Central Intelligence Agency," declassified in 2013 (CIA 1953). The second is the 1991 "Glass Ceiling Study Summary," declassified in 2006 (CIA 1991). The third is a 1994 interview transcript with several female CIA Directorate of Operations officers, called "Divine Secrets of the RYBAT Sisterhood," declassified in 2013 (CIA 1994).

Ethnographic observations and data from 20 in-depth interviews come from a year of research at the National Counterterrorism Center (NCTC). During the interview phase, I aimed to get a relatively diverse sample with regard to the analysts' home agencies to get as many perspectives as possible. Official demographic information was not available, but my perception is that the

---

[1] I acknowledge that not all women are, can be, or want to be mothers, and that not all mothers identify as women. This research is not intended to be trans-exclusionary. The data on which this chapter is based does not acknowledge trans identities in its considerations of gender, an omission I hope to rectify in future research.

population of analysts in the wider IC is not particularly diverse on measures of race, gender, and age, so there is some, but not much, variation on these measures in my interview sample. The average age of the interview participants was 31.8 years, with a range of 24 to 47 and a median of 31.5. All but three of the participants identified as white; 13 identified as female, and seven as male. The average amount of time served at NCTC was 2.48 years, with a range of four months to six years and a median of two years. The average amount of time served in the federal government was 7.7 years, with a range of two years to 15 years and a median of 7.5 years. 13 of the participants had at least one graduate-level degree, usually a master's degree. 13 of the participants claimed CIA as their home organization; seven of the longer-serving participants claimed more than one home organization throughout their careers. Based on my observations and experiences, my sample reflects the analyst population writ large, with the possible exception of the gender breakdown. I sensed that most analysts were male, but again, I cannot be sure because official demographics are not available; in any case, there is still an overwhelmingly white and male atmosphere to both CIA and NCTC, which analysts have reported and with which my own experience was commensurate (Jones 2016).

I intentionally pair up data sources that do not necessarily align with each other neatly: historical documents and declassified documents tend to focus more on operational work, for instance, whereas my data focuses on present-day analysts. Further, my data draws from the experiences of not only CIA analysts but also analysts from other agencies such as ODNI, FBI, NSA, and NGA. The data also covers different timeframes, which parallel evolutions in the discourse about the culture of gender norms in the broader society. Given the challenges with secrecy and cover status, creating a data set purely aligned with either operations or analysis proves difficult. Instead, I see these historical and contemporary data sources as complementary. There is little research in intelligence studies on issues of race, class, gender, and other forms of inequality, and future research can tackle each of the issues presented here in greater depth. My goal in this chapter is to conceptualize theories of gender in the IC broadly—across organizations, missions, and decades.

The CIA as a gendered organization: From petticoats to trench coats

The Central Intelligence Agency (CIA) is similar to other large formal organizations and, therefore bears many of the same characteristics: bureaucracy, red tape, inefficiency. But the CIA is also unique in its mission— to disrupt and pre-empt threats, collect intelligence, and conduct covert action—and in its operational capabilities to achieve that mission. The public knows many stories of the CIA's creativity and ingenuity in achieving its goals: from its collection of espionage gadgets to stories of now-declassified operations, the organization is a marvel at thinking outside the box and using anything at its disposal—and inventing whatever else it needs—to put that mission first. Indeed, the organization describes itself as "agile, responsive, and consequential" (CIA 2022)—adjectives not commonly ascribed to massive government bureaucracies. At the same time, the organization has historically been sluggish in using some of the human capital right in front of its eyes: despite its stated devotion to diversity, this notorious "old boys' club" (McIntosh 1998; Jones 2016) has historically underutilized women. This paradox presents the following puzzle: given that this organization can be so nimble and creative in achieving its operational goals, why has it been so reluctant to leverage the operational advantages women provide? I find an explanation in conceptualizing the CIA as a gendered organization.

Gendered organizations

To say that an organization is "gendered" means more than collecting statistics about women's representation in positions of power and their concentration in lower-paying jobs, and it means more than whether an organization has so-called family-friendly policies or meaningful positions against sexual harassment. Looking at an organization as "gendered" means seeing past the characteristics of individual workers' bodies and examining how gender is embedded within organizational histories, structures, and practices, even though these practices are usually presented as gender-neutral. Joan Acker's theory of gendered organizations offers the classic definition:

> To say that an organization, or any other analytic unit, is gendered means that advantage and disadvantage, exploitation and control, action and emotion, meaning and identity, are patterned through and in terms of a distinction between male and female, masculine and feminine. Gender is not an addition to ongoing processes, conceived as gender-neutral. Rather, it is an integral part of those processes, which cannot be properly understood without an analysis of gender. (Acker 1990, 146)

Gender is something we perform as individuals (Connell 1987; West and Zimmerman 1987), but it is also a fundamental feature of the organization of social life. Acker (1990, 146-147) suggests that gendered organizations get that way primarily as a result of five dynamic and co-occurring processes: the gendered division of labor; constructions of symbols and images that construct, explain, and normalize divisions; interactions among men and women, women and women, and men and men; gendered components of individual identity; and the ongoing processes of creating and conceptualizing social structures.

Gendered division of labor

It should come as no surprise that women have historically been underrepresented in positions of power and overrepresented in clerical and administrative positions at the CIA. There has been just one female Director of the Central Intelligence Agency (DCIA, formerly DCI [Director of Central Intelligence]), but further granularity is available in declassified documents. The actual personnel numbers are classified, but the reports provide percentages that paint a bleak picture. In the 1953 so-called Petticoat Panel, the report on overt professional positions showed that there were no women in the GS-14 pay grade, and women represented less than 21% of professional employees. In all but one job category, the highest pay grades women held were one to four levels below the highest grades held by men. Women represented 86% of overt clerical positions. The Petticoat Panel shows that in all age groups, men's GS level is higher on average, with men 60-64 years of age peaking at a GS-14 and women 65-69 peaking at a GS-7. Very little data for the Directorate of Operations (DO) was included in this report, but since the DO has a reputation for being even more male-dominated than the other CIA directorates, the picture is likely to have been even more skewed.

Qualitatively, Agency officials expressed the following opinions in 1953:

- "Women are not qualified to perform in those positions which they do not now occupy."

- "Women won't travel. Men are necessary for Departmental jobs since they must be used as replacements for overseas personnel."

- "Women can't work under the pressures of urgency and special considerations inherent in much of the Agency's work."

- "Women are undesirable candidates for long-range employment because they frequently interrupt or terminate their employment for marriage or family reasons."

- "Women are more emotional and less objective in their approach to problems than men. They are not sufficiently aggressive."

- "Men dislike working under the supervision of women and are reluctant to accept them on an equal basis as professional associates."

- "The economic responsibilities of women are not as great as those of men... Women should not be employed in higher-paying positions and deprive men of these opportunities. Women should not be employed at all when men are in need of employment." (CIA 1953)

Though the panel tries to refute these sentiments, some of the refutations reveal further entrenched notions of gender. For instance, in response to the objection that women are not qualified for jobs they do not already perform, the panel writes:

> Since there are some women in practically every type of position in the Agency, this argument from the viewpoint of any one individual office seems questionable. At least, it would be necessary to ascertain whether the aspects of a specific job make a woman ill-fitted for the position rather than the category of profession. It is reasonable to assume that there are specific positions requiring traits or specialized training that women are unlikely to possess. (CIA 1953)

In reply to the objection that men do not like working for women, the panel says, "It is probably offensive to many men to find a woman occupying positions superior or even equivalent to theirs. It is also probable that many women prefer to work for men" (CIA 1953), and then the refutation consists mostly of the "hope" that those attitudes will go away, without any real recommendations for how the organization can facilitate that change. By 1976, according to the CIA's history staff, only one of the Agency's 98 key officials was a woman (Martin 2015).

By the time the 1991 Glass Ceiling study was conducted, things had improved for women at the Agency, but the picture of inequality was still stark. The study shows a comparison of FY 1980 and FY 1991, where a higher percentage of women are in higher GS levels—approximately 2% of female employees were a GS 15 in 1980, but that number was about 5% in 1991; in 1980, about 5% of female employees were at a GS-14, and in 1991 that number about 8%. The curve shifts to higher GS grades—but it shifts for men, too: in 1980, about 12% of male employees were at a GS-15, and in 1991, that number was almost 20%. Overall, the number of women at higher GS levels grew, but it grew faster for men (CIA 1991). Though the data are grouped differently, Hsieh and Winslow (2006, 282) show with data from the year 2000 that in the federal government writ large, men still dominate at GS-12 and above, with about 75% of GS-14-15 workers being men. The CIA garnered national attention in the mid-1990s for some of these issues when a group of women filed a class action lawsuit against the Agency for sexual discrimination and systematic denial of promotions to women (Pear 1995).

Symbols, images, and narrative

Ely and Meyerson (2000, 117) show that narratives can take oppressive forms and that they serve a primary role in gendering organizations. Narratives and the social interactions in which they are told and retold often constitute what workers "know" about an organization and what they "know" about each other and themselves within that organization. Thus, these narratives are not just static stories but rather dynamic "social practices that are constitutive of social contexts"; narratives, therefore, actively construct what we think of as organizational "reality" (Ely and Meyerson 2000, 117).

Many organizations rely on stories about founders, oral histories, and "FOAF tales" ("friend of a friend" tales) to construct meaningful shared understandings of what constitutes success and failure, good and bad, and right and wrong in that organizational context (Mickolus 2011, 119). These narratives are often presented as gender-neutral or are gendered in ways that go unacknowledged. When the CIA tells stories about OSS Director "Wild" Bill Donovan or about successful operational activities, these stories often foreground as valuable those traits that are stereotypically coded as masculine: daring, technical competence, heroism, courage, and strength. These narratives usually fail to mention the support provided by innumerable staff members, whose work— often referred to as "behind the scenes" and therefore rendered invisible— makes the leader's noteworthy behavior possible (Ely and Meyerson 2000, 109). Indeed, General Donovan himself characterized women's role in the OSS as the "invisible apron strings" of the organization (McIntosh 1998). Multiplied over millions of interactions and retellings through the decades, support work typically done by women is marginalized in favor of underscoring masculine-coded traits as superior.

The 1991 Glass Ceiling study finds concrete qualitative evidence for the kinds of narratives that explicitly value stereotypically masculine qualities. The study found evidence that the Agency had constructed its own "model for success" and states explicitly that "white men in the upper levels are perceived to fit this model for success most closely, and women and minorities who rise to these levels are perceived to demonstrate some of the same characteristics as their successful white male peers." "Playing the game" to achieve success in the organization required demonstrating such qualities as "being aggressive, putting their careers first, not being afraid of making mistakes, having good communication skills, and displaying self-confidence." Entrenched attitudes concerning women's "family responsibilities"—whether women were married and/or had children or not—were still pervasive, and in a familiar catch-22, women were described as "both too assertive and not assertive enough" (CIA 1991).

The CIA Museum is the primary way in which the Agency preserves its history and continues to tell stories about itself (Geertz 1973). A look at some of the tangible artifacts preserved in the museum—and the official narratives about those items—demonstrate how deeply the organization is gendered. For instance, the museum displays Cold War-era spy gadgets, almost all of which were created for a male body participating in traditionally masculine activities: a compass hidden in cufflinks, a radio receiver concealed in a pipe, a camera obscured in a tobacco pouch. In her memoir *Sisterhood of Spies: Women of the OSS*, McIntosh shows that the equipment for OSS parachuters was designed for a certain kind of body:

> Some women did attend OSS parachute schools commanded by Col. Lucius O. Rucker, a veteran of 119 jumps himself. He trained thirty-eight hundred men … and thirty-eight women. In the more than twenty thousand jumps that he supervised, only fifty trainees refused when the time came to jump. Not one of those was a woman. The only complaint the women had was the extensive bruises they sustained when the parachute harnesses snapped roughly against their breasts in jumping. (McIntosh 1998, 13)

The museum houses a blade tool designed for these parachuters as well, which parachuters would carry in case the parachuters landed in a tree and had to cut themselves out. The official narrative of this object states that the blade was designed to go "in the breast pocket," meaning that the tool is assumed to go into a pocket typical of a man's shirt. Though there are some exceptions—a code disguised in the mirror of a "lady's" makeup compact, for instance—the overwhelming trend in the museum artifacts is to memorialize and reify narratives and objects relating the story of men: men's boots, gloves, and uniforms; a "spittoon" issued by the OSS to its geographer that was then passed down from officer to officer; even a hollowed-out silver dollar, meant to conceal film, is described as "pocket change"—a phrase used to refer to the loose change men carry in their pockets, since women's clothing, particularly decades ago, would not have featured pockets under the assumption that women would be carrying purses.

A particularly interesting artifact in the museum is the U-2 spy plane pilot's suit, which had to be form-fitting and pressurized to protect the pilots from the risks to the body of flying at high altitudes without artificial air pressure. The caption for the suit says: "If the suit looks something like an old-fashioned girdle, there is a reason for that: CIA contracted with the David Clark Corset and Brassiere Manufacturer for its construction" (CIA n.d.). There is an irony in the fact that this organization can be creative enough to come up with the idea of contracting a women's underwear company to design pilot suits for men but simultaneously has notions of gender so deeply embedded in it that it does not actually put women in the suits. This absence is not for lack of supply, either; even women with better qualifications than their male counterparts were systematically held back, as McIntosh (1998, 34) tells us: "Many women with doctorates, former professors and even college department heads, found themselves working for younger men who generally lacked their experience and equivalent academic credentials." These organizational practices were normalized and naturalized, such as when a chief of the station from the 1960s said, "We had no female case officers in my station. Women were responsible for support operations such as research, analysis, and office management. I feel women are just not as stable as men in critical positions" (quoted in McIntosh 1998, 242).

Interpersonal interactions

There can hardly be any doubt that women in American organizations have historically been subordinate to men, and the CIA is no exception. What is surprising is that the CIA has historically been less willing to leverage this subordination for its gain than one might expect for such an agile and flexible agency. Historically, even from the days of the American Revolution, women have certainly been willing and eager to subvert their lower status to achieve operational goals. For instance, Martin (2015) details the ways in which American colonial women used the "non-threatening traditional nature of housewives" to acquire secrets: women were recruited as domestic workers, such as cooks or maids, to eavesdrop on military personnel without raising suspicion, and others would use laundry hanging on a clothesline to send and receive messages. During the Civil War, women hid messages in their hair ribbons or their many layers of clothes, while World War I marked a transition for women to take more overt roles as linguists and codebreakers (Martin 2015). In the modern age, the theme persists that women are excellent in more powerful positions in this line of work—particularly as overseas operators— precisely because of their subordinated social position. For example, the "RYBAT Sisterhood" report suggests that women are better at detecting surveillance because they are socialized to be more aware of their surroundings, ostensibly as a way of protecting themselves against robbery and/or assault. They are also socialized to pay attention to clothing and are accepted without question in public spaces dedicated to shopping. A former DO officer named "Patty" says:

> I can tell you that the spouses—and they were usually women. In fact, they were all women—were terrific because they had no preconceived notions and they inevitably—this is me being a female chauvinist—were much better at detecting surveillants on foot. I always put that down to women [being] more sensitive [to] who's near or in their space, for physical protection. You know, if somebody moves in on you, you're going to want to know. But they were great at picking up surveillants on

foot and in stores. Because surveillants don't shop well, they just can't fake it. (CIA 1994)

Patty's colleague Meredith adds:

I always said if I ever wrote a book, I would start it with, "You could tell 'em by their socks." You would always know surveillants [redacted] at the time by the socks and the shoes. We digress here, but with all the [redacted] having such horrible clothing and horrible shoes and socks, the surveillants had good ones. That would never occur to my husband to look at it. (CIA 1994)

There is also evidence that leveraging cultural ideas of women's supposed limitations could prove useful for the Agency. The RYBAT sisterhood relays some of the ways in which this might be effective:

Meredith: I think each of us played the female part of it and really used it as the *best* way to recruit. *Very* high-level NE targets, in fact, and we were each successful at it.

Patty: ... women recruit very differently than men recruit, number one. Number two: [in] the files, however, you could never tell it was a female case officer if you took it away because we reported like a man would report it because we knew how to survive in the system. But the biggest advantage for women in recruiting ... was that men, foreign men, will tell women darned near anything ... because we are the "nurturing" part of the equation, we are non-threatening, [and] if we play our cover at all, they assume that we're not intelligence officers. I recruited an ambassador once, and, of course, you want to give them the cover, and I said, "Of course, you knew all along I was an intelligence officer." Oh yeah, *right*, he figured it out! Of course, he did. Bull...!

Carla: ... I was sort of the "Dumb Dora" personality to survive, and "Golly!" "Gee!" and "Wow!" And this [redacted] that was it, he would seek me out. "Oh, could we talk?" He would tell me, "I just love talking to you because you're not very bright." And I would just sit like this [makes an innocent expression], and ... it worked. ... He just told me everything, and I got tons of intel out of him without ever getting to break cover or anything because I was just this woman who wasn't very bright. (CIA 1994)

What is even more intriguing about these women's subversion of gendered expectations to gain access to and transmit sensitive information is that this work is coded as masculine and is today the most male-dominated directorate of the CIA, even though it relies heavily on stereotypically feminized traits such as cultivating relationships, empathy, and other "expressive" qualities. This echoes Leidner's findings in her research on insurance agents (Leidner 1991; Leidner 1993): although the work demanded qualities and interpersonal skills that are traditionally defined as feminine, the men in those jobs redefined those qualities in stereotypically masculine ways—for instance, as a love of competition and having an aggressive "killer" instinct (Leidner 1993). This shows that the jobs themselves are malleable and that their content is flexible for interpretation. Leidner (1991, 174) writes: "The actual features of the jobs do not themselves determine whether the work will be defined as most appropriate for men or women. Rather, these job features are resources for interpretation that can be drawn on by workers, their superiors, and other audiences."

Gendered components of individual identity

The social construction of gendered norms and expectations is evident in the CIA's use of these symbols, images, and narratives, as well as in popular culture's depiction of who embodies the spy or intelligence officer. These portrayals inform and reflect gendered components of individual identity. The default and normalized body is male; the most popular movies are about male fictional espionage/intelligence officers, as in the James Bond, Jason Bourne, and Jack Ryan films; *24*'s Jack Bauer; and other stand-alone films such as *Tinker Tailor Soldier Spy*, *The Good Shepherd*, *Spy Game*, and so on. Film portrayals of real people, such as Ben Affleck's take on Tony Mendez in *Argo*, are also popular. When women are portrayed as intelligence officers or case officers, they are usually presented either as hypersexualized femme fatales whose primary modus operandi is the honey trap or as unstable and crazed. Notable examples of the former include Pussy Galore from *Goldfinger*, Sarah from *Chuck*, and Nikita Taylor from *La Femme Nikita*; examples of the latter include Claire Danes's *Homeland* character Carrie Mathison, who lives with bipolar disorder, and Katherine Heigl's character in the NBC drama *State of Affairs*. When women appear in male-focused media, they are nearly non-existent or else presented as auxiliaries or as prizes for the successful man to win.[2] "The problem is that they portray women in such a one-dimensional way; whatever the character flaw is, that's all they are… it can leave a very distinct understanding of women at the Agency," says career intelligence officer Gina Bennett (quoted in Dowd 2015).

---

[2] A notable exception to this pattern is Jessica Chastain's portrayal of Maya in the film *Zero Dark Thirty*.

It is easy to think that the CIA would dismiss Hollywood's imaginings out of hand, but a series of *Newsweek* interviews with seven CIA women shows that the CIA does, on some level, embrace its Hollywood portrayal: the CIA's Office of Public Affairs is reportedly decorated with framed posters of the movies *Clear and Present Danger, Patriot Games,* and *Spy Games* (Jones 2016). "People treat it as only men have a calling to serve their country, and it's unnatural for women to do it," according to Bennett (Dowd 2015). Jones (2016) says that "we don't picture ... a woman, a mom" when we think about who is doing the work of keeping the nation safe. Moreover, the CIA reportedly asked for the *New York Times* to do a piece featuring Agency women expressly to balance the skewed Hollywood image (Dowd 2015). When I asked my interview subjects to describe how they thought of people from the intelligence agencies, I found that their default image was also a man. For instance, people described FBI officers as wearing "dark suits, white shirts" and as having "tight haircuts." Another colleague said that at the CIA, "everyone thinks they have a 16-inch cock"; someone else once joked that if the CIA had a perfume, it would smell like "Viagra and $100 bills." These comments clearly, if crudely, illustrate how the employees themselves reproduce an abstract notion of the worker that is not gender-neutral but is, in fact, a man—a hegemonically masculine and virile man, which in these narratives is deployed as a kind of short-hand code for competence.

Creating and conceptualizing social structures: Organizational logic

Gender inequality exists and persists at the CIA, at least in part because the organization perpetuates that inequality above and beyond what people enact at the level of the individual. Though organizational logic is often presented and conceptualized by its practitioners as gender-neutral, in actual reality, the worker who comes closest to fulfilling the ideals of that abstract job is usually a man. This idea is reflected in the institution's organizational logic in ways that overlap with the other categories discussed in this chapter. For instance, organizational logic refers to written rules, contracts, managerial directives, and other tools for managing large bureaucracies, such as systems of job evaluation and promotion, that rationalize and justify organization. This results in the gender inequality in GS levels found throughout the CIA's history despite the mitigating strategies of recent decades.

When notions of gender are deeply entrenched, they creep into evaluations of whether workers should advance to higher echelons. The abstract worker, in organizational logic, cannot have competing demands on their time; at least, those competing demands cannot be included in the definition of the job (Acker 1990). The higher the position, the more of oneself a worker is assumed to devote to the job; thus, a certain kind of gendered division of labor is implicitly assumed in the abstract idea of the job. Acker (1990) reminds us that hierarchies are gendered because they are constructed on these underlying assumptions. In reality, though, workers are "bodied" rather than "disembodied," and the bodied worker is much more likely to represent one demographic of person rather than a universal being.

Gender, embodiment, and the social construction of the worker

The previous section demonstrates that intelligence agencies can and do operate in gendered ways, even when organizational practices are presented as gender-neutral. In this section, I discuss the ways in which these organizational practices affect gendered workers differently, with a particular focus on the social construction of the intelligence officer.

The social construction of the body

What does it mean to say that a body is socially constructed? We are generally taught to believe that the body is solely physical, a matter of biology. But we know that factors other than genetics—nutrition, prevention and treatment of illness, exercise, quality of water and air, etc.—comprise another large part of physiological development. Beyond those factors, sociology tells us that members of a society are taught to shape their bodies in ways that comply with their culture's expectations for how bodies should look and act. While this perspective does not deny the material elements of a body and each physical body's distinctiveness, it does emphasize that society, not genes or biology, determines the "proper" shape of a body. Thus, we know that social and cultural factors—the attitudes and values attached to gendered body practices— produce bodies that one's social group considers properly masculine or feminine (Lorber and Martin 2007).

People undertake many practices in pursuit of a certain kind of body—plastic surgery, hormones, supplements, diet and exercise regimens, and more—and we know that bodies matter for appearance and success. On the surface, we say that intellect, ability, and effort count for more than anything else, especially physical appearance. At the same time, for instance, only a handful of American presidents have been shorter than six feet tall (Collins and Zebrowitz 1995), and corporate research shows that about 10% of a man's earnings can be attributed to height (Hensley and Cooper 1987). Attributes of "success" and "competence" in many other fields are similarly displayed on the face and in the body. For example, though hard to believe at first blush, Lorber and Martin (2007, 229) present a compelling overview of the jaw shapes of World War I British military officers on display at the National Portrait Gallery in London. Mueller and Mazur (1996) similarly demonstrate that the shape of a man's jaw is a determining factor in being chosen for high-ranking military office, and they show that so-called "weak-faced" men are rarely advanced to the highest ranks.

Cultural views about the body are more than aesthetic; they are often also moral judgments. For instance, when a person's body falls outside the socially accepted norms for weight or shape, that person may be considered lazy or lacking in self-control. Conversely, people whose bodies conform to norms are praised and held up as examples to be emulated. By judging, rewarding, and punishing people with varying body types and shapes, members of social groups encourage each other to aspire to and attain socially acceptable bodies.

The relevant take-away message from this literature is this: it may be normative to think that the functions of bodies stem from their physiological and anatomical makeup, but the social construction view argues that ideal types of bodies are products of a society's gendered beliefs and systems. This does not mean there is no variation in types of bodies, but rather that these norms are much more powerful and pervasive than the average person believes. Moreover, to the extent that these norms are generally recognized, people tend to normalize them as products of biology rather than society. Though physical standards may be pervasive in a country, a culture, or a racial/ethnic group, standards can vary widely within much smaller groups as well. The easiest examples can be found in athletics, where variations in body types and modification practices encourage athletes to concentrate on various sports: a body well-suited to and trained specifically for gymnastics is typically not a good fit for basketball.

It is less common to think about the social construction of the body in the work/organization context. Although some research exists to delineate physical differences *between* types of jobs—blue collar vs. white collar, for example—substantially less research has foregrounded variation *within* a single organizational context. In the next section, I turn to a discussion of some of the organizational practices that construct intelligence officers and the ways in which those practices become embodied.

Organizational practices: Constructing analysts

Like most workplace ethnographers, I collected a substantial amount of data relating to acculturation processes or the ways in which people are brought into the organization. Unlike most workplace ethnographers, I also point the arrow in the other direction and examine the ways in which the organization gets into its people. I conceptualize this process as the social and organizational construction of the intelligence officer. This work primarily looks at intelligence analysts, but coupled with the data from the declassified CIA documents, we can get a sense of how these processes work with officers from other directorates as well.

Sociology provides useful perspectives for conceptualizing intelligence as an organization. For instance, Erving Goffman and Lewis Coser coined terms that can help us understand how organizations can get into their employees' heads and encourage behavior among the workers that performs and reproduces inequality. In his book *Asylums* on Psychiatric Hospitals, Goffman (1961) introduced the concept of the "total institution"—an organization that has 24-7 physical control over its members. In addition to hospitals, we might think of institutions like prisons or the military as total institutions; each member is beholden to all the organization's rules and regulations, and upon entering, the institution makes many demands of each member, which has the effect of radically altering that person's behavior. Coser (1974) built on Goffman's notion of the total institution to coin the term "greedy institution"—an organization that does not have 24-7 physical control over its members but nonetheless makes many demands and engenders great loyalty among its participants. The greedy institution does not go as far as the total institution, but it still makes substantial demands of its members that go above and beyond those required of a more normative, less greedy institution. Rather than physical control, the grip that a greedy institution has on its members tends to be more psychological and emotional; the greedy institution engenders great loyalty from its members by reducing competing demands on time, attention, and other resources and making the organization the central focus of its members' lives.

Elsewhere (Nolan 2019), I have argued that the CIA operates as a greedy institution. The CIA is "greedy" even before it makes the offer of employment: its onboarding processes require an applicant to give their whole life over to the Agency with no guarantee of a payoff. Once inside, several key elements of the way the U.S. does intelligence work create "greedy" demands on the officers. These include information overload, incompatible technology systems (or "stovepiping"), the pressure on analysts to publish papers, and the pressure on operators to recruit assets, develop leads, and craft requirements. The CIA is a greedy and dominant organization in the sense that it has the power to reshape individuals dramatically (Adler and Adler 1998). Its employees come to identify strongly with the organization, and while this has the effect of strengthening the boundary between insiders and outsiders, it also has the effect of weakening the boundary between the individual and the organization. "In so far as one identifies himself with a whole," says Cooley (1909, 38), "loyalty to that whole is loyalty to himself." Because the organization and the self become mutually constitutive, the organization is able to offload some of its practices onto the officers, who, in turn, begin to practice measures of self-surveillance. The organization's opaqueness enables this internalization. Because they are never sure when they are being watched, officers must assume they are being watched all the time: it is an invisible panopticon (Foucault 1979). We assumed everything we did on the computers was being monitored, as well as everything we said on the phone (both open and classified lines). This internalization can, in turn, lead to some of the overwhelmed analysts' experience, for instance, in the post-9/11 tendency to send and read emails to and from the entire DI "out of mortal terror of missing something," as one of my interview subjects put it.

Officers submit to all of this voluntarily but with no idea of what kinds of information are waiting for them once they have a Top Secret clearance. There is, by definition, no way to know until you know. This access unquestionably shaped me and my colleagues; I distinctly recall a colleague's comments in my first weeks at the Agency that they could tell by the look on my face that I had been "read in"—that is, that I had learned Top Secret information. I related to Masco's (2014, 441) discussion of secrecy's "distorting effects" and Daniel Ellsberg's (2002) reflections on the psychological effects of access to classified information in his autobiography. That access has static and dynamic elements; once you know something, you know it, but the maintenance of that information requires obfuscation, occasional lying, and many kinds of keeping track, all of which is invisible labor that takes a toll physically and psychologically. In other words, what initially seems diffuse in the abstract notion of the organization is eventually located in the body.

Gendered consequences

The processes of constructing the intelligence officer up to now are common to everyone in the organization. But because the organization is gendered and because people occupy gendered bodies, I turn now to the question of how organizational processes that seem to affect everyone equally actually affect women differently. The demands of this greedy institution—including its requirement that its employees are "like a machine" and must turn off the "squishy" parts of the brain—result in, among other things, what I call the social erasure of the female body. For many female CIA officers, that CIA identity becomes what sociologists call a master status: a social identity that becomes the primary identifying characteristic for an individual. The conflict is that in contemporary American culture, "mother" is also assumed to be a master status: we still think of a "good" mother as a mother who is always available to her children. When these master statuses conflict, something must give. This conflict affects women who have never expressed an interest in motherhood as well because organizations tend to see women as potential mothers or future mothers. Because of the pervasive attitude that women face promotion obstacles because of their perceived status as future mothers—regardless of their actual status—there is evidence that some CIA women have lied about their reproductive plans or else conflated their personal and professional lives to the point where the former is subsumed under the latter. For instance, in "Divine Secrets of the RYBAT Sisterhood," a former operations officer named "Meredith" delivers the following narrative of her experience in roughly the 1980s:

[Name redacted] was Deputy Chief of Europe, and he said to me, "I really don't believe in women being ops officers." I said, "I don't understand, [redacted]. Why is that?" And he said, "Well, because you know they'll have families." And I said, "You know, almost all of your male ops officers have families, too." "No, no, no," he said, "You might get pregnant. First of all, you can't be an ops officer while you're pregnant, and secondly, you'll have to take all that time off." I had two children at the time. And I said, "Well, it's okay [redacted] because I'm fixed." And immediately, he said, "Well, okay, you seem like a reasonable candidate. We'll put you in for that." So I went ahead... I was lying. It was clear to me that I wasn't going to get in without it, so I went out and promptly on my first tour got pregnant again. But I felt so compelled—we were talking before this, about sacrifices women—and yeah, men, too—were willing to undergo at the time to have opportunities to do that. I was [redacted] [for my] first tour and got pregnant and came back to Washington a couple weeks before the baby was born, [knowing] it was going to have to be a caesarean. Went in, worked up until the day the baby was born, had the baby, had the caesarean, and was back on the street [redacted] in seven days. And I wasn't the only one that was doing that—all of us, you really felt like you couldn't take off and do that. (CIA 1994, 4)

Though more recent workers have suggested that this kind of contempt for women's bodies is not as prevalent as it used to be, it is still true that when the public and private spheres clash for women, "they clash hard," according to a *New York Times* article titled "Good Riddance, Carrie Mathison" (Dowd 2015). Gina Bennett, one subject of a 2016 *Newsweek* article on women in the CIA (Jones 2016), is featured in this *New York Times* article as well and is the author of *National Security Mom*. Bennett talks about how she conceptualizes her children in terms of the international crisis she was dealing with at work at the time—her "9/11 baby," her "Fallujah baby"—and how she briefed Condoleeza Rice while in labor. There is a sense that it is still more acceptable for a man to leave his family to travel overseas for work than it is for a woman to do it. For instance, Jennifer Matthews, the CIA station chief who was killed in the 2009 bombing at Khost, was evidently "excoriated" by relatives for leaving her family to take that post (Dowd 2015).

Valerie Plame, the former undercover officer and author of *Fair Game*, says that while the women of the Agency are talented and smart, "they had stepchildren. They had not raised their children. Or they were divorced. Or they went home to cats" (quoted in Jones 2016). Susie, part of the RYBAT Sisterhood, confesses that she "sold [her] soul" to become a case officer: "The motherhood that I insisted on became kind of secondary" (CIA 1994, 6). The 1991 Glass Ceiling Study supports this: it reports that 33% of Hispanic women at the

Agency had children compared with 58% of Hispanic men; 38% of white Senior Intelligence Service (SIS) women had children compared with 89% of white SIS men; and women in every racial category reported being treated differently because of their family responsibilities (CIA 1991, 16).

Thus, although there are so-called family-friendly leave policies in place now, the pressure some women feel to lie about or minimize the biological functions of their bodies as they interact with their colleagues suggests that although it is presented as gender-neutral, the abstract notion of a "worker" is actually a man—a man who is available to the job at all times because the gendered division of labor is assumed. As Acker writes:

> The closest the disembodied worker doing the abstract job comes to a real worker is the male worker whose life centers on his full-time, life-long job while his wife or another woman takes care of his personal needs and his children. ... The worker with "a job" is the same universal "individual" who, in actual social reality, is a man. The concept of a universal worker excludes and marginalizes women who cannot, almost by definition, achieve the qualities of a real worker because to do so is to become like a man. (Acker 1990, 149-50)

Further underscoring this point is the organization's role in managing the emotions of its workers in ways that are gendered. Jones (2016) reports that analysts "must be able to compartmentalize their emotions at precisely the most horrifying moments." This emphasis on steely rationality rather than emotions is gendered as these are qualities most likely to have been socialized in men, which further contributes to the devaluation and erasure of the feminine in the organization. The Glass Ceiling Survey states this explicitly, saying that "White women also reported having to say things in an unemotional way because being labeled as 'too emotional' will significantly damage their careers" (CIA 1991, 20). These findings echo other work in which women in masculinized environments face constrained choices in their approach to the work, as when female litigators in "Rambo-like" environments feel the pull to take on the attributes of their successful male colleagues (Britton, 2000). Moreover, we know that women who appear to be "naturals" at jobs that require emotional labor also run the risk of having their hard work rendered invisible since their labor does not show as labor but rather is essentialized and explained away as being due to their femaleness (Mastracci, Newman, and Guy 2006). In other words, social groups, including organizations, create and then essentialize gender differences:

> Claims about gender, which include bodies, fit into the social arrangements and cultural beliefs that constitute gender as a social

institution. As a social institution, gender produces two categories of people, "men" and "women," with different characteristics, skills, personalities, and body types. These gendered attributes, which we call "manliness" or "masculinity" and "womanliness" or "femininity," are designed to fit people into adult social roles, such as "mother," "father," "nurse," or "construction worker." ...

There are racial, ethnic, and class differences among women and men, but gender similarities still exist. These similarities are socially produced, but their pervasiveness makes it seem as if they are biologically linked. Thus, women's learned emotional sensitiveness will be considered as evidence that they are naturally maternal, and men's learned coolness and objectivity will be considered as evidence that they are naturally logical and scientific. Yet recent events have shown that men do cry, and women can be heroes, warriors, or terrorists. (Lorber and Martin 2007, 255)

In other words, we often assume biological explanations for social and organizational patterns that are actually the products of gendered belief systems. These patterns, in turn, have gendered consequences that hit women harder as they try to resolve the master status conflict that their participation in gendered greedy institutions creates.

Conclusion

This chapter uses declassified documents, ethnographic data, and interviews to weave together two bodies of literature that seldom intersect: the sociology of work and organizations and the social construction of the body. In doing so, I find that intelligence organizations construct officers in ways that are presented as gender-neutral but actually have gendered consequences for individual workers. For instance, I highlight what I call the social erasure of the female body, in which women lie about, minimize, or otherwise reconceptualize their participation in motherhood and other kinds of care work in an individual-level attempt to resolve the conflict that arises when they try to occupy two master status roles simultaneously. The "greediness" of the intelligence community makes considerable demands on its workers that affect these workers in gendered ways.

Although inequality is woven into the tapestry of the organization itself, most of the advice offered to combat the problem is given at the level of the individual. For instance, the women of the RYBAT Sisterhood acknowledge that "[discrimination] wasn't just a person, it really was a system" (CIA 1994, 9), and then just a few pages later state that the way forward "boils down to choices. ...

You have to make choices. When you don't, when you're not willing to sacrifice, then don't blame the system" (21). Similarly, a 2013 report from the CIA Director's Advisory Group on Women in Leadership explicitly states that "employees must more fully understand and embrace the impact of the personal choices they make" (CIA 2013, 1) and "take ownership of their careers" (15), at the same time that it offers vague organizational-level suggestions such as "valu[ing] diverse paths" to promotion (1).

Acker (2000, 630) reminds us that this disconnect is not surprising; the idea that organizations are gender-neutral actually enables an individualistic focus on and explanation for success and failure. Research suggests that individual-level solutions are not enough, however, and structural change is needed (Hult 1995). Because we know that organizations' gendered practices are not a function of representation but rather deeply engrained in the abstract conception of roles and expectations in the organization itself, it is similarly not enough to look to increase the representation of women at the highest levels. As Mastracci and Arreola (2016) tell us, "We can no longer use statistics on the growth of women in full-time employment or examples of women in upper management as proxies for fairer and more humane workplaces." Because the utilization of a diverse workforce is an explicitly stated organizational goal as well as the right thing to do, the Agency should take steps beyond the level of the individual worker to reorganize and rethink the workplace and its expectations of its employees more broadly.

References

Acker, Joan. 1990. "Hierarchies, Jobs, Bodies: A Theory of Gendered Organizations." Gender and Society 4 (2): 139-158.

———. 2000. *Revisiting Class: Thinking from Gender, Race, and Organizations.* Oxford, UK: Oxford University Press.

Adler, P. A., and P. Adler. 1998. "Intense Loyalty in Organizations: A Case Study of College Athletics." *Administrative Science Quarterly* 33: 401-417.

Britton, Dana M. 2000. "The Epistemology of the Gendered Organization." *Gender and Society* 14 (3): 418-434.

Central Intelligence Agency. 1953. "Career Employment of Women in the Central Intelligence Agency." Retrieved from https://www.cia.gov/library/readingroom/docs/1953-11-01a.pdf.

Central Intelligence Agency. 1991. "Glass Ceiling Study Summary." Retrieved from https://www.cia.gov/library/readingroom/document/526e4e95993294098d5176d4.

Central Intelligence Agency. 1994. "Divine Secrets of the RYBAT Sisterhood: Four Senior Women of the Directorate of Operations Discuss Their Careers." Retrieved from https://www.cia.gov/library/readingroom/document/526e4e95993294098d51767d.

Central Intelligence Agency. 2013. "Director's Advisory Group on Women in Leadership Unclassified Report." Retrieved from https://www.cia.gov/static/825c79d82205d8b8e0045a8dd87fc614/CIA_Women_In_Leadership_March2013.pdf.

Central Intelligence Agency. 2022. "CIA Vision, Mission, Ethos, and Challenges," accessed February 27, 2022, from https://www.cia.gov/about/mission-vision/

Central Intelligence Agency. N.d. "CIA Museum: Inform, Instruct, Inspire." Retrieved from https://www.cia.gov/about-cia/cia-museum.

Collins, M. A., and L. A. Zebrowitz. 1995. "The Contributions of Appearance to Occupational Outcomes in Civilian and Military Settings." *Journal of Applied Social Psychology* 25 (2): 129-163.

Connell, R. W. 1987. *Gender and Power.* Stanford, CA: Stanford University Press.

Cooley, C. H. 1909. *Social Organization.* New York: Charles Scribner's Sons.

Coser, L. 1974. *Greedy Institutions: Patterns of Undivided Commitment.* New York: Free Press.

Dowd, Maureen. 2015, April 4. "Good Riddance, Carrie Mathison." *New York Times.* Retrieved from https://www.nytimes.com/2015/04/05/opinion/sunday/maureen-dowd-good-riddance-carrie-mathison.html.

Ellsberg, Daniel. 2002. *Secrets: A Memoir of Vietnam and the Pentagon Papers.* New York: Penguin.

Ely, Robin J., and Debra E. Meyerson. 2000. "Theories of Gender in Organizations: A New Approach to Organizational Analysis and Change." *Research in Organizational Behavior* 22: 103-151.

Foucault, M. 1979. *Discipline and Punish: The Birth of the Prison.* New York: Random House.

Geertz, Clifford. 1973. *The Interpretation of Cultures.* New York: Basic Books.

Goffman, Erving. 1961. *Asylums: Essays on the Social Situation of Mental Patients and Other Inmates.* New York: First Anchor Books.

Hensley, W. E., and R. Cooper. 1987. "Height and Occupational Success: A Review and Critique." *Psychological Reports* 60 (3, Pt. 1): 843-849.

Hsieh, Chih-Wei, and Elizabeth Winslow. 2006. "Gender Representation in the Federal Workforce: A Comparison Among Groups." *Review of Public Personnel Administration* 26 (3): 276-294.

Hult, Karen M. 1995. "Feminist Organization Theories and Government Organizations." *Public Productivity & Management Review* 19 (2): 128-142.

Jones, A. 2016, September 21. "Women of the CIA: The Hidden History of American Spycraft." *Newsweek.* Retrieved from http://www.newsweek.com/2016/09/30/cia-women-national-security-500312.html.

Leidner, Robin. 1991. "Selling Hamburgers and Selling Insurance: Gender, Work, and Identity in Interactive Service Jobs." *Gender & Society* 5: 154-77.

Leidner, Robin. 1993. *Fast Food, Fast Talk: Service Work and the Routinization of Everyday Life.* Berkeley: University of California Press.

Lorber, Judith, and Patricia Yancey Martin. 2012. "The Socially Constructed Body: Insights from Feminist Theory." In *Illuminating Social Life: Classical and Contemporary Theory Revisited,* edited by Peter Kivisto. 6th ed. Los Angeles, CA: Pine Forge Press.

Martin, Amy. 2015. "America's Evolution of Women and Their Roles in the Intelligence Community." *Journal of Strategic Security* 8 (5): 99-109.

Masco, Joseph. 2014. *The Theater of Operations: National Security Affect from the Cold War to the War on Terror.* Durham, NC: Duke University Press.

Mastracci, Sharon, and Veronica I. Arreola. 2016. "Gendered Organizations: How Human Resource Management Practices Produce and Reproduce Administrative Man." *Administrative Theory & Praxis* 38 (2): 137-149.

Mastracci, Sharon H., Meredith A. Newman, and Mary E. Guy. 2006. "Appraising Emotion Work: Determining Whether Emotional Labor Is Valued in Government Jobs." *American Review of Public Administration* 36 (2): 123-138.

Mueller, Ulrich, and Allan Mazur. 1996. "Facial Dominance of West Point Cadets as a Predictor of Later Military Rank." *Social Forces* 74 (3): 823-850.

McIntosh, Elizabeth. 1998. *Sisterhood of Spies: Women of the OSS.* Annapolis, MD: Naval Institute Press.

Mickolus, Ed. 2011. *The Secret Book of CIA Humor.* Gretna, LA: Pelican Publishing.

Nolan, Bridget Rose. 2019. "Lessons Learned: How Sociology Can Contribute to the Study of Intelligence." In *Researching National Security Intelligence: A Reader,* edited by S. J. Coulthart and D. Van Puyvelde. Washington, DC: Georgetown University Press.

Pear, Robert. 1995, March 30. "CIA Settles Suit on Sex Bias." *New York Times.* Retrieved from https://www.nytimes.com/1995/03/30/us/cia-settles-suit-on-sex-bias.html#:~:text=The%20Central%20Intelligence%20Agency%20said,clandestine%20operations%20around%20the%20world.

West, Candice, and Don. H. Zimmerman. 1987. "Doing Gender." *Gender and Society* 1: 125-151.

Chapter 5

Analysis, collection, counterintelligence, and covert action, oh my...: Evaluating coverage of the intelligence disciplines in academic journals

Doug Patteson

University of New Hampshire

Abstract: Doug Patteson presents the result of a survey of academic national security intelligence journals from 2001 to 2021. Intelligence articles are divided into four categories: collection, counterintelligence, covert action, and analysis. The dominant intelligence topic covered in these journals was analysis, followed by covert action. Under studied is collection. Patteson concludes that broadening the literature on intelligence to include more on collection is a fundamental step in increasing our overall knowledge of intelligence.

Keywords: Analysis, collection, HUMINT, intelligence studies, OSINT

***

Introduction

This chapter presents the results of a survey of academic national security intelligence journals from 2001 to 2021. Our analysis shows that there are more articles focused on analysis than on the other three elements of intelligence: collection, counterintelligence and covert action. We identify gaps in collection research, which may help researchers identify subjects for further exploration and add to the foundational understanding of intelligence studies.

History of intelligence studies

Historically, intelligence studies as an academic subject have been treated as a subset of more traditional liberal arts disciplines such as political science

(Jackson and Scott 2005, 174). Moran and Murphy (2013) note that in "both the United States and the United Kingdom, the field of intelligence studies represents one of the fastest growing subsets of international history, political science and strategic studies." Michael Goodman (2006) writes that "the United States ... has a longer tradition than the United Kingdom for the teaching and study of intelligence."

Intelligence classes are taught at many colleges and universities, whether as special subjects, minors, or a growing number of undergraduate and graduate degree options. In the United Kingdom, the University of Salford was the first to offer a degree program in intelligence studies, with a master's in Intelligence and Security Studies (Goodman 2006, 8). Mercyhurst University (n.d.) established the first intelligence studies program in the United States in 1992. Several other colleges and universities have followed with both undergraduate and graduate studies programs in intelligence studies, including Johns Hopkins, the Institute for World Politics, Embrey Riddle, The Citadel and The University of New Hampshire, among others. The Office of the Director of National Intelligence operates a Centers for Academic Excellence (IC CAE) Program. The IC CAE program currently funds active partnerships with over 40 academic institutions and maintains relationships with at least another 30 (ODNI n.d.).

The federal government operates the National Intelligence University, which focuses on both entry-level and mid-career intelligence community employees (National Intelligence University, n.d.). With the creation of the U.S. Defense Intelligence Agency in the early 1960s, the Department of Defense recognized the need for a consolidated approach to professional intelligence education to support the military's needs. The Defense Intelligence School was first established in 1962 and five years later added civilian instructors. By 1980, the school was authorized by President Jimmy Carter to award a graduate degree, the Master of Science in Strategic Intelligence (MSSI). The school would go through several name changes over the succeeding years and, in 1997 began to award a Bachelor of Science in Intelligence (BSI). In 2011, the organization morphed into its current form, the National Intelligence University and is now administered by the Office of the Director of National Intelligence.[1]

Faculty at these and other institutions produce academic scholarship in an emerging discipline called intelligence studies. Until the mid-1990s traditional

---

[1] See National Intelligence University, n.d. NIU's mission is to prepare Intelligence Community leaders for tomorrow's challenges. As such, some of its curriculum is focused on intelligence studies, but not all. Much of it is focused on developing and/or strengthening practitioners for work in Intelligence. All students must be from the US Armed Forces or federal government and possess an active security clearance. It is thus not a pathway for many students/academics.

academic journals in disciplines such as history, psychology, and political science were the primary outlet for authors interested in intelligence. With the creation of journals specific to intelligence studies, such as *Intelligence and National Security* and the *International Journal of Intelligence and CounterIntelligence*, scholars had domain-specific journals to publish their work (Taylor & Francis, "Intelligence ...: Journal Overview," n.d.; Taylor & Francis, "International Journal ...: Current Issue," n.d.).

Intelligence, as a phenomenon for academic study, encompasses many areas. Shulsky and Schmitt (2002) subdivide national security intelligence into four elements: collection, analysis, counterintelligence, and covert action. Each of these elements deserves careful study by academics to advance the knowledge in this important field. Does the literature demonstrate equal study in practice?

A cursory review of the scholarly works contained in the existing academic journals on intelligence reveals that many of the articles are focused on the analytic world. Yet, the study of the world of intelligence collection is growing although with significant challenges. One challenge is that many sources are shielded by government secrecy. Current literature is largely a study of failures, historical action, or oversight and administrative issues. Some academics have begun to peel back the veil on collection; however, no clear research agenda has been published to guide their work.

Intelligence analysis and intelligence collection are both important components of the intelligence process. At the practitioner level, they require different skill sets and approaches. Intelligence collection involves gathering and processing raw data and information from a variety of sources, while intelligence analysis involves interpreting and synthesizing that information to produce intelligence products that inform decision-makers.

A review of both the *Journal of Intelligence and Security* and the *International Journal of Intelligence and CounterIntelligence* suggests that there is a greater emphasis on intelligence analysis in the academic literature compared to intelligence collection, counterintelligence, and covert action. It also appears that there has been a growing recognition in recent years of the importance of intelligence collection, counterintelligence, and covert action in the academic literature. Many scholars and practitioners are working to develop a better understanding of these apparently lesser-studied aspects of the intelligence process. There has also been increased interest in the role of technology in intelligence collection and how new tools and techniques can be used to improve collection efforts. Overall, while there may be more articles written on intelligence analysis in the academic literature, it is critical to recognize all the elements of intelligence in the intelligence process. Are academics working toward a balanced and comprehensive understanding of all aspects of intelligence work?

Marrin (2016) suggests there are five stages of intelligence studies as an academic discipline: documenting the known, evaluating the known for gaps or deficiencies, filling those gaps in knowledge, ensuring the new knowledge is available to those who need it, and institutionalizing this process. Our goal in this paper is to focus on the first two stages in Marrin's process: documenting the known and conducting a gap analysis. In this paper, we focus on the following research hypothesis: There are more academic journal articles on analysis than on collection, covert action, and counterintelligence. We analyze existing academic and professional literature and identify gaps in collection research.

Methodology

We collected data from two academic journals and one professional journal from 2001 to 2021. We categorized each of the articles as primarily focusing on the collection, analysis, counterintelligence, covert action or other. We generated basic descriptive statistics and then performed a gap analysis. The following paragraphs provide details on each of these steps.

In evaluating the intelligence studies literature, we looked at prominent academic and professional intelligence journals. Coulthart and Marrin (2023) provide a useful evaluation of intelligence journals. They delineate the differences between academic and professional journals and provide data on their relative impact. Based on their work, we selected *Intelligence and National Security* (*INS*) and the *International Journal of Intelligence and CounterIntelligence* (*IJIC*) for inclusion in this study. We also selected the Central Intelligence Agency's *Studies in Intelligence* (*SI*) professional journal for study (CIA n.d.). All three are peer-reviewed journals. Other journals, edited volumes, websites, and blogs were omitted from this study due to time and resource limitations.

INS, founded in 1986, publishes seven issues a year and is currently edited by Stephen Marrin and Mark Pythian. In 2022, *INS* articles were viewed/ downloaded 362,000 times (Taylor & Francis, "Intelligence and National Security: Journal Metrics," n.d.). *IJIC*, also founded in 1986, publishes four issues a year and is edited by Jan Goldman. In 2022, *IJIC* articles were viewed/downloaded 200,000 times (Taylor & Francis, "International Journal …: Journal Metrics," n.d.). *SI* is unique in that it contains both classified and unclassified articles. It was founded in 1955 by Sherman Kent and is now edited by Joseph Gartin. *SI* is published quarterly, and the number of views or downloads is not publicly available. Even the total number of articles published is not publicly known, though Nicholas Dujmovic noted in his 2005 retrospective on the first 50 years of *SI* there were "more than 1,200 article-length contributions" (Dujmovic 2005). Data on the most-viewed articles or the most cited is not available. We did not, for this study, differentiate between articles that had previously been classified but have since been declassified and articles that had been unclassified originally.

We established that the data set would encompass the years 2001 to 2021, 20 years of data. In setting this timeframe, we recognized that paralleling the growth in intelligence, the field of intelligence studies had grown in prominence post-9/11. This focus on a defined post-9/11 timeframe provided the best opportunity to test our theory. Additionally, we wanted to be able to search the data online, and all articles from this timeframe are available online. We closed our search parameters at the end of 2021, as the most recent 18 months of articles are not necessarily available online.

It is important to note that while some articles were published online during the 2001-2021 timeframe, they may have been published in print earlier than that and were brought online in the process of digitizing past issues. For this article, we choose to only use articles with original publication dates (in print and online) within our timeframe. Additionally, using Taylor and Francis's native search capabilities, we collected the top 30 most-cited articles of the last three years and of all time from each publication, likewise reducing them to articles within our study timeframe.

Using R, a statistical programming language, we gathered data on *INS* and *IJIC* articles. All analyses were performed using R Statistical Software (version 4.3.1) (R Core Team 2021).

Data on journal articles from the CIA's webpage for *Studies in Intelligence* was collected manually. The Center for the Study of Intelligence lists 586 unclassified articles by title, going back to the mid-1950s. We used a historical version of the CIA's SI website to identify 274 unclassified articles in the study timeframe. We believe there is a significant number of classified articles that would meet the requirements of this study; however, the articles are not available for unclassified research. We collected the article title, DOI or URL, volume number, issue number, date published in print, date published online, article type, and total number of views for each journal article. Some data was not available for some articles.

Using Shulsky and Schmitt's (2002) model, subdividing national security intelligence into four elements—collection, analysis, counterintelligence, and covert action—we categorized scholarly works from the three journals from 2001 to 2021. Each article was reviewed by a researcher and categorized as focusing primarily on the collection, analysis, counterintelligence, covert action, or other. We employed the definitions outlined in the following paragraphs.

An article was categorized as *collection* if the primary topic was information gathered via human intelligence (HUMINT), technical intelligence (TECHINT), or Open Sources (OSINT). We defined TECHINT broadly to include intercepted signals and communications (radio, electronic, and telemetry), photographs and images, and measurements and signatures. Reviewers also included articles about liaison relationships or intelligence-sharing partnerships in the category of collection. We argue that liaison channels are primarily a collection funnel, whether raw information or analysis. Articles about ethics also tended to fit in more than one potential category, though they predominantly fit in either collection or other.

An article was categorized as *analysis* if the primary topic was the process of transforming raw information into finished products. Articles that discussed the methods of analysis or that evaluated the effectiveness of analysis in the case of a specific event were both included in this category. Articles that were in and of themselves analytical pieces but which were not about analysis per se were not.

An article was categorized as *counterintelligence* if the primary topic was information gathered and activities conducted to protect against espionage or other intelligence activities conducted by or on behalf of foreign governments, foreign organizations, foreign persons, or international terrorist activities. Articles that focused on protection against other internal threats or on the mechanisms of defense against an adversary's efforts were also categorized as counterintelligence.

An article was categorized as *covert action* if the primary topic was about government activities to influence political, economic, or military conditions abroad, where it is intended that the role of the government will not be apparent or acknowledged publicly.

We employed a category called "other" that was primarily focused on oversight, organizational history, intelligence in broad historical contexts, administrative/ demographic, or other activities related to the intelligence community (IC) but not directly connected to the primary objectives of the IC.

There were an insignificant number of articles that could have been categorized into multiple categories—for example, both analysis and collection—or, based on the reviewer's perception of the article's primary focus, could have fit into one or another category. In these cases, the reviewers made judgment calls on the primary focus of the article and allocated it to that category.

Taylor and Francis provide data on the number of times each article has been cited and viewed for both *Intelligence and National Security* and the *International Journal of Intelligence and CounterIntelligence*. We used R to gather the data on article views for all articles in our study timeframe and sorted the data in Excel. We did not use Taylor and Francis's list of most-read articles as it only included the top 30 from the last year and the top 30 of all time. Additionally, Taylor and Francis lists the 30 most cited articles from the last three years as well as the 30 most cited of all time in the "Journal Metrics" section of each journal's website. We excluded from these lists any articles from outside our study's timeframe.

Results

Our data set comprised 1,852 journal articles across the three journals. The initial data collection for *INS* returned 2,391 articles, and for *IJIC*, 1,734 articles. After removing non-academic articles such as special-issue introductions, letters to the editor, editorials, obituaries, and the like, as well as removing articles outside our desired timeframe, our data set was reduced to 918 *INS*, 667 *IJIC*, and 267 *SI* articles.

As seen in Table 5.1, there were 534 (28.8%) articles focused on analysis, 338 (18.2%) focused on collection, 167 (9%) focused on counterintelligence, and 131 (7.1%) articles focused on covert action. The other category contained 682 (36.8%) of the articles collected.[2]

Table 5.1. Categorized journal articles

Category	Journal			
	Intelligence and National Security (INS)	**International Journal of Intelligence and Counterintelligence (IJIC)**	**Studies in Intelligence (SI)**	**All Journals**
Analysis	234	200	100	534
Collection	197	92	49	338
Counterintelligence	61	79	27	167
Covert Action	62	35	34	131
Other	364	261	57	682
Total	918	667	267	1852

We gathered annual publication data from *INS* and *IJIC*. We did not collect annual publication data for *SI*. As seen in Figure 5.1, on average, 72 journal articles of all categories were published per year by *INS* and *IJIC* collectively. Figure 5.1 shows that there were a minimum of 41 and a maximum of 97 total articles published each year by *INS* and *IJIC* from 2001 to 2021.

---

[2] A more in-depth analysis of this category is certainly warranted. While a cursory review revealed these articles to be distributed across three or four subcategories, it would be helpful to see if one subcategory stands out more than others.

Figure 5.1. Articles published per year by the journals intelligence and national security (INS) and the international journal of intelligence and counterIntelligence (IJIC)

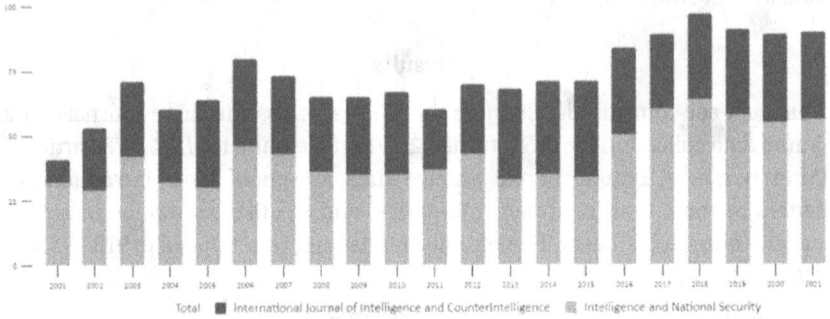

Figure 5.2 presents data on the categories of journal articles per year. From 2001 to 2021, there were, on average, 20 analysis articles, 13 collection articles, 6 counterintelligence articles, 4 covert action articles, and 29 articles of other types published by *INS* and *IJIC*.

Figure 5.2. Journal articles by year and category

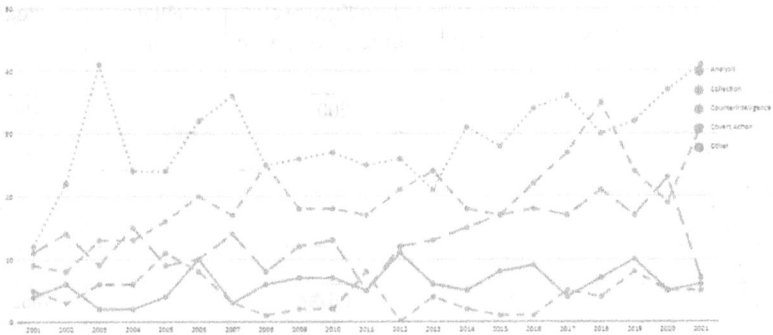

Discussion

Our review of these data indicates that, excluding the "Other" category, analysis is the most frequently occurring category of intelligence journal articles from 2001 to 2021 in the three journals included in this study: *INS*, *IJIC*, and *SI*. We evaluated the frequency of publication of each article type using the figures presented in Table 5.1. Based on those calculations, articles about analysis were published 1.58 times more frequently than collection and 3.2 and 4.1 times more often than articles about counterintelligence and covert action, respectively.

Collection articles were published less frequently than articles about analysis in all years of the study period except four (2001, 2002, 2004, and 2020). Articles about counterintelligence or covert action never surpassed the volume of analysis-oriented articles. In 2005 and 2011, the number of articles on covert action surpassed the number of collection articles published.

Figure 5.3. Word cloud of journal article titles

As seen in Figure 5.3, a word cloud of the titles of each journal article from the study period may be used to identify the prominent frequency in which the word *analysis* appears. The larger the word, the more frequently it occurs in the titles of the journals. Among the 1,852 titles, the word *analysis* is the fourth most-used word, only outweighed by *intelligence, war,* and *security.*[3]

Why do articles on analysis appear more frequently than articles on the three other elements of intelligence? It is the author's opinion that this frequency bias is not intentional; rather, it may be explained by structural impediments or reflect the authors' inherent foci or experiences. Intelligence studies are often a study of failure, both of collection and analysis. In a 1961 speech at CIA headquarters, President John F. Kennedy said, "Your successes are unheralded —your failures are trumpeted."[4] And in failure, it is the analysis and decision-making process that often bears the brunt of public examination. It is harder for intelligence community outsiders to study success, particularly when it's protected by classification.

---

[3] *British* is the fifth most frequent term used in the article titles. The prominence of the font in the word cloud in figure 5.3 above makes it appear as if it surpasses analysis, but it is just behind it in count.

[4] John F. Kennedy, remarks upon presenting an award to Allen W. Dulles, November 28, 1961.

Intelligence analysis (or, at least, its use in policy circles) is more visible and, thus, potentially easier to study than intelligence collection, which is often more fiercely protected by classification and secrecy. One of the core tenets of intelligence collection is the need to protect "sources and methods." Collection practitioners' emphasis on protecting sources and methods may make it difficult to unpack the collection process or operations for study. Additionally, most collection practitioners are undercover while engaging in their collection activity, while analysts largely are overt employees. This difference in secrecy may also add to the partiality toward analysis. Another possible explanation could be that intelligence analysis is often more closely akin to academic pursuits, and the bulk of intelligence studies professors with IC experience seem to have come from the analytic side of the community.

Does the unequal coverage of the four disciplines in academic journal articles matter? In our estimation, it does. As Marrin (2016) noted in "Improving Intelligence Studies," a body of study should be cumulative, built upon the work performed by earlier academics. If the body of work is biased in one direction, then the work built upon it may continue to expand on and potentially exaggerate that bias.

While it may not be possible, or even advisable, for each of the four categories identified by Shulsky and Schmitt to receive equal treatment in academia, the size of the gap indicates a need for increased study in the fields of collection, counterintelligence and covert action. Recognizing the gaps and identifying specific research lacunae will point toward a research agenda.

As seen in Figure 5.4, we used a word cloud to identify terms frequently used in the titles of intelligence articles in our dataset on collection. Of the 338 articles that focus on collection, the most prevalent topics seem to be collections within the context of warfare. Among the words used most frequently are *war* (appearing 38 times), *British* (24 occurrences), and *Cold War* (19 occurrences). *Signals collection/ SIGINT* (33), *HUMINT/ Human Intelligence* (16), and *liaison/ cooperation* (24) also occur frequently.

Figure 5.4. Word cloud of journal article titles focused on collection

The word cloud presented in Figure 5.4 points to a prevalence of articles on wartime collection, technical collection, the Cold War, and liaison relationships or cooperation between agencies. A review of the titles and abstracts from *INS*, as well as the titles and introductory paragraphs from *IJIC* (*IJIC* does not provide abstracts) and titles of the collection-focused articles in *SI* (again, no abstracts), gives some insight into the nature of the articles about intelligence collection. Two aspects struck us as significant in assessing the prevalence of specific topics. First, approximately one-third of all the collection-oriented articles explicitly talk about collection via technical means, whether in the early days of cryptography or modern satellites and the impacts of the information age. Additionally, almost a quarter of the articles focus on collection in the context of war or other armed conflicts.

Roughly 15% of the articles discuss some aspect of intelligence cooperation, both in peace and war. And about 10% of the articles discuss collection issues within a Cold War context. The bulk of the articles are weighted toward historically distant subjects, which makes sense given declassification issues and timeframes. More recent articles tend toward newer aspects of the collection, such as OSINT and social media collection, or are about intelligence revelations such as those of Edward Snowden and the policy discussions that arose.

A relatively small number of articles discuss the psychology of HUMINT, or why spies spy. A similar small number focus on the ethics of intelligence collection or collection via interrogation. In each case fewer than 5% of the articles touch on those issues. Overt collection is largely ignored except for specific issues around OSINT in the modern context. One article discusses the concept of overt collection in the diplomatic context, though even that title confuses the issue by calling it "Diplomatic Spying."

What's missing? Articles about the economics of collection are largely missing. In fact, the only articles expressly discussing financial impacts focus on terror funding. Missing, too, are articles that discuss the impact intelligence collection may have on day-to-day government policy in trade negotiations, arms sales, energy negotiations and the like. Intelligence collection informs decision-makers in more than just wartime or on defense-connected issues.

In addition to these recommendations, we believe there is room for more articles that look at the mechanics of collection. What methods are chosen, and why? How are those decisions made and executed? What are the cost/benefit analyses for collection for different operations?

Another area where more research can be performed is the psychology of spying. While there have been a few excellent articles on motivations, there are multiple cases that could serve as case studies yet to be explored, including cases like Ana Montes, who spied for Cuba, and Jack Barsky, a former Soviet illegal who refused to return to the USSR, among others. Exploring cultural differences and how those influence motivations likewise deserve study. For example, the approaches to exploiting the diaspora for collection likely differ between the Russians and Chinese or Israelis. Lastly, connecting collection to counterintelligence is a lacuna in current published materials that demands study. Counterintelligence is often closely linked to collection and, as such, may have considerable overlap potential.

An area of considerable contemporary interest is the collection of OSINT data by the private sector. The war in Ukraine has demonstrated the utility of commercial space-based sensors for military intelligence ("Ukraine War," 2023). Scholars could and should study the changes in OSINT to help deepen the body of knowledge in this area.

Lastly, many journals, edited volumes, websites, and blogs were omitted from this study due to time and resource limitations. Without question, these resources have made important contributions to the intelligence studies literature. Scholars should identify work in these publications on collection.

Related to this study, a deeper review of the "other" category should be conducted in order to identify categories of research. For example, "the administration of intelligence"—that is, oversight and administration, policy and policy changes, and other topics—may warrant investigation and discussion as additional categories of intelligence studies worth investigating. One category may be private-sector intelligence in all of its derivatives.

Conclusion

Using Shulsky and Schmitt's model subdividing national security intelligence into four elements—collection, analysis, counterintelligence, and covert action—we categorized scholarly works from three journals from 2001 to 2021. While analysis has been the dominant topic of scholars over these 20 years, the collection is the second most frequently published article topic.

There is more work to be done in examining the types of research conducted by intelligence scholars. More can and should be written to broaden our knowledge and inquiry into the elements of collection, counterintelligence, and covert action, all of which fall broadly within the world of intelligence operations. Additionally, each element has subcategories that are worth exploring (types and use of analysis, the various INTs within the collection, etc.) in order to ensure we are approaching the subject of intelligence studies as a phenomenon. As this research indicates, more study of the mechanics of collection, how and why collection choices are made, and their cost/benefit analysis would broaden our understanding of this critical element of intelligence.

Acknowledgments

I would like to thank Dr. Andrew Macpherson for his guidance, mentorship and thought leadership in helping define this project. Additionally, his R coding skills were invaluable. Nora Conrad was absolutely critical in reviewing the literature and categorizing the articles. Without her assistance, we would not have been able to deliver this product anywhere near on time.

Bibliography

CIA. N.d. "Center for the Study of Intelligence—Studies in Intelligence." Accessed July 19, 2023. https://www.cia.gov/resources/csi/studies-in-intelligence/.

Coulthart, Stephen, and Stephen Marrin. 2023. "Where to Submit: A Guide to Publishing Intelligence Studies Articles." *Intelligence and National Security* 38 (4): 643-653. DOI: 10.1080/02684527.2022.2144278.

Dujmovic, Nicholas. 2005. "Fifty Years of *Studies in Intelligence*: Building an 'Intelligence Literature.'" *Studies in Intelligence* 49 (4).

Goodman, Michael S. 2006. "Studying and Teaching about Intelligence: The Approach in the United Kingdom." *Studies in Intelligence* 50 (2).

Jackson, Peter, and Len Scott. 2005. "Intelligence." In *Palgrave Advances in International History*, ed. Patrick Finney. London: Palgrave Macmillan UK.

Marrin, Stephen. 2016, February 23. "Improving Intelligence Studies as an Academic Discipline." *Intelligence and National Security* 31 (2): 266-279.

Mercyhurst University. N.d. "Intelligence Bachelor of Arts." Accessed May 26, 2023. https://www.mercyhurst.edu/academics/intelligence-studies.

Moran, Christopher R., and Christopher J. Murphy, eds. 2013. *Intelligence Studies in Britain and the US: Historiography Since 1945*. Edinburgh University Press.

National Intelligence University. N.d. "NIU History." Accessed May 26, 2023, from https://ni-u.edu/wp/about-niu/niu-history.

Office of the Director of National Intelligence (ODNI). N.d. "Intelligence Community Centers for Academic Excellence." Accessed June 6, 2023. https://www.dni.gov/index.php/iccae.

R Core Team. 2021. *R: A Language and Environment for Statistical Computing*. Vienna, Austria: R Foundation for Statistical Computing. https://www.R-project.org/. R version 4.3.1.

Shulsky, Abram, and Gary J. Schmitt. 2002. *Silent Warfare: Understanding the World of Intelligence*. 3d ed., rev. Ed. Dulles, VA: Potomac Books.

Taylor & Francis Online. N.d. "Intelligence and National Security: Journal Metrics." Accessed May 29, 2023. https://www.tandfonline.com/action/journalInformation?show=journalMetrics&journalCode=fint20.

Taylor & Francis Online. N.d. "Intelligence and National Security: Journal Overview." Accessed July 19, 2023. https://www.tandfonline.com/journals/fint20.

Taylor & Francis Online. N.d. "International Journal of Intelligence and CounterIntelligence: Current Issue." Accessed July 19, 2023. https://www.tandfonline.com/toc/ujic20/current.

Taylor & Francis Online. N.d. "International Journal of Intelligence and CounterIntelligence: Journal Metrics." Accessed 29 May 2023. https://www.tandfonline.com/action/journalInformation?show=journalMetrics&journalCode=ujic20.

"Ukraine War: Offensive Use of Satellite Tech a Sign of How Conflict Is Increasingly Moving into Space." 2023, June 15. *The Conversation.* https://theconversation.com/ukraine-war-offensive-use-of-satellite-tech-a-sign-of-how-conflict-is-increasingly-moving-into-space-207641.

Chapter 6

Advancing the intelligence profession: The case for accreditation in intelligence studies

James D. Ramsay
Macquarie University

Barry A. Zulauf
President of IAFIE

Abstract: James D. Ramsay and Barry A. Zulauf present an argument for the standardization of college-level intelligence studies through the process of accreditation and organized around outcome-based education. Accreditation is held to be necessary to ensure that intelligence studies programs offer quality assurance, legitimacy, and professionalism. They begin by reviewing arguments for and against doing so and then build their case around the academic and programmatic underpinnings of well-established professions such as medicine and law.

Keywords: Accreditation, continuous improvement, educational standards, intelligence studies, occupational closure, workforce

***

Introduction

All professions start as occupations. Some resemble medieval guilds, where apprentices learn skills not available in the classroom at the side of a master, eventually becoming journeymen after working for a time still under the supervision of a master. Finally, they become masters themselves, taking on fresh apprentices. There is little or no educational foundation for the guild, and the master members of the guild oversee the only boundaries. Over time, some mature into sovereign professions—that is, professions that have an identity tied to educational underpinnings and the hegemony to define practice boundaries, determining who can and who cannot practice. Professions also provide for some standardization wherever the education takes place and wherever the work gets accomplished, often achieved through accreditation of the educational institution or the workplace. Although the roadmap to professionalization is generally understood, there is no one route that all occupations seem to take. That being said, several well-accepted characteristics define professions—such as medicine and the law—including 1) a common set of educational standards that are uniformly adopted by academic programs residing in institutions of higher education, 2) professional certifications, 3) continuing professional education processes which are themselves closely coupled to the education standards and include things like peer-reviewed journals and conferences, 4) a common understanding and use of terms regarding job descriptions, 5) a code of professional ethics and the mechanisms to enforce it and 6) occupational closure which forms barriers to entry. The intelligence discipline finds itself well along the road to professionalization with clear examples of many, though not all, the above criteria.

Regarding security studies education generally and homeland security education specifically, there continues to be a robust discussion and strong feelings around what, *exactly*, it is and what it may not be (Bellavista 2008, 2012; Ramsay and Renda-Tanali 2018; Ramsay, Cutrer, and Raffel 2010). As a major component of security studies writ large, intelligence studies also tend to be less defined than one might expect it to be this long after the Intelligence Reform and Terrorism Prevention Act of 2004 (IRTPA 2004). Some have argued that it is not really an academic major on its own but one heavily borrowing from another discipline, such as international relations or political science (Lowenthal 2013), while still others argue that it is (Ramsay and Macpherson 2022). Regardless of whether intelligence is regarded as an academic discipline, there are numerous intelligence studies programs in the United States and abroad with fully developed curricula (Zulauf 2023) reflecting consumer requirements and producing graduates, many of whom join intelligence as a profession. Anecdotally, the very nature of the intelligence discipline is occasionally brought into question. Is it art or science? Are intelligence analysts the product of higher education or on-the-job training and tradecraft? And if an intelligence analyst is best produced by on-the-job training, what role does higher education play, if any? For example, the notion that academic degree programs are central to a well-educated workforce is not universally accepted. Dujmovic (2017), a former historian at the CIA, argues that intelligence agencies "don't want new hires to have majored in intelligence."

Similarly, Lowenthal (2013) states: "Intelligence can be a minor, but it cannot be a major." It seems that the baseline argument is that intelligence agencies hire analysts with domain expertise in the areas in which they will be collecting and analyzing intelligence, such as other countries, languages, or expertise in weapons systems. Proponents of this argument state that the intelligence community does not need an intelligence studies degree as a credential for employment any more than a politician needs a political science degree to run for office. Going further, Dujmovic (2017) writes, "The intelligence agencies themselves prefer to teach the 'how to' intelligence analysis to new employees." He further contends that academic degree programs in intelligence "fail to clearly deliver a demonstrable advantage" and, in fact, could keep a student from "majoring in something that might actually get him or her hired" by the intelligence community. This position amounts to the rejection of the hands of intelligence studies programs on the claim they cannot, by definition, produce good graduates. A better approach would be to address the design and quality of the programs to produce graduates with the needed mix of education and skills.

In contrast, other scholars argue that intelligence studies programs have intrinsic value to the students who complete them as well as to society. Specifically, Riehle (2021) notes that at a very basic level, intelligence studies classes create a more informed public. In a 2019 point-counterpoint article for the CIA's journal *Studies in Intelligence*, Thomas debates Dujmovic (Thomas and Dujmovic 2019). Thomas writes that "students majoring in intelligence studies master data-mining, critical thinking, and writing skills. ... [T]hey can use this knowledge to quickly assimilate into the IC workforce and provide it with much-needed analytic agility."

Since the events of 9/11, however, intelligence studies programs have been growing in both number and scope in the U.S. (Coulthart and Crosston 2015; Landon-Murray and Coulthart 2020). There is an interesting set of market forces at work supporting this trend. For instance, Ramsay and Macpherson (2023) point out that, despite the debate amongst some academics and analysts about the role intelligence studies programs play in developing a capable and qualified workforce, the U.S. federal government clearly appreciates and supports academic intelligence education. In support of this observation, they state: "Since 2004, the Intelligence Community Centers for Academic Excellence (IC CAE) Program Office show a total of 73 educational institutions (Legacy plus subsidiary institutions) that have received IC CAE funding (Current Grant and Legacy, n.d.). Since not all intelligence programs are funded as CAEs, we can make a conservative estimate that there must be well over 100 intelligence programs at this time." Some independent research has confirmed this guestimate. IAFIE's "Project Universe," for example, has identified 144 intelligence programs in the U.S. alone across 90 institutions with at least something like an intelligence program (either an undergraduate or graduate degree with intelligence as a core focus or with intelligence in the program title)

(Zulauf 2023). These programs range from a handful of courses embedded in a security studies or international relations program to a complete range of undergraduate and graduate degrees in intelligence.

There is a significant amount of academic literature developed over the years discussing the "academization" of intelligence (Andrew 2004; Marrin 2003, 2009, 2012, 2016; Collier 2013; Barna 2014; Van Puyvelde and Curtis 2016; Bean 2018; Coulthart 2019; Michael and Kornbluth 2019; Van Puyvelde et al. 2020; Arcos, Drumhiller and Phythian 2022). Much of this material begins with intelligence training and spans the distance into university-based academic programs. This literature is relevant to further discussions regarding the development of accreditation of these existing programs. Andrew (2004), for example, observed that more and more intelligence material is entering the public domain each year as post-Cold War declassification proceeds. More mainstream disciplines, like international relations and comparative politics, must take greater account of the role of intelligence in international affairs, such as the importance of signals intelligence in winning the Cold War. As a result, intelligence needs to be built more centrally into international relations theory and the interpretations of contemporary world events.

Marrin (2003) wrote about the CIA's Sherman Kent School and the creation of the "first comprehensive program for professional intelligence analysis" in the CIA's Career Analyst Program (CAP). The genesis for the Kent School and the CAP program was rooted in agency self-reflection and charges of "lack of critical thinking and analytic rigor" in an investigation into intelligence failings leading up to the Indian Nuclear test in 1998 led by Admiral David Jeremiah. His findings included that "it was crucial to hire more analysts, improve their training and increase their contact with outside experts in order to enhance their conventional wisdom." Obviously, improving analysis would imply the value of commonly agreed-upon standards. Certainly, within government training, there has long been an effort to provide standards, for example, through the Analytic Standards and Analytic Tradecraft Standards adopted in the wake of another set of intelligence failures connected with 9/11 and the Iraq WMD situation. The main thrust of the argument here, however, is to extend the call for standardization to academic intelligence programs through an accreditation program. Bean (2018) argues for advancing intelligence studies beyond the publications that have been geared toward problem-solving in the interests of practitioners and focused on a healthy debate about transforming intelligence theory through new ontologies (what can be known) and epistemologies (how to produce new knowledge). Pythian (2022) would argue that intelligence studies must expand beyond the concerns of practitioners as the academic field matures. Likewise, Rubén Arcos, Nicole K. Drumhiller, and Mark Pythian (2022) cover the growth of the intelligence studies discipline, the variety of academic and practitioner interactions, and the case for bringing more scientific rigor to the evaluation of intelligence activities.

Just as the attempts to improve intelligence training, cited by Marrin, focused heavily on analysis, this argument also focuses on analysis in an academic setting. The intelligence community (IC) looks to academia to provide education in vital skills. Collier (2013) examined how academic programs have responded to the IC's need for students with critical and creative thinking skills. With Coulthart (2019), the circle comes completely around, considering how the product of intelligence studies makes it beyond the ivory tower of academics and into the hands of government officials, who may have resisted the knowledge transfer due to the inapplicability of academic research to public issues or challenges of communicating research findings to policy audiences. Academic intelligence studies can bridge this knowledge gap if one accepts the premise that academic knowledge can improve policy and practice.

Ultimately, there can be no doubt that the rise in intelligence studies degree programs represents a healthy and growing discipline, supported by both the public and private sectors who employ graduates and by the students and parents who invest in academic degree programs. Additionally, there is a wide array of employers who clearly value the skill sets of students from intelligence programs. Specifically, the public sector requires intelligence analysts for security and risk analyses at essentially all levels of government, and the private sector[1] requires virtually the same set of analytical skills inherent in an intelligence studies curriculum for jobs including critical infrastructure risk analyses, law enforcement, emergency management/ services, cybersecurity analyses, finance, business/marketing, healthcare, and retail services. In addition, both public- and private-sector employers in the European Union employ security analysts to support decision-making in agencies and organizations where international considerations are key to business and operations.

While most intelligence practitioners and academics alike would agree that intelligence is a vital governmental and private-sector function, whether an academic degree in intelligence studies is a preferred route to producing a qualified workforce has not been settled. For this chapter, we argue that intelligence studies programs are a vital component to the production of a capable and qualified national workforce for both the public and private sectors. However, if this premise is correct, the question then arises: if intelligence studies programs are essential to national and domestic security, as well as to private-sector security and risk management, how are academic

---

[1] *Competitive intelligence* is a term used to describe the ethical and legal use of national security intelligence analytical approaches in the business world (i.e., private sector).

degree programs structured, monitored, or even held accountable to maintain an appropriate curriculum? Unlike medicine, there is as yet no single authority like the AMA to govern the intelligence profession or what/how it is taught. Consequently, there are no consensus standards for intelligence education. However, as we argue, education standards are the most reasonable basis of a profession's identity and practice boundaries.

Education standards and occupational closure define professions.

Historically, mature, well-established (i.e., sovereign) disciplines become professions only after they develop a consensus set of learning outcomes that define their professional identity and upon which academic degree programs are based. Unlike occupations (e.g., plumbing), professions (e.g., medicine) require an advanced set of skills and capabilities and are, therefore, based on a widely disseminated and uniformly adopted set of education standards. Education standards (or student learning outcomes) are statements that define the knowledge, skills and abilities accomplished by students as they progress through a degree program. Clearly, without some sort of superordinate structure, one might expect variability in the education standards across academic degree programs. Typically, the best mechanism to widely disseminate education standards across degree-granting programs is referred to as *program-level, recognized accreditation*. Program-level accreditation is currently a required component of many mature disciplines, including medicine, engineering, law, dentistry, nursing, et cetera. However, there is no specific accreditation of degree programs currently part of academic intelligence education. Intelligence studies programs have their degree programs accredited as part of their overall accreditation of their authority to grant any degree. As a result, and by contrast to medicine, intelligence curricula, as well as faculty credentials, vary widely across degree programs (Ramsay and Macpherson, 2022). While accreditation is arguably the best established and most effective means to accomplish such dissemination and integration, it is not the final or only step in the road to the professionalization of a discipline.

The route to professionalization requires more than accreditation. After recognized program-level accreditation has been integrated into the delivery of an academic degree program, an effective mechanism to ensure uniform adoption of education standards in a workforce is referred to as "occupational closure," a phenomenon that defines the practice boundaries of professions by excluding those from practicing who are inappropriately educated and trained according to the standards set by the profession itself. Perhaps the most common methods of occupational closure include professional registration, professional certification, and licensure. For instance, lawyers, professional engineers, and physicians need to be licensed to practice, but dieticians need to be registered. Both licensure and registration typically result in a credential based upon successfully passing a professional licensure examination.

Interestingly, eligibility for either certification, registration or often taking a professional licensure examination is predicated on having graduated from an accredited academic degree program in an accredited institution of higher education. Logically, we would expect the absence of accreditation, and subsequent absence of licensure or certification would produce a workforce with irregular levels of skill and varying degrees of knowledge, which together would weaken the credibility and could not offer quality assurance, resulting in diminished consumer confidence. Hence, bona fide professions all seek occupational closure—using both accreditation and licensure/registration—primarily to assure the public of the skills, knowledge, and capabilities of its practitioners.

To establish occupational closure, it is imperative that a discipline first develop a consensus set of educational standards (student learning outcomes) that are based on research and best practices. They next need to identify a way to widely disseminate and integrate those standards into academic degree programs. Accreditation of the degrees and certification of the content are two conceptually different functions. Admittedly, divining a consensus set of educational outcomes that can be integrated across all intelligence studies programs is hampered by the fact that neither the practice nor the educational components of the intelligence discipline are standardized, and the faculty come from a wide variety of disciplines and often do not have a degree in intelligence. Regardless, the authors observe that after nearly 70 years of practice in a formalized intelligence community since the National Security Act of 1947 and over 30 years of academic experience, intelligence studies have matured enough to be able to identify and support a distinct set of student learning outcomes—knowledge, skills, and attitudes—that can both characterize and define the discipline. It is possible to identify a common set of these learning outcomes, recommend that they be adopted by any intelligence studies program hoping to be successful, and assess intelligence studies programs against these outcomes.

Ultimately, occupational closure works to protect the integrity of a profession by ensuring that its professional workforce is both appropriately trained and adequately educated to perform their duties. Herein lies the connection between occupational closure and accreditation. Closure provides critical protection for both consumers and purchasers of a given degree program, which in turn is based on education standards. In this way, accreditation lies at the heart of occupational closure as it is linked to the creation of professional boundaries and barriers to entry. For example, programs that cannot demonstrate that their core curricula teach a prescribed set of outcomes cannot become accredited, and consequently, graduates of such programs cannot become licensed to practice. The AMA performs this function for medicine. Yet, there is no institution or organization with the power or recognition to do so for intelligence analysis. If the intelligence community decides to create such an institution, it could, in principle, be based on the existing IAFIE certification program, which peer reviews and ensures courses and programs in intelligence education meet content standards established by IAFIE.[2]

As described above, program-level academic accreditation requires a discipline to have identified and vetted a set of student learning outcomes. Academic programs, in turn, integrate this set of outcomes into their core curriculum, and students of a given discipline acquire a common set of knowledge, skills, and attitudes deemed central to their discipline regardless of where they are educated. In this way, program-level accreditation works proactively and continuously to address questions about degree integrity, professional competence, truth in advertising, professional boundaries, occupational closure, quality improvement and assurance. Without accreditation, it remains extremely difficult for a discipline to demonstrate legitimacy since its curriculum would not be peer-reviewed, its faculty credentials would remain unchecked, and its learning outcomes could be anything the program determined. Taken together, this consumer confidence is minimized, as neither students nor employers would have adequate quality assurance.

Further, for true professional legitimacy to become established, even when a discipline can identify, develop, and define a set of student learning outcomes, it is the process of accreditation that is still required for those standards to be effectual across all higher education degree programs. Ultimately, to develop the legitimacy, quality assurance, and continuous improvement enjoyed by mature disciplines, the intelligence academic community, along with its primary stakeholders, needs to develop and implement a robust system of recognized, program-level accreditation and ultimately establish some level of occupational closure. Without both, it will be nearly impossible to mature and legitimize intelligence studies and, subsequently, the intelligence profession.

Consequently, the main challenge to advancing the intelligence profession is first the establishment of a consensus set of education standards and then the establishment of a bona fide, recognized program-level accreditation system. Only then can closure occur. Indeed, the intelligence discipline is not totally devoid of standards. Standards for intelligence analytic tradecraft are outlined in sections 1017, 1019, and 1020 of the Intelligence Reform and Terrorism

---

[2] For more information on the IAFIE certification program, see https://www.iafie.org/page/IAFIECertification.

Prevention Act (IRTPA 2004). Analytic products are assessed against these standards in a formalized process overseen by the Office of Analytic Integrity and Standards (AIS) in the Office of the Director of National Intelligence. Is there an AIS-like body that could oversee educational standards for intelligence studies programs?

This chapter will attempt to build a case for outcomes-based, program-level accreditation—or at least certification of content and outcomes—in academic intelligence studies programs. Not accreditation of degree-granting, per se. What follows is a brief discussion about outcomes-based education and the nature of program-level accreditation; the chapter will present a summarized list of the salient, positive attributes and characteristics that program-level accreditation can offer and, consequently, why it is logical and prudent to build program-level accreditation architecture into academic intelligence studies programs. The chapter concludes with a set of questions to guide future research in intelligence studies education.

Outcomes-based education enables outcomes-based accreditation.

Academic program accreditation is perhaps best defended in higher education as a quality assurance measure because it is based on an external peer review of all aspects of a degree program, including faculty credentials, curricula, and all degree-granting processes. Peer review, though itself not perfect, provides legitimacy and credibility because it subjects the program to the review of others who ostensibly have no stake in the outcome (ABET 2023; Council for Higher Education Accreditation 2023). However, *accreditation* is a very broad term and includes many types and levels of application. There could be a level of accreditation that focuses on a particular content area, in the case with which we are concerned here, the content of intelligence studies programs. Consequently, accreditation means different things to different people. In addition, the term is known to engender thoughts of elitism, excess expense and effort, and undue barriers to entry and exclusion to some, while to others, it might indicate a measure of sanctification, somewhat like the "USDA" stamp of approval for high-quality programs.

It is important to keep in mind that the authors do not consider accreditation a perfect device or a panacea to the challenges that face intelligence education as it continues to grow, evolve, and mature. This is mainly because, like most social constructs, accreditation has its limits. However, one might observe from more mature professions that program-level accreditation can enable faculty, programs, and students to more efficiently obtain the abilities, skills, and knowledge required by their profession. This efficiency stems from free market economics. In this way, accreditation allows for more perfect information exchanges between the suppliers of education (i.e., academic programs and faculty) and the consumers of education (employers in the private and public sectors) as well as the purchasers of education (i.e., students). Certification of the content of intelligence studies programs can ensure a better match between the consumers—IC Agencies—and the suppliers in academia. In addition, accreditation optimizes market efficiency in at least four ways. First, programs can be more efficient because accreditation lessens the likelihood of a program developing courses or majors that are not of interest to the consumers. Second, consumers can act more efficiently in the marketplace since they hire graduates who are more likely to be more completely and appropriately educated and who are better trained. Third, suppliers know clearly how best to align their faculty credentials and program curricula to the knowledge, skills, and abilities most desired in the marketplace. As a result, the accreditation process facilitates continuous quality improvement in higher education by virtue of inherent peer review and reporting requirements, which in turn keep the faculty appropriately credentialed and the outcomes current and relevant. Fourth, in disciplines that are inherently dynamic and complex, such as intelligence studies, accreditation produces a better workforce since it would require programs to integrate new science and new best practices into curricula, thus maintaining a higher level of currency in graduates from accredited programs than those from unaccredited programs.

Like all social processes, education and accreditation have evolved together. Over the last twenty years and echoing the goals of both primary and secondary education, education is now centered on outcomes, as opposed to a required set of courses. This is referred to as outcomes-based education (Spady 1994). Similarly, academic accreditation has also grown, improved, and has moved away from a rigid process orientation (i.e., a required list of courses) and toward a set of learning outcomes that represent behaviors, skills, and knowledge that practitioners need to possess to function effectively in their profession. As a basis of accreditation, outcomes-based education is now referred to as outcomes-based accreditation. To devise a set of accreditation outcomes for a professional degree program, professions such as law, engineering, medicine, and nursing have engaged both the literature and practitioners as well as regulators/policymakers when devising student learning outcomes which they intend to use as the basis of their discipline's identity. Consequently, accreditation brings the knowledge, skills, and abilities that matter to practitioners and employers to the core of an academic program. Accreditation, then, is legitimated by its basis in outcomes-based education, its connectedness to employer needs, which optimize and sustain program relevance, and its use of a peer review process to adjudicate the degree to which a program and its faculty are in alignment with employer expectations and needs.

Outcomes-based education (OBE), also known as standards-based or performance-based education, is well-established (Boyer and Bucklew, 2019; Ramsay, Cutrer, and Raffel, 2010; Ramsay and Renda-Tanali, 2018). OBE has been referred to as standards-based education since it essentially creates specific, concrete, measurable standards in an integrated curriculum framework. These standards then apply across the curriculum of a degree program. Traditional curricula may have been more subject-based in the past; however, the transition to more competency-based approaches is beginning to take place within the university sector (Edgren 2006; Boyer and Bucklew 2019). As a result of this close relationship between practitioners and educators, the underlying premise of outcomes-based accreditation in higher education is that it is a powerful means of ensuring degree integrity and quality (Harden, Crosby, and Davis 1999). In other words, this relationship fosters academia's ability to know what they should be teaching students. For example, while developing a core competency model for a graduate degree program in public health, Calhoun et al. (2008) found that educators across diverse disciplines agreed that competency- or outcomes-based education could improve individual performance, enhance communication and coordination across courses, and provide an impetus for curriculum development.

Accreditation has many forms.

Historically, accreditation has been and continues to be considered a critical quality assurance component of the U.S. educational system. Above, we established that accreditation could occur at either the program level (specialized accreditation) or the institutional level. That is, like programs, institutions of higher education can be accredited by organizations or agencies that are recognized by either the U.S. Department of Education (US DoE) or the Council for Higher Education Accreditation (CHEA). CHEA, for example, recognizes regional accrediting bodies, such as the North Central Association of Colleges and Schools or the Southern Association of Colleges and Schools, to function as institutions of higher education. Like program accreditation, institutional accreditation creates a level of consumer confidence and quality assurance.[3]

Institutional accreditation does not concern itself with individual degree programs that occur within the aegis of an institution of higher education. Like the regional accrediting bodies mentioned above, many organizations are

---

[3] See Council for Higher Education Accreditation (CHEA), https://www.chea.org/reg ional-accrediting-organizations, for a more detailed discussion of regional accreditation recognized by CHEA. See also CHEA, "Degree and Accreditation Mills," retrieved from http://www.chea.org/.

recognized to perform accreditation of individual academic degree programs. For example, one such program-level accrediting organization is ABET, Inc. ABET is a nongovernmental organization dedicated to accreditation of post-secondary academic degree programs within regionally accredited institutions of higher education (ABET 2023). NASPAA.org is another. While ABET accredits engineering and technology programs (ABET 2023), NASPAA accredits public policy or administration programs (NASPAA 2023). Enhancing the reliability and credibility of the program accreditation process, these organizations can themselves seek recognition to become an accrediting organization through either the U.S. DoE or CHEA. Recognition is, therefore, a term of art used by either of the two main accrediting bodies in the U.S., either the U.S. DoE or CHEA, that refers to an accrediting organization that has achieved several complex objectives required to responsibly carry out accreditation. These objectives include internal procedures that assure open, transparent, and consistent processes, in addition to having the administrative and financial viability to reliably engage in accreditation.[4] ABET, Inc. and NASPAA.org, for example, are each recognized to perform specialized accreditation by CHEA. Once an organization has been recognized, it can legitimately pursue and conduct specialized accreditation with academic programs. Therefore, recognition is a critical qualification in the accreditation process, which serves the public interest because it indicates that the organization performing accreditation is itself qualified and legitimate. In addition, there are also accredited professional credentials, such as the Certified Information Systems Security Professional (CISSP), a more thorough discussion of which is beyond the scope of this paper. The discussion that follows refers entirely to specialized accreditation of college/university degree programs in intelligence and homeland security sciences.

Program-level accreditation is both a structure and process that attempts to demonstrate a measure of public accountability that students who graduate from an accredited program have mastered a baseline set of outcomes (e.g., knowledge, behaviors, and skills) to function as required by their profession in specific professional venues. According to CHEA (2023), "Accreditation is a process of external quality review used by higher education to scrutinize colleges, universities, and educational programs for quality assurance and quality improvement." According to the U.S. Department of Education (USDoE): "The goal of accreditation is to ensure that education provided by institutions of higher education meets acceptable levels of quality. Accrediting

---

[4] For more on US DoE recognition requirements, see: https://www.ed.gov/accreditation or for CHEA requirements, see: https://www.chea.org/sites/default/files/2021-08/CHEA_Standards_and_Procedures-Call%20for%20Comment.pdf

agencies, which are private educational associations of regional or national scope, develop evaluation criteria and conduct peer evaluations to assess whether or not those criteria are met" (US Department of Education, 2023). Going further, accreditation at both the institutional level and program level is considered a central component in preserving degree integrity and the fight against diploma mills (CHEA 2023).

Interestingly, both institutional and program-level accreditation are outcomes-based and centered on continuous quality improvement. The main difference between institutional and program-level accreditation is the set of outcomes used. With institutional accreditation, the accrediting organization identifies the structures, fiscal conditions, and organizational practices that an institution should have in place to accomplish responsible and quality education, regardless of discipline. At the program level, it is the profession itself that develops and vets the accreditation outcomes that are reflective of that profession's best practices. Thus, it is critical to note that institutional accreditation not only has limited interest in program-level accreditation or profession-specific outcomes, but it is also not designed or intended to offer appropriate content to the program-level outcomes of a specific discipline. IAFIE's certification program is, however, specifically designed to do just that for intelligence studies courses and programs. Ultimately, the accrediting process creates a mutually reinforcing network of practitioners, regulators, academic institutions, and scholars to work together in the definition of a profession.

Characteristics of accredited programs

Specific examples of healthy, effective, and successful program-level accreditation abound. According to Ramsay, Sorrell, and Hartz:

> It is an objective reality that well-respected and well-established professions such as medicine, law, engineering, nursing, dentistry, nutrition, etc., not only embrace institutional and program accreditation, but they are also highly motivated to protect and maintain it. While there are social, regulatory, and economic pressures that may contribute to the social demand for program accreditation within a discipline, there can also be pressure within the discipline to move toward program accreditation as a mechanism to further define itself or to protect its scope of professional operations. For example, just as there are legal requirements for physicians or lawyers to be licensed or dieticians to be registered or certified in order to practice, these same professions actively set, maintain, and disseminate their student learning outcomes ostensibly to provide assurances that best practices in the field are taught

to students before graduating. The obverse is true as well. Unless a student has acquired the stated set of learning outcomes from an accredited program, that student cannot call themself a practitioner of the discipline. (Ramsay, Sorrell, and Hartz, 2015)

Professional disciplines that are based on accredited degree programs tend to demonstrate several characteristics that collectively support the nature and aspirations of academic accreditation. For instance, "they have well-established and active research and development activities, peer-reviewed journals that seek and publish contributions to the discipline's body of knowledge, and conferences designed to share information and provide opportunities for scholars, regulators and practitioners to network, opportunities for students to hone their professional development" (Ramsay, Sorrell, and Hartz 2015). Indeed, the notion of continuous quality improvement inherent to accreditation means the accreditation standards reflect both the best practices of a discipline on an ongoing basis, whether those arise from practitioners or, scholars or regulators, as well as current scholarship in the discipline. Incidentally, the continuous quality management aspect of accreditation does not mean that learning outcomes are not inviolable or permanent but rather that they should be subject to change as the needs of a program's constituents change, as practice or regulatory environments change, or as the body of knowledge evolves.

In practice, program accreditation is designed to be progressive and supportive, not restrictive. It should not stunt or limit academic freedom but rather act as a guide and resource against which programs can assure quality and impact. Quality assurance from program-level accreditation arises because the accreditation process requires a minimum set of outcomes to be common to all graduates of a program and all programs of a discipline. Implied in this is that the outcomes are indeed the thoughtful products of a healthy relationship between academia and the public and private sectors, including practitioners, policymakers, and employers. This does not imply that all the learning outcomes accomplished within a core curriculum should be directed by accreditation.

On the contrary, while each program needs to integrate and accomplish the published set of accreditation outcomes, these are the minimum set of outcomes any program should seek to achieve. Accreditation purposely allows the bandwidth for additional and more program-specific outcomes. Program-specific outcomes often include things unique to a program's faculty strengths or unique to the preferences or requirements of a program's constituents (Ramsay, Sorrell, and Hartz, 2018). Hence, individual programs remain able to create graduates in their image by moving through and then beyond the minimum set of standards required by accreditation.

A roadmap to advancing the intelligence profession through accreditation

We can think of accreditation as a strategy with a distinct end state. Accreditation then, can form the basis of a roadmap whereby occupations become professions. In this way, accreditation specifies the ends, while academic programs provide the means and ways that enhance the achievement of the ends. When those ends are collectively defined by a community of scholars, practitioners, policymakers, and other stakeholders, accreditation becomes a logical and attainable basis for a discipline's professional identity. Accreditation also becomes the basis of a discipline's educational accountability and gives a clear sense of quality assurance to the consumers of the degree program (Ramsay, Sorrell, and Hartz, 2018). The following set of steps provides a roadmap, of sorts, as to how the intelligence discipline might advance to a bona fide, mature profession.

1. **Develop a consensus set of program-level learning outcomes**. Learning outcomes form the basis for all modern academic disciplines. When there is enough agreement between practitioners, academics, and other major stakeholders about what future graduates need to know, and be able to do, a consensus set of outcomes can be formed. How a discipline might produce a consensus set of outcomes is well described by Ramsay, Cutrer, and Raffel (2010) and Ramsay and Renda-Tanali (2018). Achieving a consensus on the learning outcomes helps to integrate and disseminate the learning outcomes across academic degree programs. It also lends credibility to the outcomes as being real, current, and valued among stakeholders and employers (that is, consumers of higher education). It is often the case that achieving consensus among stakeholders is a key step in building an accreditation system because accreditation is itself dependent upon a discipline's ability to prescribe a uniform, consensus set of learning outcomes.

2. **Develop a code of ethics and professional conduct**. Most, if not all, mature professions have developed a code of ethics and a set of explicit expectations that govern professional behavior. Codes of ethics can include statements about the intent, purpose and mission of the organization or discipline. These statements are there to broadcast a profession's intentionality as well as to protect the profession's image, reputation, stakeholders, and constituents from poor or immoral decision-making by practitioners. Other organizations and individuals may also have similar codes of ethics. Not only would an established code of ethics further reflect the coherence required of a true profession,

but it would also be a target academic programs would have as they taught about professional conduct and ethics in their curricula. In addition, it would be required for the profession to establish occupational closure.

3. **Achieve outcomes-based, recognized accreditation.** Unless required by licensure or the government, program-level accreditation acts like a voluntary system of accountability that ensures a baseline level of quality, reliability, and validity among academic programs in the marketplace. Quality occurs because the accreditation system requires that programs show what their student learning outcomes are, how they are achieved and what they do to modify and enhance the program when students are not achieving the specified set of outcomes. Reliability occurs when accreditation outcomes are integrated across all programs. Validity occurs when outcomes are reliable and when the discipline works with the government, policymakers, employers, and academics to identify and vet outcomes characteristic of that discipline. This is especially true in disciplines such as homeland security, which are complex and rapidly changing (dynamic) and where best practices may change often.

   a. Program-level accreditation facilitates continuous quality improvement by both the institution and the program by integrating research into practice and best practices into accreditation standards and outcomes. In turn, this process amplifies communication and integration between academia, the government, and practitioners, which is critical in complex and dynamic fields.

   b. There is no evidence that accreditation harms restricts, or endangers any of the professions that currently embrace it. Programs typically have ample room in the curriculum to integrate outcomes of interest to the faculty or constituents that are not accreditation outcomes. Further, the professions that have embraced program-level or specialized accreditation (e.g., medicine, law, engineering, et cetera) have not reported harm to the quality of their education or limitations on their practice that are attributable to accreditation.

   c. Program-level accreditation supports the transferability and articulation of academic credit to other institutions. This is an increasingly important characteristic given the growth in intelligence studies programs.

   d. Accreditation instills consumer confidence and acknowledges competence. Because accreditation requires an organization to have numerous management controls in place related to accountability, education practices, student services and efficient, effective use of available resources in providing services, it plays a significant role in fostering public confidence in the educational enterprise, in maintaining standards, in enhancing institutional effectiveness, and in improving higher education, by providing the basis on which colleges and universities can assure that their institutions have complied with a common set of requirements and standards.

4. **Use accreditation to maintain flexibility, currency, and quality assurance through external peer review, and to widely disseminate consensus education outcomes intelligence curricula.** The global security environment has never been more complex and dynamic than today. From climate change to public health (i.e., pandemics) to transnational crime and extremism to cybersecurity, the knowledge base of today's intelligence analyst is broad and rapidly changing. Program-level accreditation allows educational and programmatic flexibility while providing inherent accountability as well as a built-in mechanism to upskill curricular rapidly and comprehensively. As a result, accreditation provides a ready vehicle for continuous quality improvement. Subsequently, flexibility arises because programs that integrate accreditation outcomes have superior agility and ample room to create unique niches in the market by institutionalizing characteristics, experiences, skills, and other outcomes specific to them and the needs of their constituents (such as public health intelligence expertise). As a result, programs can maintain and engage an industry advisory panel with whom the program works on curriculum development, internship and job placement, and regular engagement with students to determine the strengths and weaknesses of the curriculum.

These advantages do not come without challenges. Probably the biggest disadvantage to accreditation may be the extra costs associated with the accreditation process. In addition, opponents will point out that accreditation may stifle creativity or individuality in a program. Worse, others may claim that accreditation could stifle academic freedom.

However, we would point out that program-level accreditation merely aims to specify a minimum set of student learning outcomes in the curriculum. For example, consider a typical 36-credit major composed of 12 three-credit courses and that each course syllabus contains 7–9 student learning outcomes. Such a program would, therefore, require approximately 84–108 student outcomes represented in each core curriculum. It is not uncommon for recognized accreditation systems to require around 10–15 student learning outcomes. Hence, in proportion to the total number of outcomes students in a major need to achieve to graduate, the number required by accreditation tends to account for less than half, thus preserving much of any given curriculum to be the specific domain of each program whereby it meets the needs of its constituents and affords bandwidth for individual faculty academic freedom.

It is important to point out that institutional accreditation is radically different from program-level accreditation.[5] While institutional accreditation is also legitimated by being recognized, it purely focuses on the processes, systems, and structures of the institution and not the academic degree programs that occur within the institution. In this sense, institutional accreditation is not/cannot be a proxy for program-level accreditation.[6] Indeed, it is not uncommon to have as a requirement of program-level accreditation that the program resides administratively in an institution of higher education that is itself accredited. Not only does such a requirement tend to ensure that the program has access to the resources and structures needed to sustain a professional and continuously improving program, but it also serves to indicate that institutional accreditation as a process does not contribute to the set of student learning outcomes derived by a professional discipline and required by program-level accreditation.

5. **Achieve professional identity through outcomes-based education**. An outcomes-based educational structure that joins with program-level accreditation reinforces how professions define themselves. In this way, professionals use the outcomes taught in their academic degree programs to be able to declare what they do, who they are and—perhaps more importantly—what they do not do.

6. **Achieve occupational closure**. Program-level accreditation greatly enhances degree integrity (Volkwein et al. 2007) and reduces diploma mills (Spellings 2006). Licensure, certifications, and accreditation function together to create barriers to (unwanted) entry in each discipline—that is, they work in symphony to create occupational closure. Professional legitimacy requires an element of "truth in advertising" but also the notion that if any program can be an intelligence program, and any graduate calls him or herself an intelligence professional, the credibility of the intelligence discipline is diminished, and the practice becomes at risk of being perceived as questionable. Accreditation enables that, at a minimum, students graduating from an

---

[5] For an example of a program-level accreditation, see IAFIE's educational certification program: iafie_certification_program.pdf (ymaws.com)

[6] For more on regional accreditation in the US, see https://www.chea.org/regional-accrediting-organizations.

accredited program have accomplished a given set of outcomes that represent, to some degree, a common understanding of the knowledge, skills, and attitudes that characterize a discipline. Occupational closure works to ensure that unqualified workers cannot work as intelligence professionals, thus legitimizing professional practice. There is, at present, no AMA-like authority in the intelligence profession with the power to fulfill the closure function. That authority rests with the individual hiring agencies.

Conclusions and the future of the roadmap

The academic and programmatic underpinnings of the well-established professions (e.g., medicine, law, engineering, etc.) are clearly much older and, therefore, better established than those of intelligence studies. Some might argue that specialized accreditation is most appropriate in disciplines that are mature and already established or that have a robust body of knowledge and clearly identified practice boundaries. The challenge for intelligence education is whether it should try to mature passively or take its future in hand and pursue a true outcomes basis and engage in peer review of its programs to demonstrate legitimacy to its stakeholders. At some point, medicine determined that enough definition and commonality existed for it to adopt a minimum set of outcomes for education and, therefore, accreditation (a considerable feat when one considers that medical education includes multiple complex sub-disciplines). When medicine decided it was mature enough to standardize its curriculum base and pursue occupational closure to protect society from witch doctors, charlatans, and brigands, it immediately pursued accreditation to ensure its sovereignty and legitimacy. This move took place after 1910 when Andrew Carnegie commissioned the Flexner Report on Medical Education (Flexner 1910). Carnegie was attempting to minimize poor and widely variable medical practice patterns and deception and replace these with a scientifically based, consistent, and transparent educational and credentialing process to legitimize both the education and practice of medicine. Those disciplines that lean on science and best practices and use peer review and accreditation will be better able to facilitate the integration of research practices and best practices into education. As a result, these disciplines will engender more legitimacy and be better able to produce a robust and qualified workforce.

Despite the obvious and continuous improvement in academic intelligence education and evidence that intelligence education continues to mature and remain vital to both the public and private sectors, we can expect that debate about its legitimacy and its role in producing a workforce may continue. In addition to the immediate call for intelligence to adopt outcomes-based education and accreditation as described in the roadmap above, it seems apparent that the following questions still need to be addressed:

1. What are the intellectual boundaries of the academic intelligence construct?

2. What role should theory play versus basic and applied scholarship in the development of a consensus set of student learning outcomes (and, by extension, the learning outcomes of an academic degree program)?

3. Should intelligence analysts seek licensure? Occupational closure is the gold standard for how mature professions sanctify themselves, but is it important to the maintenance of a robust and appropriately educated workforce in intelligence analysis? Or is it a bridge too far?

4. Given the central role intelligence analysis plays in both domestic and national security, the private sector (i.e., 'competitive intelligence'), as well as its emergent roles in cybersecurity and public health, what role should the Federal Government play in the accreditation process?

5. While it is certainly possible to "certify" academic courses in intelligence as IAFIE has done for years, should there be a professional certification for intelligence analysts? Such is typical in the ongoing professional education and training of medicine, nursing, engineering, law, dentistry, et cetera. Given the wicked nature of the problem set intelligence analysts face daily, does it make sense to create a professional credential that qualifies graduates to practice and which requires continuing professional education?

6. What are the consequences if the academic, practitioner and policy communities in intelligence fail to define the boundaries of their profession with a consensus set of learning outcomes, no professional certifications, no closure, and no accreditation?

We conclude that the only way for intelligence studies to evolve, mature, and advance as a profession is through a formally adopted and widely disseminated set of education outcomes upon which program-level, recognized accreditation would depend. Only then would academic degree programs be able to offer clear quality assurance, legitimacy, and professionalism. In fact, given its role and the social changes already underway globally, one might argue that accreditation in intelligence studies is ultimately a matter of national security.

References

ABET, Inc. 2023. "Why Accreditation Matters to the Public." ABET. Retrieved from http://www.abet.org/accreditation-matters-public/.

Andrew, Christopher. 2004. "Intelligence, International Relations and 'Under-Theorisation.'" *Intelligence and National Security* 19 (2): 170-184.

Arcos, Rubén, Nicole K. Drumhiller, and Mark Phythian, eds. 2022. *The Academic-Practitioner Divide in Intelligence Studies.* Lanham, MD: Rowman & Littlefield Publishers. https://rowman.com/ISBN/9781538144466/The-Academic-Practitioner-Divide-in-Intelligence-Studies.

Bean, Hamilton. 2018. "Intelligence Theory from the Margins: Questions Ignored and Debates Not Had." *Intelligence and National Security* 33 (4): 527-540. https://doi.org/10.1080/02684527.2018.1452544.

Bellavita, Christopher. 2008. "Changing Homeland Security: What Is Homeland Security?" *Homeland Security Affairs Journal* 4 (2): 1-30.

———. 2012. "Waiting for Homeland Security." *Homeland Security Affairs Journal* 8 (16): 1-39.

Boyer, Naomi, and Kathy Bucklew. 2019. "Competency-based Education and Higher Education Enterprise Systems." *Journal of Competency-based Education* 4 (1). https://doi.org/10.1002/cbe2.1180.

Calhoun, Judith G., Kalpana Ramiah, Elizabeth McGean Weist, and Stephen M. Shortell. 2008. "Development of a Core Competency Model for the Master of Public Health Degree." *American Journal of Public Health* 98 (9): 1598-1607. DOI: 10.2105/AJPH.2007.117978.

Collier, Michael W. 2013. "Critical Thinking Instruction in Academia: What Can the U.S. Intelligence Community Expect?" *Journal of Strategic Security* 6 (3): 61-64.

Coulthart, Stephen. 2019. "From Laboratory to the WMD Commission: How Academic Research Influences Intelligence Agencies." *Intelligence and National Security* 34 (6): 818-832. https://doi.org/10.1080/02684527.2019.1620547.

Coulthart, Stephen, and Matthew Crosston. 2015. "Terra Incognita: Mapping American Intelligence Education Curriculum." *Journal of Strategic Security* 8 (3): 46-68. DOI: 10.5038/1944-0472.8.3.1459.

Council for Higher Education Accreditation (CHEA). 2023. "The Fundamentals of Accreditation." Retrieved from http://www.chea.org/.

Dujmovic, Nick. 2017. "Less Is More and More Professional: Reflections on Building an 'Ideal' Intelligence Program." *Intelligence and National Security* 32 (7): 935-943. DOI: 10.1080/02684527.2017.1328822.

Edgren, Gudrun. 2006. "Developing a Competence-Based Core Curriculum in Biomedical Laboratory Science: A Delphi Study." *Medical Teacher* 28 (5): 409-417. DOI: 10.1080/01421590600711146.

Flexner, Abraham. 1910. "Medical Education in the United States and Canada: A Report to the Carnegie Foundation for the Advancement of Teaching." Retrieved from http://www.carnegiefoundation.org/publications/medical-education-united-states-and-canada-bulletin-number-four-flexner-report-0.

Harden, Ronald, Jennifer Crosby, and Miriam Davis. 1999. "An Introduction to Outcome-Based Education: AMEE Guide No. 14." *Medical Teacher* 21 (1): 7-14. DOI: 10.1080/01421599979969.

Intelligence Reform and Terrorism Prevention Act of 2004. 2004. Public Law 108-458. 108th Congress. Washington, DC.

Landon-Murray, Michael, and Stephen Coulthart. 2020. "Intelligence Studies Programs as US Public Policy: A Survey of IC CAE Grant Recipients."

Intelligence and National Security 35 (2): 269-282. DOI: 10.1080/02684527. 2019.1703487.

Lowenthal, Mark. 2013. "Intelligence Education: Quo Vadimus?" *American Intelligence Journal* 31 (2): 7-11. Retrieved from http://www.jstor.org/sta ble/26202065.

Marrin, Stephen. 2003. "Improving CIA Analysis by Overcoming Institutional Obstacles." In *Bringing Intelligence About: Practitioners Reflect on Best Practices*, 41-60. Joint Military Intelligence College: Washington, DC.

———. 2009. "Training and Educating U.S. Intelligence Analysts." *International Journal of Intelligence and Counterintelligence* 22 (1): 131-146.

———. 2012. "Intelligence Studies Centers: Making Scholarship on Intelligence Analysis Useful." *Intelligence and National Security* 27 (3): 398-422. https://doi.org/10.1080/02684527.2012.668082.

———. 2016. "Improving Intelligence Studies as an Academic Discipline." *Intelligence and National Security* 31 (2): 266-279. https://doi.org/10.1080/ 02684527.2014.952932.

NASPAA. 2023. "The Global Standard in Public Service Education." Retrieved from https://www.naspaa.org/.

Ramsay, James, David Cutrer, and Robert Raffel. 2010. "Developing an Outcomes-Based Undergraduate Curriculum in Homeland Security." *Homeland Security Affairs Journal* 6 (2): 1-20.

Ramsay, James, and Andrew MacPherson. 2022. "The Integration of Statistical Learning in Intelligence Education: Is the Academy Equipping Tomorrow's Intelligence Professionals to Analyze Data-Centric Threats?" *Journal of Policing, Intelligence and Counterterrorism*. DOI: 10.1080/18335330.20 22.2048965.

Ramsay, James, and Ilene Renda-Tanali. 2018. "Development of Competency-Based Education Standards for Homeland Security Academic Programs." *Journal of Homeland Security and Emergency Management* 15 (3). https://doi.org/10.1515/jhsem-2018-0016.

Ramsay, James, Eric Sorrell, and William Hartz. 2015, February. "Advancing the Occupational Health and Safety Profession by Outcomes-Based Accreditation." *Professional Safety*, 39-48.

Riehle, Kevin. 2021. "Major or Minor?: For What Audiences Are Intelligence Studies Programs Best Suited." *Journal of Strategic Security* 14 (1): 62-77. DOI: 10.5038/1944-0472.14.1.1793.

Spady, William. 1994. *Outcome-Based Education: Critical Issues and Answers.* Arlington, VA: American Association of School Administrators. ISBN 0876521839.

Spellings, Margaret. 2006. "A Test of Leadership: Charting the Future of U.S. Higher Education." Retrieved from http://www2.ed.gov/about/bdscomm/l ist/hiedfuture/reports/pre-pub-report.pdf.

Thomas, James, and Nick Dujmovic. 2019. "Educators Consider Alternative Approaches to US College Intelligence Programs." *Studies in Intelligence* 63 (4). Retrieved from https://www.cia.gov/resources/csi/studies-in-intellige nce/volume-63-no-4/educators-consider-alternative-approaches-to-us-coll ege-intelligence-programs/.

U.S. Department of Education. 2023. Retrieved from https://www2.ed.gov/admins/finaid/accred/accreditation.html.

Van Puyvelde, Damien, and Sean Curtis. 2016. "'Standing on the Shoulders of Giants': Diversity and Scholarship in Intelligence Studies." *Intelligence and National Security* 31 (7): 1040-1054. DOI: 10.1080/02684527.2016.1185323.

Van Puyvelde, Damien, James J. Wirtz, Jean-Vincent Holeindre, Benjamin Oudet, Uri Bar-Joseph, Ken Kotani, Florina Cristiana Matei, and Antonio M. Díaz Fernández. 2020. "Comparing National Approaches to the Study of Intelligence." *International Studies Perspectives* 21 (3): 298-337. https://doi.org/10.1093/isp/ekz031.

Volkwein, J. Fredericks, Lisa L. Lattaca, Betty J. Harper, and Robert J. Domingo. 2007. "Measuring the Impact of Professional Accreditation on Student Experiences and Learning Outcomes." *Research in Higher Education* 48 (2).

Zulauf, Barry. 2023. "Teaching Analytic Objectivity in Universities: An Aspirational or Achievable Goal?" *Journal of Policing, Intelligence and Counter Terrorism*, online.

———. 2024. Personal Interview with the IAFIE President about "Project Universe." Unpublished work by the International Association for Intelligence Education (IAFIE).

Chapter 7

Official public intelligence disclosure as a tool of foreign policy

Ofek Riemer
University of Haifa

Abstract: Ofek Riemer examines the authorized disclosure of secret intelligence information and assessments as a tool of foreign policy. He notes this is not a new development but one which is becoming increasingly prevalent. Riemer asserts that while not a silver bullet, under conditions where outright warfare has not yet broken out, official public intelligence disclosure allows a state to manipulate the decision calculus and perceptions of foreign governments and publics to obtain deterrence, compellence, and legitimacy for their foreign policy.

Keywords: Disclosure, information age, coercion

***

Introduction

Russia's invasion of Ukraine in February 2022 thrust into the limelight an increasingly prevalent phenomenon in international affairs: the authorized disclosure of secret intelligence information and assessments as a tool of foreign policy. In the short period leading to the invasion, American and British intelligence services circulated over the media strategic assessments, often supported by satellite imagery, regarding Russian preparations for a military assault. They have also publicly shared intimate details on secret Russian plans to undermine the Ukrainian government and engage in deception and disinformation in preparation for the invasion. As acknowledged by Sir Jeremy Fleming (2022), Director of the British Government Communications Headquarters, "It is already a remarkable feature of this conflict just how much intelligence has been so quickly declassified." Indeed, Western intelligence revelations of Moscow's war planning and intentions rightfully attracted wide attention from scholars, pundits and practitioners alike (Dylan and Maguire 2022; Lomas 2022; London 2022; Shaaban Abdalla et al. 2022).

While the scope and granularity of the recent intelligence revelations may have been unprecedented, the practice itself is hardly a novelty in international politics. Since the emergence of modern intelligence services in the early twentieth century, states have, from time to time, engaged in public disclosure of valuable intelligence. Especially, western democracies with advanced surveillance capabilities and political cultures that value facts and truth, like the United States, Britain, and Israel, engaged in this practice, albeit in quite a sporadic and isolated manner. The Soviet Union, while also possessing strong intelligence capabilities, rarely engaged in public disclosure of reliable secret information, and when it did, genuine information was fused with forgery and disinformation (see, e.g., Rid 2020, 145-157, 180-193, 263-277).

To provide but a few notable examples of such historical incidents, in 1917, at the height of the First World War, U.S. President Woodrow Wilson disclosed to the U.S. media "the Zimmermann Telegram," a cipher sent by the German Foreign Office and decrypted by British intelligence. The public release of the cipher, which suggested that Germany may be seeking to join forces with Mexico against the United States, was meant to rally public support for the latter's intervention in the war (Boghardt 2012; Tuchman 1981). In the interbellum period, the British government, for instance, decided of its own volition to share with the national newspapers decrypted intercepts of Soviet diplomatic traffic indicating that the Soviets were subsidizing local pro-communist bodies, at a time when the two nations were engaged in trade negotiations (Andrew 2018, 577-578).

During the Second World War, given the intense fighting and the key role played by intelligence in providing military advantage, governments prioritized secrecy for strategic and operational purposes (see, e.g., Smith 2004). However, the Cold War witnessed a return to occasional public use of intelligence by states. Perhaps the most prominent example is associated with the Cuban Missile Crisis in 1962, when U.S. Ambassador to the United Nations, Adlai Stevenson, famously displayed aerial photos of the nuclear missiles the Soviets had deployed on the island of Cuba in an attempt to exert pressure on Moscow. Also related to the superpower rivalry of that time was Israel's untypical decision to publicly reveal on the Israel Defense Forces' (IDF) radio station an intercepted telephone conversation between Egyptian President Abdel Nasser and Jordanian King Hussein, held on June 6, 1967, the second day of the Six Day War. In the conversation, the two state leaders conspired to fabricate reports that the West took part in the Israeli military assault on the Arab states in a supposed attempt to draw the Soviet Union into the regional conflict (Gilboa 2013, 310-319).

While official public intelligence disclosure (OPID), that is, the purposeful, state-authorized revelation of genuine secrets of another entity for foreign policy purposes, was quite an infrequent occurrence in the past, the tide is seemingly turning. Recent years have witnessed the proliferation of OPID in both scope and number, as states seem to engage more often in intelligence disclosure campaigns. Meaning they disclose intelligence from various sources and on various platforms in a more frequent manner and over sustained periods, in order to shape the behavior of international actors and audiences.

The United States, for example, regularly reveals intelligence ranging from strategic assessments to high-resolution facts relating to the policies, operations, and military build-up of its main rivals, China (e.g., Ali and Stewart, 2020), Russia (e.g., National Intelligence Council, 2021), and North Korea (e.g., Nakashima and Warrick, 2018). Britain, on its part, has frequently engaged in revelations of intelligence on Russian—and lately Chinese—espionage and subversion in the country (e.g., Sabbagh et al., 2020; Holden and Macaskill, 2023). Several European countries that are subject to similar threats have also followed suit, although to a lesser extent (e.g., Schwirtz, 2019; Higgins and de Goeij, 2021). And again, in the context of the war in Ukraine, even after the publicly predicted invasion transpired, some governments have continued to publicly disclose reliable intelligence information in order to control the narrative, manage the escalation, and delegitimize Russian policies and actions (e.g., Schrijver, 2023; Stanley-Becker and Guinan-Bank, 2022; Stewart and Ali, 2023).

In the Middle East as well, public intelligence disclosures have been increasingly used in the context of regional conflicts, for example between Israel and Iran (Halbfinger et al., 2018; Sanger and Specia, 2018), Turkey and Saudi Arabia (Hubbard, 2018), and between the Sunni Gulf states and the Shi'ite coalition of states and armed groups (also known as the "Axis of Resistance") (e.g., Al-Jazeera, 2018; Tehran Times, 2021).

This chapter focuses on this unique and counterintuitive yet increasingly popular phenomenon in international affairs. It argues that the contemporary international security landscape, where diplomacy and warfare mostly transpire below the threshold of war and in an information-saturated environment, gives rise to OPID as an attractive tool of foreign policymaking. OPID allows states to manipulate the calculus of foreign governments and publics and to shape their attitudes, thereby allowing them to obtain deterrence, compellence, and legitimacy in accordance with their national security interests. Nevertheless, OPID is no silver bullet. Except for the inherent risks to intelligence sources, methods, and credibility, OPID has proved to have an impact when combined with other policy measures and less so when relied upon solely.

The chapter begins by exploring the reasons behind states' growing inclination toward OPID. Then, it explains the primary foreign policy objectives that states strive to achieve by resorting to this practice while using illustrations from recent cases to demonstrate its workings in practice. The chapter concludes with a discussion of the potential costs and risks involved in OPID, as well as the effectiveness of its employment.

Why OPID and why now?

Why are OPIDs becoming increasingly ubiquitous? This puzzle looms large as more and more states are joining the recent trend. Addressing this puzzling phenomenon, extant scholarly literature emphasizes domestic political incentives. Indeed, the "popularization, or publicity [of intelligence], which generates public debate over ends and means" is viewed as one indication of intelligence politicization (Ransom 1987, 26)—a term usually associated with pejorative connotations (Betts 2003; Marrin 2013). It means that parochial interests, either political, bureaucratic, or reputational, interfere with the intelligence process and determine how intelligence is used. In this regard, the run-up to the 2003 invasion of Iraq epitomizes the view of intelligence publication as politicization. That publicized Western estimates concerning Iraqi weapons of mass destruction (WMD) were proven wrong cemented the conclusion that policymakers who seek to sway public opinion and overcome opposition to promote favorable policies would often do so through the public release of "cherry-picked," distorted intelligence information and estimates (Jervis 2006 and 2010; Kaufmann 2004; Lowenthal 2010; Mandel 2009; Pillar 2010). In most cases, the policies in question are controversial and bellicose (Rovner 2011).

Against the backdrop of this pessimistic approach to OPID, Hastedt (2005) studies the phenomenon in a "value-neutral descriptive way" (Marrin 2013, 48). While recognizing that the intelligence process is fraught with politics and that OPIDs—or leaks, as he refers to them—are ipso facto political acts, Hastedt attempts to decouple intelligence politicization and "publicization." He identifies four patterns of intelligence leaks based on whether they appear in an episodic or sustained fashion and whether they are contested or not. Hastedt also suggests several hypotheses for why the U.S. discloses intelligence. However, although his typology encompasses political, bureaucratic, as well as foreign policy objectives, his explanations for the growing prominence of OPID again invoke domestic political considerations. Those include growing institutional rivalry between the legislative and the executive branches of government, the lack of foreign policy consensus, and the increased media coverage of foreign policy events that make it difficult for the government to publicly defend its policy choices. Except for pertaining to the state level, these explanations are exclusive to the American case, which takes away from their generalizability.

In light of this, I suggest two alternative explanations. The first pertains to the changing nature of the information and media environments, and the second to the changing nature of warfare. The first explanation, thus, views OPID as a performative act designed to bolster public diplomacy and project power on the international stage in keeping with the dictates of the information age and contemporary media environment. The information overload of our time has turned life "quintessentially about symbolization, about exchanging and receiving [...] messages about ourselves and others" (Webster 2006, 20). Paradoxically, however, the more we are exposed to information and signals, the less attentive we are to their meaning (ibid.).

Under these circumstances, stakeholders must do more to attract attention to themselves and their message. Put differently, social and political actors are in ever-growing need of strong performative power, as a social power to "project particular cultural meanings to public audiences in pursuit of instrumental goals" (Adler 2013, 204). Specifically on the internet—an information-saturated environment where people are constantly engaged in "self-advertisement"—scholars observe that a tradeoff has evolved between privacy and influence. Meaning, that internet users are often motivated to disclose personal information to present a unique identity on social media and accumulate social capital and greater influence vis-à-vis other users (Kramer and Haferkamp 2011; Choi and Bazarova 2015; Ellison et al. 2011). This norm has ostensibly seeped into politics as well, as politicians, for example, are rewarded for exposing private information and imagery about their personal lives with greater media coverage and public attention (Rahat and Sheafer 2007; Rahat and Kenig 2018; Stanyer 2013).

Aggregated to the international level, I argue that states—much like individuals and politicians—are also affected by the prevailing norms of the global information society and are adopting similar behavioral patterns. That international agenda is frantic due to the overflow of information and fluctuating news cycles propels states to acquire performative capabilities and apply dramatic practices in order to sell "good stories." As social actors seeking to get recognition, win favorable media coverage and raise national security issues to the international agenda, they too are encouraged to publicly employ secret information in a performative manner.

Indeed, the majority of the Israeli government officials, intelligence practitioners, and media persons I have interviewed made the connection between the information age and the ubiquity of OPIDs (Riemer 2021, 562-566). In particular, they have referred to the dramatics of disclosing intelligence as a means of reaching a vast audience and amplifying the message. A former official in the Prime Minister of Israel's Office asserted that the more confidential the matter, the more powerful "the lifting of the curtain" becomes. Indeed, dramatic revelations of secrets, especially if they are accompanied by "props" and visualizations (e.g., intercepted recordings, satellite imagery, or surveillance footage), increase the chances of making an appearance on news broadcasts worldwide. As a senior defense analyst for one of Israel's leading news channels observed, "[News] cycles are very short, and to break through, you have to bring something innovative and sparkling. [...] From a U.N. General Assembly with speeches of a hundred heads of states—yes, they do put the picture that Bibi [Benjamin Netanyahu] displays."[1]

The second explanation argues that the official release of intelligence reflects states' growing aversion to war. Since the end of the Second World War in 1945, there has been a gradual global movement away from major inter-state wars (Mueller 2021). As political scientist John Mueller (2021, 2) contends, "Developed countries (whether in Europe or not) no longer really consider war among them to be a sensible method for resolving their disputes." Instead, the international security landscape has seen the rise of intra-state wars and especially of limited wars and protracted low-intensity conflicts, often referred to as "gray zone" campaigns because of their existence "in the space between traditional diplomacy and overt military aggression" (Mazarr 2015). Constrained by escalation risks and economic interdependency, both state and non-state actors are increasingly inclined toward such campaigns that are more gradual, less violent, and less obvious.

In this context, intelligence becomes particularly valuable. Not only is it essential for uncovering ambiguous "gray zone" threats, but its public disclosure can potentially render such threats obsolete without requiring the use of force and risking military escalation. Indeed, since revisionist states and non-state actors, especially terrorist groups, tend to operate under a cloak of secrecy, publicly revealing high-resolution intelligence pertaining to their best-kept secrets can have operational and psychological effects. Therefore, OPID can be understood as an instrument by which war-averse states strategically weaponize secret information in order to shape adversaries' behavior and avert security threats below the threshold of military confrontation.

This systemic change left a great mark on the Israeli experience in recent years. As a developed, democratic state facing threats from states, but mostly

---

[1] Author's interview with Alon Ben David, on January 23, 2019. On September 27, 2018, Israeli Prime Minister Benjamin Netanyahu addressed the U.N. General Assembly, and revealed images of a warehouse in a Tehran suburb where the Iranian regime had allegedly hid equipment and material from its secret nuclear program. See Sanger and Specia (2018).

from non-state actors, Israel began to "squander" intelligence publicly at the expense of protecting and saving it for the event of war in an attempt to shape the strategic environment and prevent military escalation (Riemer 2021, 566-570). A former IDF spokesperson described it as "the maturity" of the intelligence community, which realized that "intelligence is not only to be read in secret."[2] On this point, a senior defense analyst elaborated that "in the past, conflicts were between states, which every once in a while would reach an outburst, and each side would keep the intelligence to itself so that in the moment of truth, it will have advantages and surprises. Today, since we are talking about prolonged asymmetric conflicts, in which states are reluctant to aspire for decision [...] the area of intelligence, secrets, embarrassing information, influence over consciousness and public opinion is very central."[3] A former senior official in the Israeli intelligence community referred to this as nothing less than a revolution in which the intelligence that was meant for supporting decision-making has become an agent of information and psychological warfare.

Evidently, the systemic trends mentioned above do not affect all states equally, as many, including some with apt intelligence services, still shy away from publicly disclosing secret information. Indeed, variations in international status, geopolitics, regime type, national culture, and organizational cultures of intelligence services are likely responsible for the variation in states' approach to OPID. Nonetheless, I argue that the growing need for performativity in the digital age and the pervasiveness of low-intensity conflicts contribute to the overall increasing propensity toward OPID.

What can OPIDs achieve?

There are various possible justifications for states' use of OPID. This section focuses on three main strategic justifications: (1) deterrence, (2) coercive diplomacy, and (3) domestic and international legitimacy.[4] It explains the theoretical rationale underlying the use of OPID for such strategic purposes and provides historical and contemporary examples that support the theoretical argument.

---

[2] Author's interview with Ronen Manelis, on April 10, 2019.

[3] Author's interview with Alon Ben David, on January 23, 2019.

[4] Other scholars use different typologies. Hasted (2005, 419) divides disclosures into four categories (promotional, orchestrated, warring, and entrepreneurial) based on their duration and political controversiality. Dylan and Maguire (2022, 39-44) identify five potential gains from employing OPIDs (support, action, resilience, and incrimination).

Deterrence

Deterrence is a strategy designed to prevent the target from altering its behavior toward the sender or one of its allies. There are two archetypes of deterrence: general deterrence, which seeks to preserve the long-term military balance between two rival parties, and immediate deterrence, which seeks to prevent escalation into a military confrontation in a specific time of heightened tensions. In both cases, a deterring message is supposed to communicate to the target that as long as it maintains the status quo, no harm will befall it, but if it does strive to change the status quo, it might pay a heavy price for doing so. Therefore, deterring threats can be comprised of denial, as in a message that communicates to the target its inability to achieve whatever it aspires to achieve by changing the status quo. Alternatively, they can be comprised of a punishment that presents the target with a "price tag" for every action that breaks the status quo (Art and Greenhill 2018, 4-10).

Publicly disclosing intelligence on a target can enhance the sender's deterrence toward the former. In order to enhance general deterrence, an OPID must emphasize the sender's superiority in relation to the target's inferiority. Indeed, the very disclosure of the target's most intimate secrets, which it had likely sought to keep away from the sender, is in itself a testament to the superiority of the latter. It testifies to the potency and proficiency of the sender's intelligence services and suggests that the sender is knowledgeable of the target's weaknesses that can be exploited and strengths that can be circumvented. As for the content of the OPID, this can directly point to the inferiority of the target. For instance, the target's operational plans with an emphasis on their soft spots; trends in the target's arms procurement and training that might indicate shortcomings in supply and performance; and, of course, intimate information that suggests problems in decision-making at political and military levels, such as frictions, disagreements, and mental or poor health issues.

Following the war between Israel and the Lebanese party-militia Hezbollah, which lasted for 33 days in the summer of 2006, the IDF took measures to maintain the balance of deterrence through occasional OPIDs on Hezbollah's military deployment and the relationships at the top echelons. Most notably, in a series of OPIDs in 2010 and 2011, the IDF's Northern Command in charge of the Lebanese (and Syrian) front provided Israeli and international media with maps indicating the exact locations of Hezbollah posts across southern Lebanon, that included fighting positions, launch sites, and arms depots (Katz 2010; Washington Post 2011). A few years later, in 2017, IDF Chief-of-the-General-Staff disclosed in a public speech that the Israeli army had obtained intelligence confirming that Hezbollah Secretary-General Hassan Nasrallah and Commander of the Islamic

Revolutionary Guard Corps (IRGC) Quds Force Division Qassem Soleimani ordered the assassination of a senior military commander in Hezbollah, Mustafa Badreddine, in Syria in May 2016 (Cohen 2017).

As mentioned above, OPID can also facilitate immediate deterrence. The American and British campaign exposing Russian aggressive intentions toward Ukraine, which lasted for approximately three months prior to the invasion, is the last—and probably the best—example of an attempt to generate extended deterrence in defense of an ally during a crisis using OPID, among other measures. According to Dylan and Maguire (2022, 46), the "intelligence-led exposures—combined with shuttle diplomacy, threats of heavy economic sanctions and security assistance to Ukraine—had the maximalist aim before 24 February of deterring Putin from covertly subverting President Volodymyr Zelensky's government in Kyiv or overtly invading Ukraine." These exposures were meant to demonstrate Western intelligence's superiority and ability to penetrate Russia's best-kept secrets, from the tactical to the strategic level, and thereby signal to Putin that not only was he being carefully watched but also that his plans were transparent and could be preempted. Ultimately, while this campaign did manage to preempt several subversive operations, it failed to prevent Russian aggression against Ukraine altogether.

Admittedly, we learn about deterrence mostly when it fails. In this case, however, OPID was one of several means by which the West sought to deter Russia (e.g., diplomacy, threats of economic sanctions), and it is difficult to analytically parse out its contribution to this deterrence failure. Whereas some scholars argue that "the release of information by governments should never, and can never, be seen as part of a strategy to deter an assault" (Shaaban Abdallah et al. 2022), others find that "the pre-emptive approach of using intelligence to deter or undermine Russian actions have been remarkably novel in the modern history of international statecraft" (Dylan and Maguire 2022, 34).

But when deterrence allegedly succeeds, it means that nothing has happened, and the so-called success can, therefore, be attributed to a host of other factors except for deterrence strategies. This makes it even more complicated to make a valid judgment. Nonetheless, in a different setting, Easter (2018) maintains that consistent, gradual OPID by Soviet authorities—and especially by Chairman Nikita Khrushchev—on a secret American-Turkish collusion to overthrow the pro-communist regime in Syria in the autumn of 1957 played a decisive role in preventing the collusion from materializing.

Coercive diplomacy

Whereas deterrence is designed to prevent undesirable actions and maintain the status quo, coercive diplomacy seeks to induce action and restore the status quo ante (Art and Greenhill 2018, 4-5, 13). In other words, it is a strategy designed to persuade the target to "stop and/or undo an action he is already embarked upon" (George 1991, 5). To this end, coercive diplomacy entails threats and, when necessary, limited, even symbolic, use of force in controlled increments in order to put enough pressure on the target to make it capitulate.

In this regard, OPID can also serve as a coercive instrument, analogous to both threats and "sticks" that inflict limited damage on the target. This assertion rests on the idea that various actors require at least some secrecy to maintain stability and to conduct their affairs with relative legitimacy and maneuverability. Most prominently, militaries, security agencies or violent non-state actors keep secrets from their adversaries to maintain an operational advantage. Such secrets usually pertain to plans and operations, namely surprise attacks or covert actions, whose revelation would result in steep political and military costs (Betts 2010; Brun 2010). This is especially true for plans and actions that contravene international norms (O'Rourke 2018; Poznansky 2020).

What follows is that visibility into an adversary's secrets makes it potentially vulnerable to strategic manipulation. First, an OPID can communicate a coercive threat since it unveils the sender's awareness of the security threat posed by the target and, therefore, its discontent and possibly its intent to take action to remove the security threat. In fact, the public revelation of a security threat that was previously the private knowledge of only the leadership of the two parties to the conflict is a conscious act of "tying-hands" (Fearon 1997). By publicly revealing a security threat to which the domestic public was previously unaware, the leadership is committing itself to eliminating the security threat. This is potentially signaling to the target just how much the sender is determined to confront it (Riemer and Haas, 2023).

For example, when the Commander of the IDF Intelligence Directorate publicly revealed, for the first time, that Hezbollah, with the help of the IRGC, is establishing a military industry on Lebanese soil for the manufacturing of precision-guided missiles, it stirred a sense of war scare as if Israel was poised to strike Lebanon. This led Israeli and Lebanese officials to declare shortly after that there were, at the time, no missile manufacturing facilities in Lebanon and that Iran and Hezbollah were considering locating such facilities in Syria (Riemer and Sobelman, 2023, 286). However, as it became apparent that Israel was deterred from targeting Lebanese territory and that its efforts to coerce Hezbollah to forsake its primary military buildup program were heavily reliant on OPIDs of secret sites and personnel, the latter's coercive power diminished (Ibid., 296).

Second, OPID can serve as a substitute for military force, which in coercive diplomacy is often used for saber-rattling or for gradually harming the target in order to communicate the sender's earnestness and resolve. This stems from the fact that secrecy has multiple functions. Except for military and operational purposes, actors employ secrecy to keep embarrassments and failures away from the public's eye, to hide from the central government or other competitors in case of non-state actors, and to avoid international criticism and punishment. Knowledge of such secrets can, therefore, be turned into leverage in the hands of the coercer through incremental, calculated disclosure that imposes a price on the target but at the same time alludes to the price it might continue to pay if it fails to acquiesce and the coercer reveals all that it knows.

In this exact fashion, Turkey turned to leverage its intimate information on the involvement of the Saudi Royal Court in the premeditated assassination of dissident Jamal Khashoggi in the Kingdom's consulate in Istanbul in October 2018. Over a few weeks, the Turkish government gradually disclosed incriminating intelligence pertaining to the planning and execution of the assassination, which seriously damaged the Saudi image, in order to force it to take responsibility and bear the consequences for its wrongful act. But when Riyadh persistently refused to take responsibility and instead resorted to cover-up and disinformation, the OPIDs became more focused on the U.S. media in an attempt to galvanize American public opinion and put pressure on the Trump administration to acknowledge the crimes of its close ally and penalize it for them (Riemer and Sobelman 2023, 289-293). Nevertheless, the fact that considerable U.S. and Saudi interests were at stake prevented President Trump from risking the two countries' alliance, even in the face of solid, conclusive intelligence. His administration's unexpected concessions to Turkey, in the form of diplomatic rapprochement and economic and legal benefits, were likely aimed at buying Turkish silence and preventing it from revealing the "smoking gun" and from keeping the scandal in the headlines (ibid., 294).

This case demonstrates that coercion does not necessarily have to be direct but can rather go through a third party. Indeed, often the target is resilient to the coercer but is vulnerable to a third party, which might be malleable to manipulation by the coercer (Sobelman 2022). For example, a revisionist state or a non-state actor that engages in activities that violate international norms (e.g., war crimes, nuclear proliferation, electoral fraud or intervention) has a clear interest in keeping it secret (Cohen 2001; Poznansky 2020). However, paradoxically, the guardians of the international regimes themselves often seek to keep such violations secret in order to escape hypocrisy costs and avoid escalation (Carnegie and Carson 2018; Cohen 2013; Kelley 2009). In such cases, actors whose intelligence services are privy to the violation but have no leverage over the culprit can manipulate the concerns of the guardians of international regimes for their credibility and reputation and prod them into action by publicly revealing the violation (Greenhill 2010; Nutt and Pauly 2021).

That is what the Soviet Union did in the Summer of 1977 when its intelligence discovered evidence of a South African nuclear test site. The Kremlin decided to release the evidence to the media because it assessed that the United States would not act to halt the South African nuclear program based on the evidence that was shared with the administration in private (Nutt and Pauly 2021, 34-39). This is also what Israel did in the Spring of 2013, when it had wanted the Obama administration to enforce its red line on the Syrian regime when evidence began to surface of the use of chemical weapons against civilians (Sanger and Rudoren, 2013). And this is what Israel often does against the Iranian nuclear program. Absent an independent military option to eliminate what it deems an existential security threat, the Israeli government occasionally discloses intelligence on various secret aspects of the program, thereby forcing the IAEA and the parties to the negotiations with Iran—mainly the United States—to acknowledge them, and accordingly impose sanctions on Tehran (Riemer and Sobelman 2019).

Legitimacy

One can use OPID not only to get foreign actors to act or refrain from action but also to sway their opinion and worldview in one's favor. In other words, OPID can be used for explaining and legitimizing controversial policies and for garnering foreign support before executing a policy for which one can be criticized and penalized. The best, and probably the most famous example, is the public use of intelligence by the United States and Britain in the run-up to the invasion of Iraq in 2003. At the height of their efforts to convince foreign governments and the public of the need to join forces and wage war against Saddam Hussein, the U.S. Secretary of State, Collin Powell, gave a presentation before the United Nations Security Council, which cited multiple pieces of evidence from various intelligence sources. In hindsight, the information was unreliable, and the estimates exaggerated the threat and were ultimately proven wrong, but the intent was the same: to gain legitimacy and support for war (Rovner 2011, ch. 7).

More recently, Israel has employed this tactic in its campaign against Iran's military establishment in Syria during the civil war. Given the political, economic, and military fragmentation of the Assad regime, Israel was not deterred from militarily targeting Syrian territory. However, at the time, the Russian military was already present—mainly in the western parts of the country, carrying out air strikes and operating air defense systems. Concurrently, to the east, the Americans, along with other Western and regional allies, were engaged in similar operations against Daesh. Under these circumstances, it became crucial for Israel to justify military action against Iranian elements in Syria and lay the groundwork to prevent any counter-reaction, especially from Russia. Additionally, in the event of an escalation, it was essential to mobilize Israeli public opinion in support of this strategic objective.

Consequently, Israel pursued a two-fold approach. In the initial stage, it disclosed intelligence regarding the Iranian presence and assessments of Iran's broader vision for Syria. In the second stage, the IDF took military action against targets that Israel claimed were integral to the Iranian vision. For instance, the IDF targeted a military base located south of Damascus, some 50 km (30 miles) from the Israeli border, whose existence had been exposed by the BBC less than a month prior to its destruction (Corera, 2017). Except for an immediate attempt by Syrian air defense systems to counter it, neither party retaliated nor protested against the attack.

OPID's potential costs and risks

Despite its multiple uses and evident appeal, OPID is a costly practice that also bears some risks. On the face of it, exposure contravenes a fundamental principle in intelligence work—secrecy (Lowenthal 2000, 1). Secrecy is the cornerstone of intelligence operations, as it is crucial for protecting sources, methods, and personnel (Lefebvre 2018). It allows states to operate discreetly in the shadow of international law and acquire access to the well-kept secrets of another entity, which can grant them an advantage in diplomacy, war, counterterrorism, and counterintelligence. Exposing information that has been gleaned under such circumstances, therefore, poses several political and operational risks; chief among them is the risk of alerting the opponent to the security breach, thereby jeopardizing the source of the information (Carnegie and Carson 2019). A former senior official in the Israeli intelligence community lamented that the risk of OPID is so great because it is almost impossible to speculate in advance what the damage from a single OPID might be. The official explained that "the other side is sitting there, like me, trying to put together an intelligence assessment comprised of a lot of small pieces. I do not know which pieces it holds in its hands, I do not know how many pieces it holds, and by disclosure [of intelligence], I might have given it another piece that allowed it to solve the puzzle."

However, the risk is not only to sources and methods but also to the reputation and the public trust in the intelligence services. These elements are crucial for maintaining the intelligence services' role in the decision-making process as being entrusted with professionally portraying the security situation to policymakers, who are required to use it as a basis to shape public policy and mobilize public opinion. Furthermore, reputation and public trust are essential for sustaining the image that intelligence services usually wish to project to allies and adversaries as all-knowing. Consequently, when intelligence services disclose plans and intentions of adversaries in order to deter them, there is a potential risk of the former being too successful and becoming the victims of their success. In other words, if the anticipated hostilities do not materialize due to their public disclosure, internal and international audiences may suspect that they have never existed or that intelligence analysts have misinterpreted the information, or even worse, that they have deliberately misled policymakers, and thus accuse them of being alarmist and unprofessional. This, in turn, might undermine the reliability and credibility of the intelligence services.

Certainly, there is an inherent risk in the opposite direction as well. Intelligence assessments, by nature, are incomplete and leave some room for doubt. An intelligence assessment is composed of several available fragments of information to which intelligence analysts add their interpretations. Ergo, it is always subject to questioning, deliberation, and change. In view of that, the decision to disclose intelligence information and assessments is a conscious choice that places the credibility of the intelligence community on the line, particularly if reality unfolds differently or contradicts initial assumptions. This is what happened, for example, following the 9/11 attacks, when psychological and cognitive biases, and often negligence, of intelligence analysts converged with the neoconservative, hawkish agendas of the new and surprised U.S. administration. This combination led to alarmist assessments that magnified the threat to international security posed by the Iraqi regime and helped to pave the way to the invasion in 2003 (Betts 2007; Jervis 2010; Kaufmann 2004). These assessments were eventually proven wrong, reflected poorly on the American intelligence community and damaged its reputation for years to come (Harris et al., 2022).

The fact that the domestic audience is also exposed to media publications by its national intelligence community alludes to yet another tension, one between strategy and democratic accountability. OPIDs that are intended for strategic influence usually rely on limited and carefully selected information, often mixed with disinformation designed to deceive the opponent and obscure the source of the information. Democratic governments and their intelligence services must take into account their own public's exposure to such publications and minimize the risk of corrupting domestic public opinion. Indeed, sometimes governments are required to engage in "educational" OPIDs that rely on solid and truthful evidence in order to inform the public about the security environment and foster resilience and political participation. Such democratic responsibilities often come at the expense of strategic goals. For instance, U.S. public reports on China's nuclear arsenal (e.g., Bugos and Klare 2023) or Israeli public estimates on Hezbollah's arsenal of rockets and missiles (e.g., Federman 2022) may jeopardize American and Israeli deterrence posture, respectively. Nevertheless, such public disclosures are essential for public debate over policy and resources and for the resilience of the home front.

Conclusion

Official public intelligence disclosure (OPID), as a foreign policy practice, is becoming increasingly prevalent in international affairs. The growing inclination of governments worldwide to disclose secret intelligence as a measure of projecting power and shaping other actors' mindsets and behavior is a reflection of major systemic trends. Indeed, that war and diplomacy transpire in an information-saturated global environment propels states and intelligence services to adopt new information and communication strategies. OPID is one of those strategies that allows states to defuse security threats and avoid military escalations while upholding their image and projecting their potency on the international stage.

As this chapter elucidated, states can pursue various strategic goals through OPID. They can deter adversaries from initiating offenses and challenging the status quo. They can manipulate the calculus of both adversaries and allies and coerce them into changing their behavior and acting against their stated interests. Moreover, they can enhance public diplomacy and craft strategic narratives designed to persuade domestic and international audiences of the propriety of their policies.

However, OPID is no silver bullet. As the majority of the examples given throughout this chapter demonstrate, its success is limited, and no policy or strategy should rest solely on it. The United States and Britain failed to deter a determined Russia from invading Ukraine in 2022, although their preemptive disclosures of intelligence have managed to put a spoke in its wheel by disrupting some of Moscow's covert operations and bringing together major international actors around a single clear, coherent narrative. The Turkish government, for its part, failed to force Saudi Arabia to take responsibility for Khashoggi's assassination in October 2018 and to pressure the U.S. administration into punishing its important ally for its wrongdoing. However, Ankara did manage to mend fences with Washington and extract a few valuable diplomatic and economic benefits. And Israel failed in coercing Hezbollah to abandon its primary military buildup program in Lebanon, although its repeated disclosure of operational secrets regarding the "precision project" did manage to delay and disrupt Hezbollah's plans, which in itself is not an insignificant achievement.

With this in mind, it is crucial to weigh the benefits of OPID against the risks involved, and they are numerous, from risks to sources and methods, through risks to the credibility and reputation of the intelligence community, and all the way to negative consequences to norms of intelligence work and to the marketplace of ideas, which is the cornerstone of democratic societies. For these reasons, states are usually cautious when engaging in OPID and tend to progress gradually along a spectrum stretching from implicit and deniable disclosure of low-resolution information or paraphrased assessments, on one end, to the explicit, formal public disclosure of high-resolution, compelling evidence, on the other end.

In conclusion, the proliferation of OPID as a tool of foreign policy obliges scholars and practitioners to further our understanding of the advantages and disadvantages of this unique practice. Admittedly, there remain various avenues for future investigation relating to the determinants of successful influence through OPID, to models that can help us predict risks to intelligence assets, and to the long-term implications of the growing use of OPID on policy, society, and intelligence, for example on public attitudes toward government secrecy.

References

Adler, Emanuel. 2013. "Damned if You Do, Damned if You Don't: Performative Power and the Strategy of Conventional and Nuclear Defusing." *Security Studies* 19 (2): 199-229. https://doi.org/10.1080/09636411003796002

Al-Jazeera. 2018. "Diplomatic Leaks: UAE Dissatisfied with Saudi Policies." *Al-Jazeera*. April 17, 2018. https://www.aljazeera.com/news/2018/4/17/diplomatic-leaks-uae-dissatisfied-with-saudi-policies.

Ali, Idrees, and Phil Stewart. 2020. "Pentagon Concerned by China's Nuclear Ambitions, Expects Warheads to Double." *Reuters*. September 1, 2020. https://www.reuters.com/article/us-usa-china-military-nuclear-idUSKBN25S5MB.

Andrew, Christopher. 2018. *Secret World: A History of Intelligence*. New Haven: Yale University Press.

Art, Robert J., and Kelly M. Greenhill. 2018. "Coercion: An Analytical Overview." In *Coercion: The Power to Hurt in International Politics*, edited by Kelly M. Greenhill and Peter Krause, 3-32. Oxford: Oxford University Press.

Betts, Richard K. 2003. "Politicization of Intelligence: Costs and Benefits." In *Paradoxes of Strategic Intelligence: Essays in Honor of Michael I. Handel*, edited by Richard K. Betts and Thomas G. Manhnken, 59-79. London: Routledge.

———. 2007. *Enemies of Intelligence: Knowledge and Power in American National Security*. New York: Columbia University Press.

———. 2010. *Surprise Attack: Lessons for Defense Planning*. Brookings Institute.

Boghardt, Thomas. 2012. *The Zimmermann Telegram: Intelligence, Diplomacy, and America's Entry into World War I*. Annapolis, MD: Naval Institute Press.

Brun, Itai. 2010. "'While You're Busy Making Other Plans'—The 'Other RMA.'" *Journal of Strategic Studies* 33 (4): 535-565. https://doi.org/10.1080/01402390.2010.489708.

Bugos, Shannon, and Michael Klare. 2023. "Pentagon: Chinese Nuclear Arsenal Exceeds 400 Warheads." *Arms Control Association*. January/ February. https://www.armscontrol.org/act/2023-01/news/pentagon-chinese-nuclear-arsenal-exceeds-400-warheads

Carnegie, Allison, and Austin Carson. 2018. "The Spotlight's Harsh Glare: Rethinking Publicity and International Order." *International Organization* 72 (3): 627-657. 10.1017/S0020818318000176.

———. 2019. "The Disclosure Dilemma: Nuclear Intelligence and International Organizations." *American Journal of Political Science* 63 (2): 269-285. https://doi.org/10.1111/ajps.12426.

Choi, Yoon Hyung, and Natalya N. Bazarova. 2015. "Self-Disclosure Characteristics and Motivations in Social Media: Extending the Functional Model to Multiple Social Network Sites." *Human Communication Research* 41 (4): 480-500. https://doi.org/10.1111/hcre.12053

Cohen, Avner. 2013. *The Worst-Kept Secret: Israel's Bargain with the Bomb*. New York: Columbia University Press.

Cohen, Gili. 2017. "Israel's Army Chief: Hezbollah Commander Mustafa Badreddine Killed by His Own Men." *Haaretz*. March 22. https://www.haaretz.com/israel-news/2017-03-22/ty-article/israels-army-chief-hezbollah-top-commander-killed-by-his-own-men/0000017f-e07b-d75c-a7ff-fcff17500000.

Cohen, Stanley. 2001. *States of Denial: Knowing About Atrocities and Suffering*. Cambridge: Polity.

Corera, Gordon. 2017, November 10. "Iran Building Permanent Military Base in Syria–Claim." BBC. https://www.bbc.com/news/world-middle-east-41945189.

Dylan, Huw, and Thomas J. Maguire. 2022. "Secret Intelligence and Public Diplomacy in the Ukraine War." *Survival* 64 (4): 33-74. https://doi.org/10.1080/00396338.2022.2103257.

Easter, David. 2018. "Soviet Intelligence and the 1957 Syrian Crisis." *Intelligence and National Security* 33 (2): 227-240. https://doi.org/10.1080/02684527.2017.1370072.

Ellison, Nicole B., Jessica Vitak, Charles Steinfield, Rebecca Gray, and Cliff Lampe. 2011. "Negotiating Privacy Concerns and Social Capital Needs in a Social Media Environment." In *Privacy Online*, edited by Sabine Trepte and Leonard Reinecke, 19-32. New York: Springer.

Fearon, James D. 1997. "Signaling Foreign Policy Interests: Tying Hands versus Sinking Costs." *Journal of Conflict Resolution* 41 (1): 68-90. https://doi.org/10.1177/0022002797041001004.

Federman, Josef. 2022. "Israeli General Readies to Lead the Charge against Hezbollah." Associated Press. September 9, 2022. https://apnews.com/article/middle-east-israel-lebanon-militant-groups-hezbollah-85a053e07d9c03a6d0b5a03aeb3d2a9d.

Fleming, Jeremy. 2022. "Director GCHQ's Speech on Global Security Amid War in Ukraine." *GCHQ*. March 31, 2022. https://www.gchq.gov.uk/speech/director-gchq-global-security-amid-russia-invasion-of-ukraine.

George, Alexander L. 1991. *Forceful Persuasion: Coercive Diplomacy as an Alternative to War*. Washington, DC: United States Institute of Peace.

Gilboa, Amos. 2013. *Mr. Intelligence: Ahrale Yariv*. Tel Aviv: Miskal [Hebrew].

Greenhill, Kelly M. 2010. *Weapons of Mass Migration*. Ithaca, NY: Cornell University Press.

Halbfinger, David M., David E. Sanger, and Ronen Bergman. 2018. "Israel Says Secret Files Detail Iran's Nuclear Subterfuge." *New York Times*. April 30, 2018. https://www.nytimes.com/2018/04/30/world/middleeast/israel-iran-nucle ar-netanyahu.html?module=inline.

Harris, Shane, Karen DeYoung, Isabelle Khurshudyan, Ashley Parker, and Liz Sly. 2022. "Road to War: U.S. Struggled to Convince Allies, and Zelensky, of Risk of Invasion." *Washington Post*. August 16. https://www.washingtonpo st.com/national-security/interactive/2022/ukraine-road-to-war/.

Hastedt, Glenn. 2005. "Public Intelligence: Leaks as Policy Instruments—The Case of the Iraq War." *Intelligence and National Security* 20 (3): 419-439.

Higgins, Andrew, and Hana de Goeij. 2021. "Czechs Blame 2014 Blasts at Ammunition Depots on Elite Russian Spy Unit." *New York Times*. April 17. https://www.nytimes.com/2021/04/17/world/europe/czech-republic-skirp al-russia-gru.html.

Holden, Michael, and Andrew Macaskill. 2023. "British Approach to China Risk 'Completely Inadequate,' Committee Says." Reuters. July 13. https://www.r euters.com/world/uk-governments-strategy-china-risk-completely-inadequ ate-committee-2023-07-13/.

Hubbard, Ben. 2018. "One Killing, Two Accounts: What We Know About Jamal Khashoggi's Death." *New York Times*. October 20, 2018. https://www.nytime s.com/2018/10/20/world/middleeast/khashoggi-turkey-saudi-narratives.html.

Jervis, Robert. 2006. "Reports, Politics, and Intelligence Failures: The Case of Iraq." *Journal of Strategic Studies* 29 (1): 3-52. https://doi.org/10.1080/ 01402390600566282

———. 2010. *Why Intelligence Fails: Lessons from the Iranian Revolution and the Iraq War*. Ithaca: Cornell University Press.

Katz, Yaakov. 2010. "IDF Reveals Hizbullah Positions." *Jerusalem Post*. July 7, 2010. https://www.jpost.com/israel/idf-reveals-hizbullah-positions.

Kaufmann, Chaim. 2004. "Threat Inflation and the Failure of the Marketplace of Ideas." *International Security* 29 (1): 5-48. https://www.jstor.org/stable/ 4137546.

Kelley, Judith. 2009. "D-Minus Elections: The Politics and Norms of International Election Observation." *International Organization* 63 (4): 765-787. https://www.jstor.org/stable/40345955.

Kramer, Nicole C., and Nina Haferkamp. 2011. "Online Self-Presentation: Balancing Privacy Concerns and Impression Construction on Social Networking Sites." In *Privacy Online: Perspectives on Privacy and Self-Disclosure in the Social Web*, edited by Sabine Trepte and Leonard Reinecke, 127-142. New York: Springer.

Lefebvre, Stéphane. 2018. "Why Are State Secrets Protected from Disclosure? The Discourse of Secret Keepers." *International Journal of Intelligence, Security, and Public Affairs* 20 (3): 204-229. https://doi.org/10.1080/23800 992.2018.1532184.

Lomas, Dan. 2022. "To Brief, or Not to Brief: UK Intelligence and Public Disclosure." *RUSI.* February 2. https://rusi.org/explore-our-research/publicat ions/commentary/brief-or-not-brief-uk-intelligence-and-public-disclosure.

London, Douglas. 2022. "To Reveal, or Not to Reveal: The Calculus Behind U.S. Intelligence Disclosures." *Foreign Affairs.* February 15. https://www.foreign affairs.com/articles/ukraine/2022-02-15/reveal-or-not-reveal.

Lowenthal, Mark M. 2000. *Intelligence: From Secrets to Policy.* Washington, DC: CQ Press.

————. 2010. "The Policymaker-Intelligence Relationship." In *The Oxford Handbook of National Security Intelligence,* edited by Loch K. Johnson, 438-451. Oxford: Oxford University Press.

Mandel, Robert. 2009. "On Estimating Post-Cold War Enemy Intention." *Intelligence and National Security* 24 (2): 194-215. https://doi.org/10.108 0/02684520902819610

Marrin, Stephen. 2013. "Rethinking Analytic Politicization." *Intelligence and National Security* 28 (1): 32-54. https://doi.org/10.1080/02684527.2012. 749064

Mazarr, Michael J. 2015. "Struggle in the Gray Zone and World Order." *War on the Rocks.* December 22. https://warontherocks.com/2015/12/struggle-in-the-gray-zone-and-world-order/.

Mueller, John. 2021. *The Stupidity of War: American Foreign Policy and the Case for Complacency.* Cambridge University Press.

Nakashima, Ellen, and Joby Warrick. 2018. "U.S. Spy Agencies: North Korea Is Working on New Missiles." *Washington Post.* July 30. https://www.washingto npost.com/world/national-security/us-spy-agencies-north-korea-is-workin g-on-new-missiles/2018/07/30/b3542696-940d-11e8-a679-b09212fb69c2_st ory.html

National Intelligence Council. 2021. "Intelligence Community Estimate: Foreign Threats to the 2020 U.S. Federal Elections." *Director of National Intelligence.* March 10. https://www.dni.gov/index.php/newsroom/reports-publications/reports-publications-2021/3521-intelligence-community-asse ssment-on-foreign-threats-to-the-2020-u-s-federal-elections.

Nutt, Cullen G., and Reid B. C. Pauly. 2021. "Caught Red-Handed: How States Wield Proof to Coerce Wrongdoers." *International Security* 46 (2): 7-50. https://doi.org/10.1162/isec_a_00421.

O'Rourke, Lindsey A. 2018. *Covert Regime Change: America's Secret Cold War.* Ithaca: Cornell University Press.

Pillar, Paul R. 2010. "The Perils of Politicization." In *The Oxford Handbook of National Security Intelligence,* edited by Loch K. Johnson, 473-484. Oxford: Oxford University Press.

Poznansky, Michael. 2020. *In the Shadow of International Law: Secrecy and Regime Change in the Postwar World.* Oxford University Press.

Rahat, Gideon, and Ofer Kenig. 2018. *From Party Politics to Personalized Politics?: Party Change and Political Personalization in Democracies.* Oxford University Press.

Rahat, Gideon, and Tamir Sheafer. 2007. "The Personalization(s) of Politics: Israel, 1949–2003." *Political Communication* 24 (1): 65-80. https://doi.org/10.1080/10584600601128739

Ransom, Harry Howe. 1987. "The Politicization of Intelligence." In *Intelligence and Intelligence Policy in a Democratic Society,* edited by Stephen J. Cimbala, 25-46. Dobbs Ferry, NY: Transnational Publishers.

Rid, Thomas. 2020. *Active Measures: The Secret History of Disinformation and Political Warfare.* London: Profile Books.

Riemer, Ofek. 2021. "Politics Is Not Everything: New Perspectives on the Public Disclosure of Intelligence by States." *Contemporary Security Policy* 42 (4): 554-583. https://doi.org/10.1080/13523260.2021.1994238.

Riemer, Ofek, and Daniel Sobelman. 2019. "Coercive Disclosure: Israel's Weaponization of Intelligence for Coercion." *War on the Rocks.* August 30. https://warontherocks.com/2019/08/coercive-disclosure-israels-weaponization-of-intelligence/.

———. 2023. "Coercive Disclosure: The Weaponization of Public Intelligence Revelation in International Relations." *Contemporary Security Policy* 44 (2): 276-307. https://doi.org/10.1080/13523260.2022.2164122.

Riemer, Ofek, and Melinda H. Haas. 2023. "Let Everybody Know: Public Intelligence Disclosure, Audience Costs, and Credible Threats." *Paper presented at the American Political Science Association Annual Meeting & Exhibition, Los Angeles, CA, August 31-September 3, 2023.*

Rovner, Joshua. 2011. *Fixing the Facts: National Security and the Politics of Intelligence.* Ithaca, NY: Cornell University Press.

Sabbagh, Dan, Luke Harding, and Andrew Roth. 2020. "Russia Report Reveals UK Government Failed to Investigate Kremlin Interference." *The Guardian.* July 21. https://www.theguardian.com/world/2020/jul/21/russia-report-reveals-uk-government-failed-to-address-kremlin-interference-scottish-referendum-brexit.

Sanger, David, and Jodi Rudoren. 2013. "Israel Says It Has Proof That Syria Has Used Chemical Weapons." *New York Times.* April 23. https://www.nytimes.com/2013/04/24/world/middleeast/israel-says-syria-has-used-chemical-weapons.html.

Sanger, David E., and Megan Specia. 2018. "Israeli Leader Claims Iran Has 'Secret Atomic Warehouse.'" *New York Times.* September 27. https://www.nytimes.com/2018/09/27/world/middleeast/israel-iran-nuclear-agreement.html

Schrijver, Peter. 2023. "'The Wise Man Will Be Master of the Stars': The Use of Twitter by the Ukrainian Military Intelligence Service." *Irregular Warfare Initiative.* June 27, 2023. https://irregularwarfare.org/articles/the-wise-man-will-be-master-of-the-stars-the-use-of-twitter-by-the-ukrainian-military-intelligence-service/.

Schwirtz, Michael. 2018. "Top Secret Russian Unit Seeks to Destabilize Europe, Security Officials Say." *New York Times.* October 8. https://www.nytimes.com/2019/10/08/world/europe/unit-29155-russia-gru.html.

Shaaban Abdalla, Neveen, Philip H. J. Davies, Kristian Gustafson, Dan Lomas, and Steven Wagner. 2022. "Intelligence and the War in Ukraine: Part 1." *War on the Rock.* May 11, 2022. https://warontherocks.com/2022/05/intelligence-and-the-war-in-ukraine-part-1/.

Smith, Michael. 2004. "Bletchley Park and the Holocaust." *Intelligence and National Security* 19 (2): 262-274. https://doi.org/10.1080/0268452042000302994

Sobelman, Daniel. 2022. "Re-Conceptualizing Triangular Coercion in International Relations." *Cooperation and Conflict* [published online]. https://doi.org/10.1177/00108367221098494.

Stanley-Becker, Isaac, and Vanessa Guinan-Bank. 2022. "Germany Intercepts Russian Talk of Indiscriminate Killings in Ukraine." *Washington Post.* April 7. https://www.washingtonpost.com/world/2022/04/07/bucha-german-intelligence-radio-bnd-russia/.

Stanyer, James. 2013. *Intimate Politics: Publicity, Privacy and the Personal Lives of Politicians in Media Saturated Democracies.* Cambridge: Polity.

Stewart, Phil, and Idrees Ali. 2023. "Russia 'Very Unlikely' to Use Nuclear Weapons, US Intel Chief." Reuters. May 4. https://www.reuters.com/world/europe/russia-very-unlikely-use-nuclear-weapons-us-intel-chief-2023-05-04/.

Tehran Times. "Leaked Documents Show Details of Failed Arab-U.S. Move to Form Anti-Iran Alliance." *Tehran Times.* May 9, 2021. https://www.tehrantimes.com/news/460766/Leaked-documents-show-details-of-failed-Arab-U-S-move-to-form.

Tuchman, Barbara W. 1981. *The Zimmermann Telegram.* London: Macmillan.

Washington Post. 2011. "Israeli Military Maps Hezbollah Bunkers." *Washington Post.* March 30, 2011. https://www.washingtonpost.com/wp-srv/special/world/Israeli-military-information-on-Hezbollah.html.

Webster, Frank V. 2006. *Theories of the Information Society.* 3rd ed. London: Routledge.

Chapter 8

The IAEA and the dynamics of intelligence sharing

Robert Reardon

North Carolina State University

Abstract: Robert Reardon examines the complicated and politically sensitive process of intelligence sharing. His focus is on the three-way relationship between the International Atomic Energy Agency (IAEA); the U.S., on which it is highly dependent for intelligence to carry out its mission; and the state that is the target of intelligence. Reardon outlines a framework to analyze this relationship and applies it to North Korea and Iran. His analysis sheds light on why cooperation here is generally higher than expected and offers guidance for policy makers in deciding the pros and cons of sharing intelligence.

Keywords: Intelligence-sharing, IAEA, open source intelligence, secrecy

***

For an international organization, the International Atomic Energy Agency (IAEA) is unusually dependent on third-party intelligence to carry out its mission. IAEA's intelligence capabilities are weak, while some of its member states—particularly the United States and its close allies—possess formidable intelligence capabilities for detecting nuclear-related activities. This chapter analyzes the three-way strategic dynamic between the United States as an intelligence provider, the IAEA as an intelligence recipient, and the state that is the target of intelligence. It suggests an analytic framework that considers the tradeoffs all three of these actors face. The United States, as an intelligence provider, weighs the need to make the intelligence it shares as compelling as possible against the need to keep sources and methods secret. The IAEA faces a tradeoff between increasing its credibility with the United States by maintaining secrecy against maintaining its credibility with the rest of the international community, which can view IAEA cooperation with the United States as a sign that the Agency is simply a U.S. policy tool. The targeted state faces pressure to cooperate when presented with compelling intelligence of suspicious activity and an incentive to resist this pressure to avoid domestic and international reputational costs. The targeted state is also incentivized to resist if it has something to hide. Secrecy can make the evidence appear to the targeted state weaker than it is, increasing its incentive to resist. However, secrecy can also lower the reputational costs of compliance.

All three actors consider their expectations of how the others respond. Suppose the United States anticipates the IAEA will not be cooperative. In that case, it may choose to act unilaterally or strike a different tradeoff between secrecy and forthcomingness if it believes doing so might increase the chances of IAEA action. It will also consider how much it thinks the IAEA can be trusted with sensitive information. The IAEA must consider the reliability of the United States, which could be viewed as higher or lower depending on previous interactions with the Agency. It also has to consider how its actions could affect future assistance from the United States or future cooperation from targeted states. The targeted state is more willing to resist inspection demands if it believes the IAEA is vulnerable to pressure and it can drive a wedge between the Agency and the United States.

This framework has important implications for both scholars and practitioners. It helps explain decisions made in important cases that have otherwise appeared puzzling. In particular, it describes why cooperation among all three actors is generally higher than expected. It also guides U.S. policymakers who must weigh the pros and cons of sharing intelligence with the IAEA and decide how much intelligence is enough. While it cannot provide a precise answer to that question, it clarifies the questions policymakers should ask themselves when making these decisions.

The chapter proceeds as follows. The next section reviews the academic literature on intelligence-sharing and how states decide when to keep intelligence secret and when to go public. As far as possible, it focuses on the relatively small literature on intelligence-sharing with the IAEA in particular. The following section provides a more detailed outline of the analytic framework and illustrates it by referencing important historical cases. The next section briefly examines how useful the framework is for understanding the cases of Iran and North Korea. The conclusion follows, which considers the limitations of the framework, possible future research, and policy implications.

Literature review

A burgeoning literature in the international relations field addresses state secrecy and, in particular, how and why states cooperate to keep secrets. The literature addresses why this cooperation is so frequent, given the benefits of transparency identified by international relations scholars (Carnegie 2021).

Scholars have focused on causal factors in two principal areas: domestic politics and international politics. In terms of domestic politics, leaders have an incentive to maintain secrecy and cooperate with other leaders in doing so when they are enacting unpopular policies (Schuessler 2010), trying to prevent escalation (Carson 2020), or seeking to negotiate without audience costs (Johns and Pelc 2016). Internationally, states may cooperate to keep secrets to facilitate intelligence sharing. States are especially concerned about protecting intelligence sources and methods (Colaresi 2014) and are more likely to share intelligence with close allies they can trust to keep secrets (Haas and Yarhi-Milo 2020) and with international organizations that have the necessary institutions to handle secret information (Carnegie and Carson 2019). States and international organizations may conspire to cover up norm violations if they believe transparency could destabilize the regime (Carnegie and Carson, 2018). Alternatively, making intelligence public can be used coercively, putting pressure on bad actors to change course or on the international community to enforce norms (Riemer and Sobelman, 2023).

Some scholars have looked specifically at intelligence sharing with the IAEA. Ogilvie-White (2014) argues that before the IAEA's intelligence debacle in Iraq, the United States was reluctant to share intelligence with the Agency. This reluctance stemmed from concerns about the Agency's ability to appropriately handle classified information, prevent leaks or theft of sensitive information, and carry out valuable analyses based on this information. As Ogilvie-White (2014) points out, the United States was essentially alone in the 1970s and 1980s advocating in favor of an enhanced IAEA intelligence capability, which was opposed by other member states (even including U.S. allies in Western Europe during this period) out of concern that they would lose influence over the Agency. The Iraq failure effectively tipped the balance in the United States' favor, allowing for the creation of an expanded intelligence apparatus, which included rules and institutional arrangements for handling third-party intelligence with secrecy. As these capabilities developed in the 1990s in response to the Iraq case, the United States became increasingly willing to share intelligence with the agency.

This, however, only partially answers why the United States would prefer to share intelligence with the Agency in the first place rather than pursue nonproliferation objectives on its own. Acton (2014) identifies several reasons. One is that the Agency commands greater international legitimacy in this area than the United States and is, therefore, more likely to be met with cooperation by the targeted states and support from the international community. However, as Acton notes, there are times when the United States has preferred to withhold intelligence from the Agency. As Nutt and Pauly (2021) argue, third-party providers of intelligence to the IAEA (specifically the United States) will keep intelligence secret if they believe they can successfully use it to pressure the target state and reveal the information publicly if they think only pressure from the broader international community can do so.

For example, U.S. and UK intelligence agencies had amassed considerable information about the A.Q. Khan network and Libya's nuclear weapons program that they chose not to share with the IAEA (Bowen 2006, 65-66). Similarly, the United States had information on Iran's nuclear efforts long before they were publicly revealed. Washington chose to allow those revelations to come from actors other than the IAEA ("NCRI" 2006). The decision to keep a lid on intelligence about Libya stemmed from Washington's preference to cut a denuclearization deal with Libya on its terms. The United States and the United Kingdom presented the evidence privately to the Libyans, making it clear they would make their case public if the Libyans did not concede (Nutt and Pauly 2021). A direct approach like this and the use of blackmail to compel Libyan compliance would have been greatly complicated by IAEA involvement.

Similarly, when the United States negotiated with North Korea in the early 1990s, its efforts to reach an accommodation by overlooking some of North Korea's past violations were often hampered by the IAEA's insistence on resolving outstanding questions about past activities (Wit, Poneman, and Gallucci 2005). In that case, Washington's and Vienna's interests diverged, as the IAEA was concerned about its reputation in the wake of the Iraq failure and sought to use the DPRK case to demonstrate the Agency had teeth. On the other hand, Washington was more interested in resolving the standoff, even if it meant ignoring the letter of the country's safeguards agreement.

Acton (2014) also notes significant differences between the capabilities and mandates of national intelligence agencies and those of the IAEA. U.S. intelligence can rely on signals intelligence and human intelligence in ways the IAEA could never do. At the same time, the IAEA has access to sites on a state's territory under its safeguards agreements, which would be unthinkable for U.S. intelligence (Acton 2014). Thus, there are benefits to working together.

The IAEA could avoid some of these dilemmas by developing its intelligence-gathering capabilities. However, there are several significant barriers to this. First, many member states generally oppose the Agency possessing intrusive intelligence capabilities. As it is, the IAEA is unique among international organizations in its ability to conduct relatively invasive and sophisticated monitoring activities on the territories of member states to certify compliance with safeguards agreements. Most of these activities are limited to what is negotiated in the safeguards agreement with that state and involve a specific set of methods employed at declared sites (Rockwood 2013). However, this is only sometimes the case: the IAEA can demand access to suspected undeclared sites and has done so numerous times. While strictly speaking, this could be considered intelligence-gathering, it differs from the sorts of monitoring capabilities the Agency could, in principle, deploy to gather intelligence remotely, clandestinely, and without the cooperation of the targeted state.

Indeed, the IAEA has several programs that fund research on remote detection and other intelligence-gathering technologies (Smartt 2022). It is doubtful, though, that the IAEA would deploy such technologies even if they were developed, given political opposition from member states. This is mainly the case given the research on these technologies is primarily conducted in the United States and Europe, as these are the places by far the most capable of doing this research. It would also be problematic because these countries would likely be unwilling to share these technologies with other member states (Ogilvie-White 2014). Second, because the technologies required for the IAEA to have a genuinely independent intelligence-gathering capacity would necessarily come from the United States and its closest allies, by adopting them, the Agency would increase its dependence on these member states. The Agency's need to maintain secrecy around these technologies and restrict access to them would also likely further a narrative that the IAEA is a pawn of the United States.

Third, regardless of its technical capacity, the agency would unlikely ever be given a mandate to carry out the sort of sweeping intelligence-gathering operations the United States does. The Agency would not intercept phone conversations, pay bribes for information, reward defectors, or many other forms of intelligence gathering a nation-state would rely on. Ultimately, the IAEA will likely always depend on third-party intelligence sharing from its most powerful and technologically sophisticated member states. The Agency will continue to possess its own. Still, these will largely be limited to radiation and isotope detection and other tools specific to nonproliferation rather than broader human and signals intelligence capabilities that are the provenance of states (Acton 2014). The Agency likewise maintains a formidable capacity to gather intelligence from open sources, which has grown as commercially available technologies and imaging have improved (Hobbs and Moran 2014).

Several important points emerge from this literature. First, the United States' decision to share intelligence with the IAEA does not rest solely on the risk of revealing sources and methods or otherwise putting U.S. security at risk. It also matters what the United States believes the IAEA will do with the information: whether it will handle it appropriately, diligently pursue inspections, or complicate negotiations that the United States thinks could yield better results if done directly with the targeted state behind closed doors. Second, the IAEA heavily relies on the United States for intelligence and maintains a capacity to work with classified materials to strengthen that cooperation. However, the IAEA is also interested in maintaining credibility with the rest of its members, who may look skeptically at the Agency's dependence on the United States and U.S.-IAEA secrecy (Carnegie and Carson 2019).

The literature, however, largely ignores the calculus of the targeted state, which is generally portrayed as a passive actor that can either give in to coercion or resist. However, the target state has choices, including ways to manipulate the IAEA. The targeted state can use the IAEA's need to maintain secrecy to its advantage by demanding to see the evidence against it and using the IAEA's refusal to do so to undermine its legitimacy. Likewise, the target state can exploit efforts to blackmail it with intelligence if it knows the information is wrong, as it can go public and embarrass the United States and IAEA for making demands based on unsound intelligence. The framework outlined in the following section suggests why we see this occur more frequently.

In the following section, I build on this literature by proposing a more ambitious framework encompassing the interactions across all three actors. This is needed because of the strategic nature of these interactions. Each actor considers not only its own interests but how the other actors are likely to respond given their interests. When these strategic interactions are considered in the literature, it is typically between two relevant actors rather than all three.

Analytic framework

The IAEA is a cornerstone of the international nonproliferation regime in verifying member states' compliance with their obligations under the Nuclear Nonproliferation Treaty (NPT). It has arguably played a critical role in limiting the number of nuclear-armed states worldwide (Miller 2014). The Agency primarily plays this role by negotiating safeguards agreements with member states that provide comprehensive monitoring and verification measures tailored to each state's nuclear facilities and practices. Its objective is to verify that nuclear materials are not diverted or used for the production of nuclear weapons. If the IAEA is unable to verify compliance with safeguards—either because it has detected activities that violate the terms of the safeguards agreement or is denied sufficient access to sites to satisfactorily conduct those verification measures—the IAEA Board of Governors may decide to forward the case to the UN Security Council, whose members can determine what actions, if any, can be taken.

The IAEA has the additional authority to demand "special inspections"—unscheduled inspections at declared or undeclared sites outside of the scope of the specific measures outlined in the safeguards agreement—to verify the "completeness" of the state's safeguards declaration (i.e., that nuclear activities are not being secretly conducted at undeclared sites in the country). The Agency has long possessed the legal authority to carry out such inspections. Still, it has been reluctant to use that authority without a state's agreement to the Additional Protocol, which specifically sets out the IAEA's ability to initiate special inspections, among other measures (Rockwood 2007).[1]

Some IAEA member states, however—and especially the United States—possess vast and sophisticated intelligence-gathering resources specifically related to the proliferation of nuclear weapons (Richelson 2006). By sharing intelligence with the IAEA, these member states can significantly enhance the Agency's ability to investigate suspected undeclared sites or potential weapons activities. However, as discussed above, the United States and others often have disincentives to provide the information they possess. The United States has approached this by weighing the benefits of giving the IAEA the information against the risks. It will share enough information to demonstrate the evidence is compelling and withhold as much information as possible to verify its trustworthiness to the United States. Alternatively, the United States could decide not to work with the IAEA if it believes unilateral action is more likely to achieve the desired outcome or that working through the IAEA could complicate negotiations (Nutt and Pauly 2021).

The IAEA must navigate between the pressure to act on third-party intelligence when doing so could undermine the Agency's credibility and its reputation for independence from the most powerful member states. The Agency must consider two very different audiences: the United States and its close allies, who represent the overwhelming share of intelligence providers, and the much larger group of states that are either the targets of this intelligence or weak member states that are sensitive to any appearance of the IAEA acting as a tool of the United States. As an institution with its own particular set of interests, the IAEA seeks to maximize its power as an international actor and elevate the perceived importance of its global mission. To accomplish this, it must maintain credibility and support from the powerful states who most strongly support the IAEA's role in nonproliferation and weaker states that are often suspicious of the Agency's willingness to act on behalf of those powerful states at the expense of the others. IAEA legitimacy (and therefore its power) stems from maintaining credibility among both groups while maintaining as much independence as an institution (Ogilvie-White 2011).

However, these incentives are at odds with one another. Credibility with one group is often bought at the expense of lost credibility with the other. And just as U.S. leaders must balance the competing interests of government institutions

---

[1] There is considerable controversy regarding the IAEA's legal mandate concerning special inspections and the verification of the completeness of states' safeguards declarations.

like the State Department and elements of the Defense Department that privilege nonproliferation goals over preserving secrecy and the intelligence community that prioritizes secrecy above all else, IAEA leaders seek a policy course that tries to please competing interest groups (Findlay 2012). A logical result is for the IAEA to underuse the third-party intelligence resources at its disposal (Ogilvie-White 2014). Even when high-quality and credible intelligence is shared with the IAEA, it may be reluctant to demand access to sites and to aggressively pursue evidence of illicit nuclear activities if doing so could put the Agency's broader legitimacy at risk.

The case of Syria's suspected nuclear activities illustrates much of this dynamic. In 2007, Israel used airstrikes to destroy a suspected nuclear reactor at al Kibar in Syria. U.S. and Israeli intelligence concluded a reactor was being constructed at the site with North Korean assistance and was part of a potential nuclear weapons program. U.S. and Israeli intelligence was reportedly quite strong, consisting of testimony from defectors, satellite imagery, and other sources. Initially, this intelligence was not shared with the IAEA. However, having low confidence in the IAEA's willingness to act assertively, the United States and Israel preferred to act outside of the organization (Simpson 2008). When intelligence was presented to Vienna after the fact, IAEA leadership was unwilling to act, even though the intelligence was compelling. The Agency now faced a cost from acting on the intelligence regardless of its quality, as it would be following the U.S. lead in the wake of military action that lacked international legitimacy (moreover, the memory of Colin Powell's testimony in 2003 was still fresh) (Simpson 2008). As a result, the Agency was reluctant to use its full authority to demand access to sites even as the Syrian government refused to allow full access voluntarily, and as of this writing, numerous important questions about Syria's activities remain unanswered (Ogilvie-White 2014). The Syrian case and others demonstrate that it is not simply a function of the quality of the intelligence that determines IAEA action. Instead, IAEA leadership has a more complex decision-making process when determining to act based on intelligence provided by the United States and other third parties that takes both the quality of the evidence and political realities into consideration. These decision-making processes—those of the United States and the IAEA—are strategically linked. U.S. decision-makers have to consider how much they have to reveal *to get the Agency to act*, not just convince the Agency leadership that their claims are true, as the IAEA may have an incentive not to act even when the intelligence is compelling.

The United States also has to take into consideration that the IAEA is under pressure to make intelligence public if they need to build a public case to maintain their credibility. The United States itself also can make evidence public to put additional pressure on the IAEA. Domestic politics becomes relevant here, as sub-state actors can choose to leak intelligence about another state's illicit nuclear facilities as a way of forcing the United States government to act. The United States demanded it be allowed to inspect the Kumchang-ri site in North Korea in 1999 despite substantial doubt across nearly all U.S. intelligence agencies about evidence suggesting it was a clandestine nuclear facility. The Defense Intelligence Agency (DIA), which was alone in its conviction that the site was part of a nuclear weapons program, leaked information to the press as a way to pressure the government into demanding North Korea allow inspections (and ultimately bribe Pyongyang into allowing them) (Wit 2019).

The targeted state has its calculus about whether to cooperate with IAEA demands to investigate claims. It must consider whether or not it actually has something to hide (i.e., whether the intelligence is correct), its relationship to the third-party provider of the intelligence (how adversarial the relationship is), how compelling the intelligence might appear to the general public both domestically and internationally (which in turn depends on how much of it is made public), and its vulnerability to domestic pressure.

The targeted state is confronted with several key dilemmas. The first is whether to cooperate with the IAEA at all by providing access to sites when special inspections are demanded. This is not entirely a binary choice. The target state can foot-drag and delay, negotiate, offer limited access, and demand to see the intelligence on which the demand for site access is based. The target state can also argue that the site is sensitive (e.g., a military installation), whether true or not, as a way to stall.[2]

Second, the target state can choose whether or not to go public. Under certain circumstances, there may be a significant payoff for publicly revealing information about demands for inspections. For example, if U.S.-provided intelligence leads the IAEA to demand inspections at a site where, in fact, there is no illicit activity taking place, the targeted state can choose to allow access to the site and then benefit by drawing attention to the IAEA's failure (and accuse Washington of duplicity) (Chinoy 2013). Doing so can make the state look like a victim of unfairness, the United States as a peddler of faulty or fabricated intelligence, and the IAEA as an illegitimate stooge of the United States. It also helps create disincentives against further requests for access, as the IAEA will likely be more skeptical of future U.S.-provided intelligence and fear further damage to its own reputation.[3] In general, the more it can be publicly revealed

---

[2] There is no legal reason why the IAEA cannot access these sites, but in practice, the Agency has tended to show deference to national security considerations (Rockwood 2007).

[3] The greatest damage to the U.S.-IAEA intelligence relationship came from the U.S. presentation of evidence of an Iraqi nuclear program in 2003.

that the IAEA is acting on flawed U.S. intelligence, the more it can be portrayed as Washington's pawn, and the more dubious claims against the target state will become in the eyes of much of the international community. The IAEA may even decide to publicly challenge U.S. intelligence claims, as the Agency did during the run-up to the Iraq War. In that case, the Bush administration and the Agency each challenged the other's legitimacy, as Washington sought its preferred policies, and Vienna sought to uphold its reputation for accuracy and independence (Pfiffner 2004). The targeted state also faces domestic political incentives that may affect its decision on whether or not to reveal information about its dealings with the IAEA. If U.S.-provided intelligence proves to be false, the target state can use this as a way to advance the narrative with its domestic audience that the United States is cynically using high-minded appeals to nonproliferation norms as cover for a more malicious agenda.[4]

However, the targeted state's incentives are not necessarily so clear-cut. The target state, for example, could decide to take a strong stance against access when the site in question is innocent despite the above incentives to do so. Denial of access, at least temporarily, could allow the target state to extract concessions (as the North Koreans were able to do over the alleged Kumchang-ri nuclear site) or could create a high-profile dispute that could prove even more embarrassing to the IAEA (and the United States) once access is allowed and it is revealed that U.S.-provided intelligence is flawed. This could lead the IAEA to demand more credible evidence from the United States in the future and make the Agency more reluctant to pursue demands for access unless it had a very high level of confidence in its intelligence. Washington would face an even more acute disclosure dilemma, as it would require the disclosure of more intelligence (and therefore more information about U.S. intelligence-gathering capabilities) to produce a desired IAEA action.

Nor is the domestic political calculus so simple for the target state. Provision of access to the IAEA, especially if it is publicly known that the IAEA's actions are based on U.S.-supplied intelligence, can make the government appear weak and could be exploited by hardline domestic political opponents. Hardliners would be able to argue that not only is the government caving to IAEA demands based on U.S. intelligence, but it is doing so even when that intelligence is demonstrably flawed (and potentially shared in bad faith). This could also create an incentive to take a more uncooperative stance toward the IAEA, even if the site in question is an innocent one. Thus, the target state's government faces competing incentives. On the one hand, allowing inspections at an innocent site could embarrass the IAEA and the United States

---

[4] This has been a common assertion in Iran (e.g., Mousavian 2012).

and potentially raise the bar for future demands for inspection.[5] On the other, accommodation can be politically damaging if it makes the government appear weak to its constituents.

The target state has another important incentive, however, to resist demands for access, even when the intelligence is flawed and there is nothing to be revealed at the suspected sites. If access is granted, the state pays a reputation cost even if there is nothing to find simply because giving in to any demand driven by U.S.-supplied intelligence risks making the state appear weak. This arms domestic critics and risks incentivizing further demands based on weak intelligence. However, secrecy can be important in this situation as well. If the United States, the IAEA, and the target state cooperate to keep the matter secret, providing site access will carry with it lower reputational costs. At a minimum, it can avoid domestic political costs. In terms of concern over future demands, the targeted state's compliance will depend on whether it believes the IAEA will act as a reliable gatekeeper by refusing to act on weak intelligence and pushing back on U.S. unilateral claims. This dynamic may, in fact, explain why there were so few high-profile refusals of inspections when the targeted state had little to hide.[6]

Much of this reasoning explains Iran's reluctance to resolve outstanding questions about its pre-2003 nuclear weapons-related activities. Iran had something to hide in this case in the sense that any thorough investigation would uncover clandestine weapons-related activities. But this is unlikely the only barrier to cooperation, as there is already little doubt about Iran's activities given the strength of existing evidence (IAEA Director General 2011). Political factors could be as important in Tehran as much of the evidence driving the IAEA's demands for access to particular sites and documentation came from Israeli, U.S., and other Western intelligence agencies, including evidence from a laptop acquired by U.S. intelligence containing designs for a uranium gas-production facility, modifications for Iranian ballistic missiles to accommodate a nuclear warhead and other evidence of an Iranian nuclear weapon program.[7] The source of the intelligence, independent of the strength of the evidence on

---

[5] It is important to note that this, too, could backfire. If pressing flawed intelligence claims does not lead the target state to become more uncooperative, this could incentivize further demands for inspections based on intelligence of low confidence.

[6] In personal correspondence, an anonymous former Egyptian diplomat who worked with the IAEA has claimed this dynamic has in fact occurred a number of times with Iran, where Iran acceded to inspections based on flawed intelligence, nothing was found, and all parties cooperated to keep the matter secret.

[7] The laptop evidence was only a part of the abundant documentation collected by Western intelligence agencies and turned over to the IAEA (Sanger and Broad 2015).

its merits, allowed the Iranian government to cast doubt on its integrity, claims that resonate with public attitudes domestically and internationally. This presented the IAEA with a dilemma, as the strength of Western intelligence on Iran created pressure to investigate suspected sites while actually doing so could negatively impact the Agency's credibility outside of the Western community, as well as undermine cooperation with Iran on more pressing issues.

The strength and credibility of the IAEA's evidence on Iran's past activities put considerable pressure on the Iranian government to accommodate Vienna's demands for access to suspected sites. By compiling a presentation of this evidence in the November 2011 IAEA safeguards report on Iran, the Agency was able to mitigate potential political problems from reliance on Western intelligence by highlighting not only the depth of evidence but also how it was drawn from a breadth of sources including numerous member states' sources that were verified by the IAEA itself (IAEA Director General 2011). However, the moderate Rouhani government also faced pressure from the country's hardliners, who could portray compromise with the IAEA as a weakness. In this case, the government sought to thread the needle through limited acquiescence to IAEA demands and foot-dragging while continuing to portray IAEA claims as Western propaganda and the evidence as fabrication (Einhorn 2015).

The IAEA, the United States, and the targeted state are all engaged in a balancing act in which each state's decisions are strategically dependent upon those of the others. The way these various incentives align or misalign can determine how much intelligence member states are willing to provide (or whether they choose to work through the Agency at all), how aggressively the IAEA is willing to act based on third-party intelligence, and the degree to which the targeted state's government is willing to cooperate with the Agency. Under certain circumstances, this can lead all the parties to cooperate to maintain secrecy. If the United States presents the IAEA with ambiguous intelligence, the IAEA may decide to move forward with it, and the targeted state may accede to demands for inspections, provided all parties agree to keep the issue out of the public eye. This way the United States and the IAEA avoid the public embarrassment and loss of credibility for acting on faulty intelligence, and the government of the target state avoids the domestic and international reputations costs that would accrue if the event were publicized. The target state can agree to this arrangement so long as doing so does not produce an increase in demands for access to suspected sites. In this case, it would still be able to go public with the false accusations.

The United States and the targeted state may also cooperate to keep knowledge of the targeted state's activities ambiguous. This is particularly the case if resolving questions about past activities could prevent agreement to curtail future actions. For example, to achieve the Agreed Framework, the

Clinton Administration proved willing to defer the resolution of outstanding questions about North Korea's past activities—despite damning evidence of the country's nuclear weapons efforts and over the IAEA's preference to more aggressively pursue the matter—in order to achieve a freeze of the DPRK's nuclear program. In essence, Washington and Pyongyang cooperated to diffuse the issue by crafting a deal that left the issue unresolved but included a pledge by the North Koreans to resolve the matter over time in cooperation with the IAEA. It is doubtful either side believed these outstanding questions would be resolved as agreed. This was cooperation to defuse an issue important to the IAEA's institutional interests and one that could be effectively exploited by domestic opponents of a deal in Washington in the absence of any pledge by Pyongyang to address it in the future (Wit, Poneman, and Gallucci 2005).

A counterintuitive dynamic can develop to address the dilemmas faced by the three parties in which they cooperate to keep inspections of undeclared sites secret, or at least take measures to limit public attention. For the United States, secrecy facilitates intelligence sharing and minimizes the potential political fallout should the intelligence turn out flawed. Thus, secrecy makes the disclosure dilemma less acute. Under conditions of relative secrecy, the United States and the IAEA will both pay a lower cost should the intelligence turn out to be flawed, as those costs are based on reputational costs that can accrue to all three parties involved. The lower those costs, the more willing the United States will be to provide lower-confidence intelligence and the freer it will feel withholding or degrading intelligence to conceal intelligence capabilities. The IAEA, for its part, benefits from secrecy because it will pay a lower reputational cost for cooperating with the United States and a lower cost should the intelligence that is provided turns out to be flawed. This makes it easier to accept U.S. intelligence and to pursue access to suspected sites in the targeted state based on intelligence that is weaker than what would be required if under public scrutiny.

The targeted state's government has a more complicated calculus, however, because there may be benefits to reneging and publicly revealing intelligence failures, as described above. The target state is more likely to maintain secrecy when the benefits of revealing failure and inflicting reputational costs on the United States and the IAEA are outweighed by the costs of appearing weak for accommodating IAEA demands based on U.S. intelligence. This is most likely to be the case when the government faces a powerful and popular hardline opposition that can effectively use revelations of inspections to undermine the government's credibility when the government lacks the means to keep special inspections away from public scrutiny, and when the target state faces high costs if it refuses access.

Figure 8.1. The analytic framework

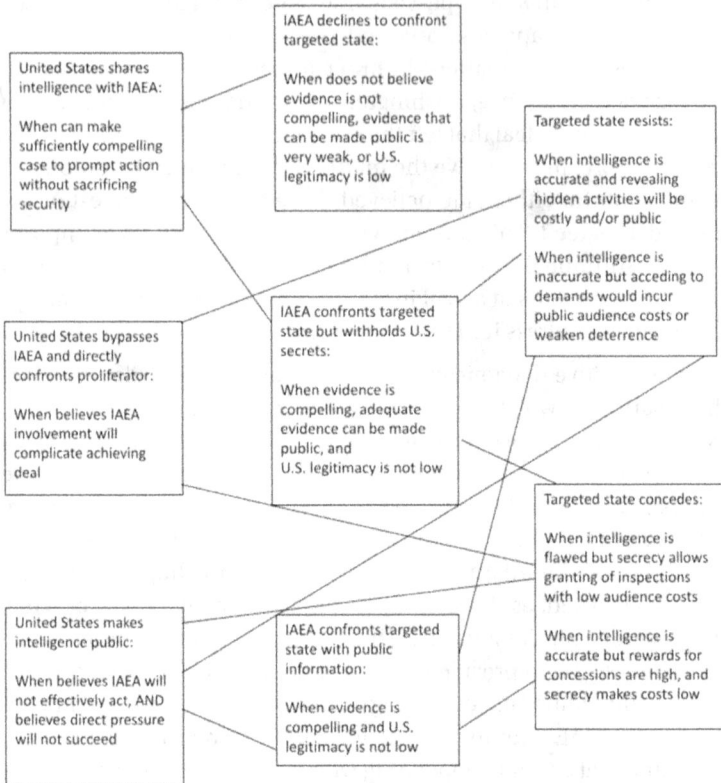

United States shares intelligence with IAEA:

When can make sufficiently compelling case to prompt action without sacrificing security

IAEA declines to confront targeted state:

When does not believe evidence is not compelling, evidence that can be made public is very weak, or U.S. legitimacy is low

Targeted state resists:

When intelligence is accurate and revealing hidden activities will be costly and/or public

When intelligence is inaccurate but acceding to demands would incur public audience costs or weaken deterrence

United States bypasses IAEA and directly confronts proliferator:

When believes IAEA involvement will complicate achieving deal

IAEA confronts targeted state but withholds U.S. secrets:

When evidence is compelling, adequate evidence can be made public, and U.S. legitimacy is not low

Targeted state concedes:

When intelligence is flawed but secrecy allows granting of inspections with low audience costs

When intelligence is accurate but rewards for concessions are high, and secrecy makes costs low

United States makes intelligence public:

When believes IAEA will not effectively act, AND believes direct pressure will not succeed

IAEA confronts targeted state with public information:

When evidence is compelling and U.S. legitimacy is not low

The analytic framework put forth in this section is illustrated in Figure 8.1. The United States and the IAEA face two key decisions: how strong an intelligence case is required to move forward with demands for inspections and whether to keep that information secret or go public with it. The targeted state decides whether to give in to demands and whether to go public or cooperate to maintain secrecy. The framework explains why the targeted state will often cooperate to maintain secrecy even if it is confronted with inaccurate intelligence. The following section illustrates this dynamic by drawing on the histories of the Iran and North Korean nonproliferation cases.

Iran and North Korea

Despite the major differences between the North Korean and Iranian cases, they are both consistent with the analytic framework outlined in the above section. The Kim regime may not be as vulnerable to attacks from the domestic right as many other regimes, but it does need to satisfy the country's military leadership, which has demonstrated a preference for a hardline position toward the United States and international organizations like the IAEA that it views as tools of U.S. coercion (Kim 2010). The regime is less susceptible to negative public perception and exercises substantial control over information access within the country. It does have an interest, though, in maintaining an international reputation for taking strong stances against the IAEA, particularly when IAEA demands for access to sites are believed to be based on U.S. intelligence. Finally, the costs of defiance for Pyongyang are relatively low. It is a pariah state with nuclear and conventional forces that can effectively deter a military response to violations of its nonproliferation obligations. It can also depend on support from China even when it is being intransigent, as Beijing has a considerable interest in preventing a collapse of the regime.

Taken together, these factors would predict that, in general, we should expect the DPRK to be quite uncooperative with the IAEA, as it has little to gain from cooperation and much more to lose. The country is also heavily dependent on its nuclear weapons program for a variety of reasons—both in terms of national security and domestic politics—and thus can be expected to be fairly risk-accepting in international diplomacy. We should expect North Korea to be less likely to cooperate with the IAEA and third-party intelligence providers despite the fact that the regime can, in general, maintain a high level of information control and, therefore, would have a considerable capacity to maintain secrecy if it chose to. The regime, however, is less capable of keeping secrets from the military than it is from the general public, and the military is the domestic audience it is far more concerned about. North Korea also depends quite heavily on its reputation for resolve in the international context, as it is a relatively small state faced with far more powerful adversaries, and it relies on the deterrent threat of nuclear use and its willingness to initiate a war on the Korean peninsula. It is likely to weigh those considerations much more highly than any potential gains from cooperating with the IAEA. We should, therefore, expect little cooperation with secrecy (and more generally) and a willingness to try to capitalize on intelligence failures by the United States.

Iran's strategic calculus differs dramatically from that of North Korea. During the Rouhani presidency, the moderates who led negotiations with the P5+1 to produce the JCPOA were vulnerable to attacks from the right by hardliners (Reardon 2012). Although Iran is far from democratic, the government still must concern itself with managing public opinion, and there would be a price to pay should the public perceive the government as weak in excessively accommodating the IAEA and the United States (Hurst 2016). There is also a general perception of the IAEA as a tool of American interests that is used to undermine Iran's position in the world in the name of upholding international law. In addition, Iran faces higher costs for noncooperation with the IAEA than does the DPRK. Iran is not a pariah to the same degree as North Korea and is far more dependent upon access to international markets and more vulnerable to military action. It possesses no nuclear deterrent and has no great-power benefactor. It could inflict costly damages in a war, but likely not at the same scale as North Korea would be able to do, given its concentration of heavy artillery along the DMZ that could target parts of Seoul. Iran could inflict costs through terrorist attacks and by interfering with shipping in the Persian Gulf, but these costs would be more limited and more easily overcome by its adversaries. Iran is also dependent on the flow of oil through the Persian Gulf. Iran's nuclear interests can largely be met, in the eyes of Iranian moderates, by maintaining a robust uranium enrichment program and missile program without necessarily acquiring weapons (Fukushima 2021). The JCPOA applied limits to the enrichment program but otherwise left major elements of the program intact. Iran, therefore, had a considerable interest in cooperating with the IAEA, at least enough to maintain the nuclear deal and avoid escalation in the form of sanctions or military force. As a result, we should expect Iran to be more cooperative than North Korea with the IAEA. Moreover, the conditions have been present in Iran to make cooperative secrecy a feasible way to facilitate inspections while lowering the costs of cooperating, especially when inspections are based on U.S.-supplied intelligence in whole or in part.

Conclusion

This chapter has explored the various incentive structures that impact the decision-making of third-party providers of intelligence to international organizations; the IAEA, which depends on the provision of intelligence from the United States and its allies; and the states that are the targets of that intelligence. The choices these actors make are strategically interrelated. The United States must consider how much intelligence must be shared with the IAEA to prompt action, whether that can be done without creating excessive risks for its intelligence assets, and whether its objectives can better be achieved by working outside of IAEA auspices. The IAEA must consider the value of third-party intelligence, maintaining its reputation of reliability with major intelligence providers, preserving its reputation for independence and objectivity with its member states overall, and its institutional interest in maintaining credibility as an effective organization capable of carrying out its mission. States that are the target of third-party intelligence must consider the costs of compliance with IAEA demands in terms of both domestic politics and the potential consequences of revealing illicit behaviors, as well as the potential benefits of complying if doing so creates a pathway toward a mutually beneficial agreement. An interesting implication of this is that the United States can use intelligence-sharing to first apply pressure on suspected states, then cooperate with the target state to downplay suspicions about past behavior—even when doing so may be contrary to the IAEA's interests as an institution—in order to achieve a deal that limits future nuclear weapons-related activities.

The framework can benefit U.S. nonproliferation policy by helping clarify the conditions when intelligence sharing with the IAEA is appropriate and most likely to succeed. Alternatively, it helps identify when bypassing the Agency and confronting a suspected proliferator directly is the more appropriate strategy. In addition, it demonstrates the importance of secrecy in many cases and suggests secrecy may be easier to maintain than is often believed, as under certain circumstances, all parties will have an incentive to cooperate to prevent public scrutiny.

There are important limitations here, however. While the cases discussed in this chapter, such as North Korea and Iran, suggest the framework has promise as an analytic tool, this is far from a robust test of its claims. At best, the evidence suggests the approach is worthy of further study. In addition, there may be numerous other factors yet to be considered that can influence whether international actors will cooperate to maintain secrecy. This chapter seeks to contribute to the important and growing literature on this topic.

References

Acton, James M. 2014. "International Verification and Intelligence." *Intelligence and National Security* 29 (3): 341-356.

Bowen, Wyn. 2006. "Libya and Nuclear Proliferation: Stepping Back from the Brink." *IISS Adelphi Paper* 46 (380): 1-103.

Carnegie, Allison. 2021. "Secrecy in International Relations and Foreign Policy." *Annual Review of Political Science* 24: 213-233.

Carnegie, Allison, and Austin Carson. 2018. "The Spotlight's Harsh Glare: Rethinking Publicity and International Order." *International Organization* 72 (3): 627-657.

———. 2019. "The Disclosure Dilemma: Nuclear Intelligence and International Organizations." *American Journal of Political Science* 63 (2): 269-285.

Carson, Austin. 2020. *Secret Wars: Covert Conflict in International Politics.* Princeton: Princeton University Press.

Chinoy, Mike. 2013, April 12. "Why North Korean Intelligence Is So Hard to Read." CNN. https://www.cnn.com/2013/04/12/world/asia/north-korea-nuclear-capabilities/index.html.

Colaresi, Michael P. 2014. *Democracy Declassified: The Secrecy Dilemma in National Security.* Oxford: Oxford University Press.

Einhorn, Robert. 2015, December 1. "An Unsatisfactory Outcome on Iran's Past Nuclear Activities Is No Reason to Derail the Nuclear Deal." Brookings Institution. https://www.brookings.edu/articles/an-unsatisfying-outcome-on-irans-past-nuclear-activities-is-no-reason-to-derail-the-nuclear-deal/.

Findlay, Trevor. 2012. *Unleashing the Nuclear Watchdog: Strengthening and Reform of the IAEA.* Waterloo, ON: Centre for International Governance Innovation.

Fukushima, Mayumi. 2021, June 28. "Why Iran May Be in No Hurry to Get Nuclear Weapons Even Without a Nuclear Deal." *National Interest.*

Haas, Melinda, and Keren Yarhi-Milo. 2020. "To Disclose or Deceive? Sharing Secret Information Between Aligned States." *International Security* 45 (3): 122-161.

Hobbs, Christopher, and Matthew Moran. 2014. "Armchair Safeguards: The Role of Open-Source Intelligence in Nuclear Proliferation Analysis." In *Open-Source Intelligence in the Twenty-First Century: New Approaches and Opportunities*, edited by Christopher Hobbs, Matthew Moran, and Daniel Salisbury. New York: Springer.

Hurst, Steven. 2016. "The Iranian Nuclear Negotiations as a Two-Level Game: The Importance of Domestic Politics." *Diplomacy & Statecraft* 27 (3): 545-567.

IAEA Director General. 2011, November 8. "Implementation of the NPT Safeguards Agreement and Relevant Provisions of Security Council Resolutions in the Islamic Republic of Iran." GOV/2011/65. https://www.armscontrol.org/system/files/IAEA_Iran_8Nov2011.pdf.

Johns, Leslie, and Krzysztof J. Pelc. 2016. "Fear of Crowds in World Trade Organization Disputes: Why Don't More Countries Participate?" *Journal of Politics* 78 (1): 88-104.

Kim, Samuel S. 2010. "North Korea's Nuclear Strategy and the Interface Between International and Domestic Politics." *Asian Perspective* 34 (1): 49-85.

Nutt, Cullen G., and Reid B. C. Pauly. 2021. "Caught Red-Handed: How States Wield Proof to Coerce Wrongdoers." *International Security* 46 (2): 7-50.

Ogilvie-White, Tanya. 2011. "Nuclear Intelligence and North-South Politics," *International Journal of Intelligence and Counterintelligence* 24: 1-21.

———. 2014. "The IAEA and the International Politics of Nuclear Intelligence." *Intelligence and National Security* 29 (3): 323-340.

Miller, Nicholas L. 2014. "The Secret Success of Nonproliferation Sanctions." *International Organization* 68 (4): 913-944.

Mousavian, Seyed Hossein. 2012. *The Iranian Nuclear Crisis: A Memoir.* Washington, DC: Brookings Institution Press.

"NCRI Did Not Discover Natanz." 2006, October 28. *Arms Control Wonk* blog. Accessed June 30, 2023. http://www.armscontrolwonn.com/1274/ncri-did-not-discover-natanz.

Pfiffner, James P. 2004. "Did President Bush Mislead the Country in His Arguments for War with Iraq?" *Presidential Studies Quarterly* 34 (1): 25-46.

Reardon, Robert J. 2012. *Containing Iran: Strategies for Addressing the Iranian Nuclear Challenge.* RAND Corporation.

Riemer, Ofek, and Daniel Sobelman. 2023. "Coercive Disclosure: The Weaponization of Public Intelligence Revelation in International Relations." *Contemporary Security Policy* 44 (2).

Richelson, Jeffrey. 2007. *Spying on the Bomb: American Nuclear Intelligence from Nazi Germany to Iran and North Korea.* New York: W. W. Norton.

Rockwood, Laura. 2007. "Safeguards and Nonproliferation: The First Half-Century from a Legal Perspective." *Journal of Nuclear Materials Management* 35 (4): 7.

———. 2013. *Legal Framework for IAEA Safeguards.* Office of Science and Technology Information.

Sanger, David E., and William J. Broad. 2015, December 2. "Nuclear Agency Says Iran Worked on Weapons Design until 2009." *New York Times.* https://www.nytimes.com/2015/12/03/world/middleeast/iran-nuclear-report-atomic-agency.html.

Schuessler, J. M. 2010. "The Deception Dividend: FDR's Undeclared War." *International Security* 34 (4): 133-165.

Simpson, Fiona. 2008. "The IAEA's Dilemma with Syria's Al-Kibar Nuclear Site." *Bulletin of the Atomic Scientists.*

Smartt, Heidi. 2022. *Remote Monitoring Systems / Remote Data Transmission for International Nuclear Safeguards.* No. SAND2022-4273. Sandia National Lab.

Wit, Joel. 2019, January 22. "What I Learned Leading America's First Nuclear Inspection in North Korea." NPR. https://www.npr.org/2019/01/22/681174887/opinion-what-i-learned-leading-americas-1st-nuclear-inspection-in-north-korea.

Wit, Joel S., Daniel Poneman, and Robert L. Gallucci. 2005. *Going Critical: The First North Korean Nuclear Crisis.* Washington, DC: Brookings Institution Press.

Contributors

Dr. John Borek completed his post-doctoral fellowship in February 2023 in the Homeland Defense and Security Issues Group at the U.S. Army War College and is currently an adjunct instructor in the National Security Intelligence Analysis Program at the University of New Hampshire. He is a former Army strategic intelligence officer and served as a civilian analyst, senior analyst, and branch chief at the National Ground Intelligence Center where he was recognized for analytic excellence on four separate occasions for both individual and team production. He was certified as a Director of National Intelligence Analytic Tradecraft Standards evaluator, and is certified by both the DoD and the Intelligence Community Joint Duty Program. John received his PhD in public policy from Walden University, an MS in strategic intelligence from the National Intelligence University, and a BS in geography from the Pennsylvania State University.

Andrew Macpherson is an Assistant Professor of security studies at the University of New Hampshire. He is the program coordinator for the UNH master's degree in National Security Intelligence Analysis and the principal investigator for the Northeast Intelligence Community Centers for Academic Excellence, a long-term partnership with the Office of the Director of National Intelligence.

Dr. Angela Lewis is an adjunct professor in Georgetown University's Applied Intelligence program and in the University of Cincinnati's School of Public and International Affairs. Dr. Lewis earned her PhD at Pepperdine University, where her dissertation focused on a systems theory approach to leveraging strategic intelligence for executive decision-making in the private sector. Dr. Lewis formerly worked in both the public and private sectors, including executive-level roles in security and intelligence with Creative Artists Agency (CAA), Nisos, and Salesforce, and building and leading the strategic intelligence team at The Walt Disney Company. She also previously served as a senior targeting officer in the Central Intelligence Agency (CIA), with multiple tours abroad.

In addition to her PhD, Dr. Lewis has an MA in international relations from American University and BAs in international relations and political science from the University of Cincinnati. She serves on the Education Committee for the Association of International Risk Intelligence Professionals (AIRIP), and she is the Private Sector Chair of the State Department's Overseas Security Advisory Council (OSAC) Middle East and North Africa (MENA) Regional Committee and a Girl Security Mentor. Dr. Lewis is passionate about strategic intelligence, organizational culture, and leadership development.

Bridget Rose Nolan is an Assistant Professor of security studies at the University of New Hampshire. She completed her bachelor's degree in psychology at Princeton University and her PhD in sociology at the University of Pennsylvania. Her research interests include organizational change and failure, intelligence analysis, international security, and diversity in government. Dr. Nolan completed a postdoctoral research fellowship at the National Security Studies Institute at the University of Texas at El Paso. She is a former counterterrorism analyst for the Central Intelligence Agency.

Doug Patteson is an adjunct professor of intelligence studies at the University of New Hampshire. He spent a decade as an Operations Officer at the CIA. He also serves as CFO for Turbocam International, a U.S.-headquartered multinational manufacturing firm, in addition to consulting on espionage-themed film and TV projects.

James Ramsay is a Professor of security studies, and Head of the Department of Security Studies and Criminology at Macquarie University in Sydney Australia. Prior to this position, he was the founding coordinator of the Homeland Security program, and the founding Chair of the Department of Security Studies at the University of New Hampshire. Earlier, he had created one of the first undergraduate programs in homeland security in the U.S. at Embry-Riddle Aeronautical University in Florida, where he also founded the Department of Security Studies and International Affairs. He has over 20 years' experience in public health, security studies, emergency management, and occupational and environmental health, building several degree programs, dozens of courses, and two departments. He has created an NSA Center of Academic Excellence in cybersecurity defense education and an ODNI CAE in intelligence education. Dr. Ramsay serves on the IAFIE board as the education practices chair, and as the editor-in-chief for the Journal of Homeland Security and Emergency Management. He also serves on the editorial boards for the Homeland Security Affairs Journal and the Journal of Policing, Intelligence and Counter Terrorism, and he co-founded and serves as associate editor for the Journal of Security, Intelligence, and Resilience Education. Dr. Ramsay's books include Environmental Security: Concepts, Challenges and Case Studies (American Meteorological Society, 2019); and Introduction to Homeland Security, Critical Issues in Homeland Security: A Casebook, and Theoretical Foundations of Homeland Security: Strategies, Operations and Structures, each published by Routledge. Dr. Ramsay was appointed by the U.S. Secretary of Health and Human Services to serve on the Board of Scientific Counselors to the Director of the National Institute of Occupational Safety and Health in the CDC, where he served for four years.

Barry Zulauf, PhD, is the president of IAFIE. Dr. Zulauf is on the intelligence faculty of Johns Hopkins, Georgetown, James Madison, Indiana, and Mercyhurst Universities. Since August 2023, he has been the Defense Intelligence Officer for Counternarcotics, Transnational Organized Crime, and Threat Finance. He was named in June 2022 as the DNI's representative at the CIA's Center for the Study of Intelligence, and was selected by DNI James Clapper to be the first ODNI Chair on the faculty of the National Intelligence University from 2012 to 2015.

Ofek Riemer is a postdoctoral research fellow with the Chaikin Chair for Geostrategy at the University of Haifa, and the coordinator of the Israeli Forum for Intelligence Studies (IFIS). He received his PhD from the Hebrew University of Jerusalem in 2022 for his work on public intelligence disclosure in international relations, which received the Israel Political Science Association Award for Best Dissertation that year. His research was published in Contemporary Security Policy, The British Journal of Politics and International Relations, Strategic Assessment, and War on the Rocks.

Robert J. Reardon is an Associate Professor in the College of Humanities and Social Sciences, at North Carolina State University. He is also the Director of the Master of International Studies in the School of Public and International Affairs.

Glenn P. Hastedt is a professor emeritus of the Justice Studies department at James Madison University (JMU), where he served as the chair. His publications include American Foreign Policy: Past, Present, and Future and numerous articles on intelligence in Intelligence and National Security and the International Journal of Intelligence and Counterintelligence. He is a former co-editor of the journal White House Studies. Dr. Hastedt supports the Northeast Intelligence Community Centers for Academic Excellence.

Katharine Cunningham. After attaining her Masters of Science in Analytics from the University of New Hampshire Katharine Cunningham joined Accenture a global leader in digital and technology transformation. As a Data Scientist in the Applied Intelligence Team, she provides innovative data solutions to clients' most complex business problems. She consults with companies across multiple industries transforming their businesses by providing key data insights.

Index

www.ingramcontent.com/pod-product-compliance
Lightning Source LLC
Chambersburg PA
CBHW062031270326
41929CB00014B/2396